OUT OF THIS WORLD

Deleuze and the Philosophy of Creation

PETER HALLWARD

VERSO

London • New York

First published by Verso 2006
© Verso 2006

1 3 5 7 9 10 8 6 4 2

Verso
UK: 6 Meard Street, London W1F 0EG
USA: 180 Varick Street, New York, NY 10014–4606
www.versobooks.com

Verso is the imprint of New Left Books

ISBN-10: 1-84467-079-6 (hardback)
ISBN-13: 978-1-84467-079-6
ISBN-10: 1-84467-555-6 (paperback)
ISBN-13: 978-1-84467-555-6

British Library Cataloguing in Publication Data
A catalogue record for this book is available from the British Library

Library of Congress Cataloging-in-Publication Data
A catalog record for this book is available from the Library of Congress

Typeset in Monotype Baskerville by Andrea Stimpson
Printed and bound in Great Britain by William Clowes Ltd, Beccles, Suffolk

Contents

Acknowledgements   v

Abbreviations   vii

Introduction   1

1   The Conditions of Creation   8

2   Actual Creatures, Virtual Creatings   27

3   Creatural Confinement   55

4   Creative Subtraction   79

5   Creation Mediated: Art and Literature   104

6   Creation Unmediated: Philosophy   127

Conclusion   159

Notes   165

Bibliography   187

Index   195

Acknowledgements

Fragments of a much earlier version of this book were published as articles in *Radical Philosophy* and *Philosophy Today* in 1997; I finished this final version in 2004–05, during research leave funded by King's College London and the Arts and Humanities Research Council (UK). I'm grateful to friends and colleagues who helped with the book's interminable revision, in particular Sinéad Rushe, Brice Halimi, Patrick ffrench, Alberto Toscano and Ray Brassier, as well as Christian Kerslake, Eric Alliez and other members of Middlesex University's Centre for Research in Modern European Philosophy. I'm especially grateful to Dan Smith for his detailed engagement with some of the more contentious aspects of the argument, and to Sebastian Budgen for gaining me the space, and the time, to carry this argument through. Verso's Tim Clark, who copy-edited the manuscript, could not have been better qualified for the task.

I dedicate this book to my mother, Clare.

'A creator who isn't grabbed around the throat by a set of impossibilities is no creator. A creator is someone who creates their own impossibilities, and thereby creates possibilities' (N, 133).

Abbreviations

Wherever possible, references are to the most easily available English translations; 'tm' stands for 'translation modified'.

B   *Le Bergsonisme*. Paris: PUF, 1966. *Bergsonism*, trans. Hugh Tomlinson and Barbara Habberjam. NY: Zone, 1988.

C1 *Cinéma 1: L'Image-mouvement*. Paris: Minuit, 1983. *Cinema 1: The Movement-Image*, trans. Hugh Tomlinson and Barbara Habberjam. Minneapolis: University of Minnesota Press, 1986.

C2 *Cinéma 2: L'Image-temps*. Paris: Minuit, 1985. *Cinema 2: The Time-Image*, trans. Hugh Tomlinson and Robert Galeta. Minneapolis: University of Minnesota Press, 1989.

CB 'Un Manifeste de moins'. Carmelo Bene and Gilles Deleuze, *Superpositions*. Paris: Minuit, 1979.

CC *Critique et clinique*. Paris, Minuit, 1993. *Essays Critical and Clinical,* trans. Daniel W. Smith and Michael A. Greco. Minneapolis: University of Minnesota Press, 1997.

D   *Dialogues*, avec Claire Parnet [1977]. Paris: Flammarion, 'Champs' 1996. *Dialogues*, trans. Hugh Tomlinson and Barbara Habberjam. NY: Columbia University Press, 1987.

DI *L'Ile déserte et autres texts: Textes et entretiens 1953–1974*. Ed. David Lapoujade. Paris: Minuit, 2002. *Desert Islands and Other Texts 1953–1974*, trans. Michael Taormina. Cambridge: Semiotext(e), 2004.

DR *Différence et répétition*. Paris: PUF, 1968. *Difference and Repetition*, trans. Paul Patton. NY: Columbia University Press, 1994.

EP *L'Idée d'expression dans la philosophie de Spinoza*. Paris: Minuit, 1968. *Expressionism in Philosophy: Spinoza*, trans. Martin Joughin. NY: Zone, 1990.

ES *Empirisme et subjectivité*. Paris: PUF, 1953. *Empiricism and Subjectivity*, trans. Constantin Boundas. NY: Columbia University Press, 1991.

FB *Francis Bacon: Logique de la sensation*, vol. 1. Paris: Editions de la Différence, 1981. *Francis Bacon: The Logic of Sensation*, trans. Daniel W. Smith. London: Continuum, 2003.

FC   *Foucault*. Paris: Minuit, 1986. *Foucault*, trans. Seán Hand. Minneapolis: University of Minnesota Press, 1988.

KP   *La Philosophie critique de Kant*. Paris: PUF, 1963. *Kant's Critical Philosophy*, trans. Hugh Tomlinson and Barbara Habberjam. Minneapolis: University of Minnesota Press 1984.

LB   *Le Pli: Leibniz et le baroque*. Paris: Minuit, 1988. *The Fold: Leibniz and the Baroque*, trans. Tom Conley. Minneapolis: University of Minnesota Press, 1993.

LS   *Logique du sens* Paris: Minuit, 1969. *The Logic of Sense*, trans. Mark Lester with Charles Stivale. NY: Columbia University Press, 1990.

N   *Pourparlers, 1972–1990.*. Paris: Minuit, 1990. *Negotiations*, trans. Martin Joughin. NY: Columbia University Press, 1995.

NP   *Nietzsche et la philosophie*. Paris: PUF, 1962. *Nietzsche and Philosophy*, trans. Hugh Tomlinson. Minneapolis: University of Minnesota Press, 1983.

PI   *Pure Immanence: Essays on a Life*, trans. Anne Boyman. NY: Zone, 2001.

PS   *Proust et les signes* [1964]. Paris: PUF, 1976 (fourth edition). *Proust and Signs*, trans. Richard Howard. London: Continuum, 2000.

PV   *Périclès et Verdi. La Philosophie de François Châtelet*. Paris: Minuit, 1988.

RF   *Deux Régimes de fous. Textes et entretiens 1975–1995*, ed. David Lapoujade. Paris: Minuit, 2003.

SM   *Présentation de Sacher-Masoch*. Paris: Minuit, 1967. *Masochism: An Interpretation of Coldness and Cruelty*, trans. Jean McNeil. NY: Zone, 1989.

SP   *Spinoza: philosophie pratique* [1970]. Paris: Minuit, 1981. *Spinoza: Practical Philosophy*, trans. Robert Hurley. San Francisco: City Light Books, 1988.

With Félix Guattari

AO   *L'Anti-Oedipe. Capitalisme et schizophrénie*. Paris: Minuit, 1972. *Anti-Oedipus. Capitalism and Schizophrenia*, trans. Robert Hurley, Mark Seem and Helen R. Lane. Minneapolis: University of Minnesota Press, 1977.

K   *Kafka: pour une littérature mineure*. Paris: Minuit, 1975. *Kafka: For a Minor Literature*, trans. Dana Polan. Minneapolis: University of Minnesota Press, 1986.

TP   *Mille plateaux. Capitalisme et schizophrénie*. Paris: Minuit, 1980. *A Thousand Plateaus. Capitalism and Schizophrenia*, trans. Brian Massumi. Minneapolis: University of Minnesota Press, 1986.

WP   *Qu'est-ce que la philosophie?* Paris: Minuit, 1991. *What is Philosophy?*, trans. Hugh Tomlinson and Graham Burchell. NY: Columbia University Press, 1994.

Introduction

'Rather than repeat what a philosopher says, the history of philosophy has to say what he must have taken for granted, what he didn't say but is nonetheless present in what he did say.'[1]

This book aims to go right to the heart of Deleuze's philosophy. It seeks to isolate and make sense of the main idea that informs virtually all his work. It's meant to be neither an introductory reader's guide nor a comprehensive monograph; rather, on the basis of a single presumption, it will try to chart one broadly consistent course through his project.

Although it may have some complicated implications, this presumption is a very simple one. Deleuze presumes that being is creativity. Creativity is what there is and it creates all that there can be. Individual facets of being are differentiated as so many distinct acts of creation. Every biological or social configuration is a creation, and so is every sensation, statement or concept. All these things are creations in their own right, immediately, and not merely on account of their interactions with other things. The merely relative differences that may exist or arise between created things stem from a deeper, more fundamental power of creative *differing*. 'Differentiation is never a negation but a creation, difference is never negative but essentially positive and creative' (B, 101).

We can only make sense of any given activity, says Deleuze, 'in terms of what it creates and its mode of creation'.[2] This is a principle that Deleuze will apply to the activity of living (the creation of ways of life) and the activity of being (the creation of beings) as much as to the activities of painting (the creation of lines and colours), speaking (the creation of sense) or philosophy (the creation of concepts). In each case, 'truth is not to be achieved, formed or reproduced; it has to be created. There is no other truth than the creation of the New' (C2, 146–7). In each case, the activity in question is precisely that – a dynamic activity or process, rather than an entity or state. And so in each case, what is primary is always the creating rather than the created: a writing rather than the written, an expressing rather than the expressed, a conceiving rather than the conceived. The language of creative activity speaks through verbs rather than nouns.[3]

The more creative the activity, the more intensely or inventively expressive of being it becomes. For reasons that may only become fully clear towards the end of this book, Deleuze further assumes that the most creative medium of our being is a form of abstract, immediate or dematerialised thought. 'Thought is creation' and 'to think is to create – there is no other creation' (WP, 55; DR, 147). From start to finish, Deleuze affirms the creative telos of thought in terms that invite comparison with what Spinoza called the 'intellectual love of God'. The subject of such thought or love is nothing other than infinite creativity or God himself, insofar as he thinks and loves through us: our 'mind's intellectual love of God is part of the infinite love by which God loves himself'.[4] As we shall see (again for good Spinozist reasons), to claim that purely creative thought becomes abstract or immaterial is not to say that such thought is then simply empty or 'non-extended', so much as liberated from any constituent relation to anything external to itself. Purely creative thought will proceed on the model of what Deleuze calls an 'abstract line', a line that traces a trajectory whose development or becoming is indifferent to any already constituted forms or shapes, whose creative flight is free from any territorial constraint. A thinking that proceeds independently of any reference to or mediation through a world or reality external to itself will prove to be our most adequate means of expressing an absolutely creative being or force.

Almost every aspect of Deleuze's philosophy is caught up with the consequences of this initial correlation of being, creativity and thought. Roughly speaking, it implies: (a) that all existent things or processes exist in just one way, as so many distinct acts of creation or so many individual *creations*; (b) that these creations are themselves aspects of a limitless and consequently singular creative power, a power that is most adequately expressed in the medium of pure thought; (c) that every creating gives rise to a deriva-tive *creature* or created thing, whose own power or creativity is limited by its material organisation, its situation, its actual capacities and relations with other creatures, and so on; (d) that the main task facing any such creature is to loosen and then dissolve these limitations in order to become a more adequate or immaterial vehicle for that virtual creating which alone individuates it. In other words, the main task facing a creature capable of thought is to learn how to think. In the process, our task is nothing less than to develop mechanisms 'that liberate man from the plane or level that is proper to him, in order to make him a creator, adequate to the whole movement of creation' (B, 111).

Deleuze's fundamental idea, in short, is that if being is creativity, it can only fully *become* so through the tendential evacuation of all actual or creaturely mediation.

This terminology – creation, creatings, creatures, and so on – is not Deleuze's own. Although it may quickly become repetitive, such repetition is hard if not impossible to avoid: the real challenge in writing about Deleuze's philosophy lies not in the remarkable diversity of materials that he considers but in the monotony of the underlying logic he invokes to understand them. The use of a recurrent set of terms may at least help, I hope, to distinguish between superficial and fundamental levels of consistency in Deleuze's work. It may also help us to consider anew various concepts and notions (rhizome, assemblage, difference, deterritorialisation, body without organs, schizophre-nia, the virtual...) that, in the recent proliferation of critical work on or around Deleuze, have become casually familiar while often remaining unhelpfully arcane. More impor-tantly, it should help formulate an argument about the overall orientation of his project – about what Deleuze 'didn't say but is nonetheless present in what he did say'.

Deleuze has most often been read as a philosopher who explores the material convolution of the world, who delights in the invention of mechanical assemblages, the science of complex multiplicities, the exuberant fertility of the social body, the tangled trajectories of cultural or political difference. The present book offers a very different understanding of his work. It will argue that Deleuze's philosophy is best described as an exercise in creative *indiscernment*, an effort to subtract the dynamics of creation from the mediation of the created. Deleuze certainly pays careful attention to the mechanics of material or actual creation, the ways in which creatural structures are consolidated, administered, represented, and so on – but he explores these things only in order to invent suitably targeted means of escaping them. His affirmation of absolute and immanent creativity certainly blocks any invocation of a transcendent 'creator', but it also implies a philosophy that seeks to escape any mediation through the categories of subjectivity, history and the world. At the limit, we'll see that *purely* creative processes can only take place in a wholly virtual dimension and must operate at a literally infinite speed.

What is really at stake in Deleuze's work, therefore, is not some sort of enhanced creatural mobility, a set of techniques that might enable more supple or more fruitful modes of actual interaction. What matters is instead the redemptive re-orientation of any particular creature towards its own dissolution. Rather than a philosopher of nature, history or the world, rather than any sort of 'fleshy materialist', Deleuze is most appropriately read as a spiritual, redemptive or subtractive thinker, a thinker preoccupied with the mechanics of *dis*-embodiment and *de*-materialisation. Deleuze's philosophy is oriented by lines of flight that lead out of the world; though not other-worldly, it is *extra*-worldly.

Deleuze's work thus proceeds in keeping with Nietzsche's prescription of a 'constant self-overcoming': 'to become what one is, one must not have the faintest notion *what* one is'.[5] Any particular creature can reorient itself in line with the virtual creating that it expresses through a series of transformations or 'becomings' directed towards what Deleuze presents as their exclusive telos: their becoming imperceptible. The value of any particular becoming (woman, animal, molecule…) varies with the degree that it acts 'to the benefit of an unformed matter of deterritorialised flux', the degree to which it carries us beyond the limits of perception, meaning and form.[6] The 'imperceptible is the immanent end of becoming, its cosmic formula'.[7] Only by becoming imperceptible can an actual individual become fully adequate to the virtual creating to which its very being attests. Beyond the organic limitations of an actual living being, 'becoming imperceptible is Life, "without cessation or condition"'. To use a metaphor adapted from Deleuze's reading of Beckett, the imperceptible subject of such a life comes to float like a cork, helpless but serene, upon a tempestuous ocean of pure movement. Abandoned to the 'cosmic and spiritual lapping' of this sea, such a subject 'no longer moves, but is in an element that moves' (CC, 26). Like all of the writers that Deleuze admires, Beckett knows that 'the aim of writing', its 'final enterprise', is a 'becoming-imperceptible'. Beckett knows that in order 'to create […] one has to lose one's identity, one has to disappear, to become unknown' (D, 45).

We will have to distinguish, as carefully as possible, such disappearing or becoming-imperceptible from annihilation pure and simple. Despite some illuminating points of convergence, Deleuze's counter-actualisation shouldn't be confused with negative processes like those that Simone Weil calls 'decreation' or Walter Benjamin 'mortification'.[8] Nevertheless, the subtractive orientation of Deleuze's philosophy is decisive. The pivotal question – how, as creatures, 'can we rid ourselves of ourselves?' (C1, 66) – finds an answer in the promise of

> imperceptibility, indiscernibility, and impersonality – the three virtues. To reduce oneself to an abstract line, a trait, in order to find one's zone of indiscernibility with other traits, and in this way enter the haecceity and impersonality of the creator. One is then like grass: one has made the whole world into a becoming because one has suppressed in oneself everything that prevents us from slipping between things (TP, 279–80).

In most of Deleuze's otherwise varied discussions (of Spinoza, Nietzsche, Bergson, Proust, Bacon, Masoch, cinema…) what is at issue is almost always a variation on this same basic sequence. For obvious reasons, the inventions of art and science are especially suited to Deleuze's conception of things, and it's not surprising that readers keen to stress the contemporary relevance of Deleuze's work tend to stress his approach to these and related topics. It's with good reason that Deleuze is now widely read by students in all branches of artistic practice, and theorists of science from Prigogine and Stengers to De Landa and Massumi have long recognised the compatibility of his differential ontology with the unabashedly speculative or 'acritical' metaphysics that underlie some recent contributions to complexity theory (a theory dedicated to tracking the unpredictable, non-linear emergence of self-ordering trajectories and 'dissipative structures' from within fields marked by turbulence, disequilibrium, delocalised resonances, and so on).[9] But preoccupation with the recent and the contemporary, may distract attention from what are clearly the most important paradigms of creation for Deleuze, namely ontology and cosmology. It is not just the work of art or science that is creative. It is all of being that is creative, in itself. Through most of the history of philosophy, of course, creative ontologies have been developed within explicitly theological frameworks, frameworks that rely on some sort of transcendent creator or God. Deleuze certainly doesn't acknowledge any transcendent idea of God. Nevertheless, in a number of important ways his work is consistent with the general logic of a cosmic pantheism, i.e. the notion that the universe and all it contains is a facet of a singular and absolute creative power (cf. EP, 333).

More specifically, I will argue that the logic of Deleuze's work tends to proceed broadly in line with a *theophanic* conception of things, whereby every individual process or thing is conceived as a manifestation or expression of God or a conceptual equivalent of God (pure creative potential, force, energy, life…). Deleuze is not the only French philosopher of his generation to think along these lines; he shares some limited though suggestive common ground with his contemporaries Henry Corbin, Michel Henry, Christian Jambet and Clément Rosset, among others.[10]

There is clearly nothing specifically contemporary about such a logic, however. On the contrary, the basic parameters of a philosophy that seeks to align itself with a singular principle of absolute creativity are very ancient. As is well known, Deleuze draws much of his inspiration from Bergson and Spinoza. But well before Bergson and even before Spinoza, the essential distinctions at issue were already clearly established in the work of a radical theophanist like John Scottus Eriugena (himself working in a Neoplatonic tradition that goes back to Pseudo-Dionysius and Plotinus).[11] Adapting the terms of Eriugena's fourfold division of nature, we might say that any singular principle of radical creativity will entail the distinction of: an uncreated and consequently unknowable or unthinkable *creator*; the immediate and adequate expression of this creator in multiple self-revelations or *creatings* (which are both created and creative); the various *creatures* (created but not creative) that lend material weight to these creatings; and finally, a virtual state beyond creaturely perception and distinction, to which whatever is eternally creative about these creatures is destined eventually to return. As Eriugena explains, if 'every creature visible and invisible can be called a theophany' or manifesting of God,[12] and if God *qua* creator can be thought only as nothing, then only nothing separates God from his creation. This is why, he goes on, 'we ought not to understand God and the creature as two things distinct from one another but as one and the same: the creature, by subsisting, is in God, and God, by manifesting himself, in a marvellous and ineffable manner creates himself in the creature'. Understood in this way, God not only 'becomes in all things all things', he 'dwells nowhere but in the nature of men and angels, to whom alone it is given to contemplate the Truth'.[13] God expresses himself in the infinite multiplicity of his creatings, God *is* only in these creatings, but these creatings remain expressive of a single creative force, 'an indivisible One, which is Principle as well as Cause and End'.[14] The Sufi philosopher Ibn al-'Arabi will arrive at much the same conclusion: 'that which there is in reality is the Creator-creature, creature in one dimension, creator in another, but the concrete whole is a single Whole'.[15] So will Meister Eckhart, when he tries to see all creatures in God and God in all creatures. And so will Spinoza: God expresses himself in all things, and all things are an expression of God.

For the same reason, the simplicity or singularity at issue here must always be distinguished from mere uniformity or homogeneity. Absolute creation involves immediate (or non-relational) forms of individuation, precisely, as opposed to both relational or dialectical forms of individuation on the one hand and sheer extinction or de-individuation on the other. A singular creative force *is* nothing other than the multiplication of singular creatings, each of which is originally and uniquely individual in its own right. The essential point is that such individuation does not itself depend on mediation through the categories of representation, objectivity, history or the world. An individual is only truly unique, according to this conception of things, if its individuation is the manifestation of an unlimited individuating power.

More crudely: you are only really an individual if God (or something like God) makes you so.

Participation in absolute creation is not the result, then, of a process of approximation or progression. It is not conditioned by trends in the world, or mediated by a complex dialectic. We *are* and have always been creation, and our awareness of being this relies, in the end, on nothing more (or less) than an original or pre-original affirmation, an affirmation which opens the field of its subsequent effects as a series of immediate implications. Preoccupation with the world as such, let alone a concern with the orderly representation of the things of the world, serves only to inhibit any such affirmation. Rather than seek to elaborate rational rules for the consistent representation *of* reality, Deleuze sees the fundamental task of philosophy as exclusively conditioned by our immediate participation *in* reality. Before he declares his well-known antipathy to Hegel, Deleuze seeks to confirm Bergson's break with the neo-Kantian configuration of modern philosophy. (In this sense it is indeed Kant who figures as the genuine antagonist of Deleuze's philosophy; Hegel is better conceived as its most dangerous *rival*). Rather than represent the world in a reliable way, Deleuze maintains that our real concern is to 'know how the individual would be able to transcend his form and his syntactical link with a world' so as to become the transparent vessel for that 'non-organic life of things which burns us [...,] which is the divine part in us, the spiritual relationship in which we are alone with God as light' (LS, 178; C1, 54). As we shall see, in many ways Deleuze's project resonates with and renews that 'Oriental intuition' which Hegel found at work in Spinoza's philosophy, 'according to which everything finite appears as something merely transient and ephemeral' – that 'oriented' conception of the absolute conceived as 'the light which illumines itself'.[16]

There are important differences, of course, between the transcendent conception of creation presumed by Eriugena and other Neoplatonists and the fully immanent conception affirmed by Deleuze, after Spinoza. Deleuze often insists on these differences. Neoplatonism orients the whole of creation towards an unknowable creator beyond creation. An immanent approach assumes, on the contrary, that creativity is only absolute or unlimited if it saturates the whole of being with no remainder. No more than Spinoza or Bergson before him, Deleuze leaves no place for an inscrutable creator-God who acts at an unthinkable distance from his creation. Needless to say, the notion of creation at issue in the present book is not a version of the transcendent 'creationism' that Deleuze attacks in his book on Spinoza so much as a reworking of the process that Deleuze himself describes and affirms in terms of 'expression'. But as we shall see, the affirmation of an expressive or creative immanence does not so much eliminate the question of transcendence as distribute it throughout creation as a whole: rather than reserved for that which exceeds creation or orients it towards its limit, an immanent conception of creativity will assign the task of self-transcendence to its every creature. Every actual creature will have as its particular task the development of its own counter-actualisation or self-transcendence, the process whereby it may become an adequate vehicle for the creating which sustains and transforms it.

I will make occasional reference to such theophanic logics to help explain various stages of the argument developed in this book, starting with a general overview of Deleuze's conception of the conditions of creation in my first chapter. The remainder of the book is organised in line with the broadly redemptive trajectory of Deleuze's own work. After a review of the mechanics of individuation or differentiation in Chapter 2, Chapter 3 considers the constraints and delusions that characterise actual (or creatural) existence. Chapters 4 and 5 go on to explore the ways that a creature might succeed in transcending these constraints, first from within the creatural dimension, and subsequently through direct participation in creatings as such. The sixth and final chapter considers Deleuze's account of philosophy as the most adequate form of such participation.

To insist in this way on the logic of creation as the primary if not exclusive focus of Deleuze's work is undeniably to simplify aspects of his thought. My goal in this book is not to engage in the detailed analysis of particular sequences or problems in Deleuze's texts, but to characterise the dominant movement of his philosophy as a whole. For the sake of clarity and economy this characterisation will pay little attention to the complexities of context or the occasional inconsistencies that must accompany the development of so large and wide-ranging a body of work. Despite these shortcomings, I think it's fair to say that this approach remains broadly in line with Deleuze's own way of reading other philosophers. Like Leibniz or Bergson, Deleuze assumes that every philosopher is animated by just one fundamental problem, and that to read a work of philosophy 'does not consist in concluding from the idea of a preceding condition the idea of the following condition, but in grasping the effort or tendency by which the following condition itself ensues from the preceding "by means of a natural force"'.[17] Every 'philosophy's power is measured by the concepts it creates', 'concepts that impose a new set of divisions on things and actions'. On the basis of the concepts they create, philosophers 'subordinate and submit things to a question in such a way that, in this forced and constrained submission, things reveal to us an essence, a nature'.[18]

The main virtue of the question to which Deleuze's project will itself be submitted in the following pages may be to reveal in a somewhat unexpected way the degree to which his work, far from engaging in a description or transformation of the world, instead seeks to escape it. The Deleuze that has long fascinated and troubled me is neither a worldly nor even a 'relational' thinker. If (after Marx and Darwin) materialism involves acceptance of the fact that actual or worldly processes inflect the course of both natural and human history, then Deleuze may not be a materialist thinker either. As Deleuze presents it, the destiny of thought will not be fundamentally affected by the mediation of society, history or the world; although Deleuze equates being with the activity of creation, he orients this activity towards a contemplative and immaterial abstraction. More than a hundred and fifty years after Marx urged us to change rather than contemplate the world, Deleuze, like so many of his philosophical contemporaries, effectively recommends instead that we settle for the alternative choice.

The real preoccupation of this book concerns the value of this advice.

1

The Conditions of Creation

'Whatever exists expresses the nature or essence of God in a certain and determinate way […]. To express is always to sing the glory of God.'[1]

Deleuze equates being with unlimited creativity. This means that all actual beings exist as facets of a single productive energy or force. An infinitely creative force expresses itself through an infinitely differentiated creation. In the next chapter we'll look at Deleuze's account of how such differentiation works; this preliminary chapter considers some of the general implications of this account and some of the assumptions that lie behind it. It will also introduce a couple of the main ideas that Deleuze adapts from his two most important predecessors, Benedict de Spinoza (1632–77) and Henri Bergson (1859–1941).

The next few pages will introduce six of the most significant aspects of Deleuze's ontology. Deleuze conceives of being as univocal (and inclusive), accessible (or intuitive), continuous (or indivisible), intensive (and vital), hierarchical (and quantitative), and as virtual (or unpresentable). To go through these aspects in sequence may facilitate the work of exposition; readers should remember, however, that they apply all at once, as parallel consequences of one inaugural affirmation.

I

The first and most far-reaching implication of Deleuze's ontology, of his equation of being and creativity, is that everything that is *is* in the same sense or way. If all is creation, this means first and foremost that there is only one way of being. Deleuze's work begins with the assertion that 'there has only ever been one ontological proposition: Being is univocal'. Being is univocal rather than equivocal or polyvocal. A univocal ontology declares that all beings 'express' their being with a single voice, and according to Deleuze, 'from Parmenides to Heidegger it is the same voice which is taken up […], a single and same voice for the whole thousand-voiced multiple, a single and same Ocean for all the drops, a single clamour of Being for all beings' (DR, 35, 304). Thoughts and things, organisms and ideas, machines and sensations – they all are in one and the same sense of the word. All individuated beings contribute to one and the same activity and articulation of being.

There is nothing obvious about this assertion. Many philosophers have adopted the opposite point of departure, and assumed an essential difference between kinds or ways of being – for instance, a difference between the way things appear and the way they really are, between the literal and the figurative, the temporal and the eternal, the contingent and the necessary, and so on. In classical philosophy and theology, the most important of these assumed differences separated the real from the ideal, the human from the divine, the mortal from the immortal. The big question that obsessed so much of pre-modern European philosophy concerns the relation between God and humanity. If the human is created in the image or likeness of God, what is the nature of this likeness? How distant or different are we from the power that creates us? Do sin and mortality condemn us to an irreducible alienation from God? What kind of reconciliation are we entitled to expect, and what kinds of institutions or practices might be required for its pursuit?

In the scholastic terms in which the distinction between univocal and equivocal conceptions of being was hammered out (for instance in the argument between Duns Scotus and Thomas Aquinas), a univocal conception of being simply meant that there was no ontological difference between the human and the divine. Univocity means there is no absolute difference between the creator and his creatures. The human is not then 'like' God in the normal, analogous sense of the term. The human cannot exist in the image of God, if this means a figurative distance from God; rather, human and God must *be* in precisely the same way. The human is simply a facet or mode of God. God is all there is, or inversely, there is nothing distinctive, nothing separate or eminent about God. The divine voice is the only voice there is, and so 'the philosopher and the pig, the criminal and the saint' all contribute to one and the same indivisible song. 'Each one chooses his pitch or his tone, perhaps his words, but the tune is certainly the same, and under all the words, in every possible tone, and in every pitch, the same tra-la-la' (DR, 83–4).

Along with theophanists like Meister Eckhart and Jacob Boehme, it was above all Spinoza who developed a fully univocal conception of being. It's because he sees in Spinoza's work the most uncompromising assertion of univocity that Deleuze considers him to be the veritable 'Christ' and 'prince of philosophers', 'philosophy incarnate'.[2] Spinoza's rationalism was often denounced (before being applauded) as atheist, since it acknowledges no privileged place for a God as separate from a universe that he creates and directs. Spinoza evacuates any place for a transcendent conception of God, and with it, any obscurely providential interpretation of history or of the human condition. However, Spinoza's philosophy can just as well be read as pantheist or at least 'panentheist', in the sense that it equates all being with being in God. Deleuze himself is perfectly happy to embrace both aspects of this Spinozist inheritance. Although he will denounce every avatar of a transcendent God, one of the reasons why Deleuze privileges Spinoza over other (less emphatically) univocal thinkers like Scotus or Leibniz is that his Spinoza fully 'accepts the truly philosophical "danger" of immanence and pantheism implicit in the notion of [univocal] expression. Indeed he throws in his lot with that danger' – as does Deleuze after him (EP, 333; cf. 67). Deleuze's own atheism does not so much secularise a bleakly disenchanted reality as intensify or indeed *resurrect* it. He certainly annuls the difference between God and world but he does this in favour of God, not world. More precisely, what he annuls is rather the world's own capacity to negate God, to say no to God, to hold God at a critical or interpretative distance from itself. Here again he follows Spinoza's lead, at least insofar as Spinoza can be read as a philosopher who refuses to 'distinguish God from the world' and who thus 'maintains that there is no such thing as what is known as the world', that left to itself 'the world has no true reality'.[3]

What then is Spinoza's essential insight? Like that of Deleuze, Spinoza's philosophy is animated by a presumption that is quite literally simplicity itself: there is only one reality, one substance (or God), and everything that is *is* or rather acts as a modifying of this one substance.

> Whatever is, is in God, and nothing can be or be conceived without God [...] From God's supreme power, or infinite nature, infinitely many things in infinitely many modes, that is, all things, have necessarily flowed, or always follow, by the same necessity and in the same way as from the nature of a triangle it follows, from eternity and to eternity, that its three angles are equal to two right angles.[4]

God or substance is an infinitely powerful or creative being, one that modifies, expresses or invents itself in an infinitely multiple variety of ways. The more creative such a modification or expression becomes, the 'more reality or perfection' it will have, the more powerfully it will tend to exist and the more adequately it will express the sole cause of all existence. This cause is again God, affirmed as perfectly self-causing or self-creating. God is the infinite cause at work in every finite cause. As Deleuze explains, 'finite beings do not exist and are not preserved by their own power, but are dependent for their existence and preservation on a being able to preserve itself and to exist through itself. Thus the power by which a finite being exists, is preserved, and acts, is the power of God himself' (EP, 89–91). Everything that exists exists as a more or less active, more or less powerful or expressive facet of a single, unlimited power of existing and acting.

Deleuze's work resounds with echoes of its univocal orientation. If all that exists exists in the same way, then there can be only one physics of creation, a single order of fully immanent causation. 'There is only one matter', 'matter equals energy', and there is no ontological distinction between 'matter and life'.[5] There is 'only one kind of production, the production of the real' (AO, 32), such that any supplementary distinctions between real, symbolic and imaginary, for instance, must themselves be more apparent than real. Rather than supervise the suitably measured representation of appearances, Deleuze orients his philosophy in line with that immediate, overwhelming participation in reality which in *Anti-Oedipus* he and Guattari attribute to the figure of the schizophrenic – a participation which 'brings the schizo as close as possible to matter, to an intense, living centre of matter', 'closest to the beating heart of reality, to an intense point identical with the production of the real'.[6]

Everything is real and everything does what it *is* in the same way. Once they have been suitably destratified or deterritorialised, chemical reactions combine with signs, genes with words, passions with electrons. All creatings proceed within a shared and infinitely ramified plane of consistency, and the plane upon which they come to consist is a plane marked by 'the abolition of all metaphor; all that consists is real' (TP, 69; cf. K, 24). Deleuze adheres in this way to Parmenides' principle that 'thinking and being are one and the same' (WP, 38). Thought and nature will co-exist as parallel expressions of a single plane of consistency or a single line of variation.

II

A second and equally Spinozist implication of Deleuze's univocal ontology concerns the sort of knowledge it is meant to enable. What can we know of beings, of the being of beings? What can we know of beings as they really are? The paradigmatic version of this metaphysical question was again: what can we know of God? How might we interpret the divine design, or decipher the signs of a divine will? What kind of access might we have to the mind of God? Immanuel Kant prescribed a new direction for philosophy when he dismissed these and related questions as beyond the legitimate exercise of reason. Kant says that although we may occasionally act in keeping with assumptions about a divine providence, as if we are endowed with an unconditional freedom and an immortal soul, nevertheless we can know nothing of either this freedom, this immortality, or this divinity. Since according to Kant the only reliable knowledge we have is of the way objects appear to us, since the only reality that we can claim to know is the one that conforms to the way our minds seem to work, so then we can have no immediate intellectual intuition of any noumenal domain beyond appearance. Kant led much of modern philosophy to adopt an essentially *critical* stance, one that rejects direct claims to a God-like power of thinking as incoherent, and much of post-Kantian philosophy has busied itself with the elaboration of internally consistent rules for the way we should represent to ourselves a universe whose essential reality we assume to be forever out of our reach.

By contrast, the most influential ontologist of the twentieth century, Martin Heidegger, revived the old metaphysical questions, but exclusively *as questions*. He confirmed that the answer to the question – what can we know of being (or God)? – is always nothing, insofar as our answer forgets the difference between a being and the activity of being. We can know no-thing of being. We know nothing of being, insofar as we seek to know being as created rather than creative, as a being rather than as be*ing* itself. But rather than dismiss such questions as Kant does, Heidegger preserves and privileges their inexhaustible interrogative power. The questioning of being is itself the most profound exercise of thought, and promises a boundless access to its essentially mysterious domain. Being veils and unveils. Every 'unconcealing' of being proceeds together with its concealing. From here we are only a short step away from the explicit revalorisation of transcendence, an affirmation of being as altogether beyond our knowledge of it, or even the affirmation of a guiding principle – such as Emmanuel

Levinas' assertion of an infinite responsibility to the infinitely other – that is altogether other than and altogether higher than being itself.

For all their differences, what Kant and Heidegger share (along with thinkers as different as Wittgenstein and Adorno) is a refusal of traditional metaphysical claims, i.e. claims that we might have an adequate conceptual knowledge of the essential nature of things, or that, in theological terms, we might have direct access to the mind of God. Together with both Spinoza and Bergson, by contrast, Deleuze lays claim to exactly this sort of knowledge. Against Kant and the neo-Kantian tradition, Deleuze always affirms 'Spinozism's most radical thesis', the thesis of 'absolute rationalism, based on the adequation of our understanding to absolute knowledge' – the thesis that presumes the 'total intelligibility of God, the key of the total intelligibility of things'.[7]

The authorisation for such knowledge comes directly from our preliminary affirmation of ontological univocity. If we are in the same way as God, if we are as God is and think as God thinks, then whatever we genuinely know of God we know immediately and adequately, rather than approximately. Our knowledge of God, or of being, or indeed of anything at all, will not be a matter of representation or figuration, or at least not a representation that would somehow 'be' in a different sense from the thing represented. What we know or think, we know as it is in itself. According to a univocal or neo-Spinozist conception of things, God (or the creative equivalent of God) does not stand beyond a universe whose inhabitants are thereby condemned to puzzle over the enigma of his transcendence. When we truly think it is God who thinks through us. If Deleuze rejects the Cartesian cogito as a viable foundation of thought it is because he affirms, instead, a Spinozist *cogitor* or being-thought.

Against Kant, Deleuze will thus assume and renew the self-evident legitimacy of immediate intellectual intuition. Since he everywhere assumes our ability directly to see or conceive the literal reality of things, to grasp the immediate nature of things, Deleuze's work is best read as a renewal or radicalisation of the affirmative naturalism he celebrates in the work of Spinoza and Leibniz in particular. The great achievement of these most uncompromising rationalists was to reverse the critical devaluation of reality or nature almost as soon as it began, and by doing so, to lay claim 'to the deepest things, the "arcana"', via an intuition or insight that 'makes man commensurate with God' (EP, 322; cf. LS, 278–9). Deleuze's own philosophy is less distinctively modern or critical so much as enthusiastically neo-Spinozist. The telos of Deleuze's philosophy will be a version of what Spinoza called a perfectly sufficient or 'intuitive knowledge' of singular things, i.e. an insight that 'proceeds from an adequate idea of the formal essence of certain attributes of God to the adequate knowledge of the essence of things'.[8]

III

Now univocity in no sense implies uniformity. On the contrary: univocity is affirmed as the basis and medium for a primordial and unlimited differentiation. For something to be at all is for it to be involved and thus consumed in a process whereby it becomes something different or new. 'Being is alteration' (DI, 25). A third implication of the assertion that all is creation concerns, therefore, the properly fundamental status of this creativity as such. Deleuze's ontology is meant to revitalise or re-energise being, to endow it with a primary and irreducible dynamism. 'Everything I've written', as Deleuze affirmed in 1988, 'is vitalistic, at least I hope it is.'[9] Being is alive, because it *is* living. Being is inventive, because it *is* invention. Being is innovative, because being innovates; being is differentiated, because being differentiates. Being and differing are one and the same.

What grounds or causes these processes, in Deleuze as much as in Spinoza, is simply the affirmation of an unconditionally self-causing power as such. What differs is a power of absolute self-differing. As Michael Hardt explains, *'causa sui* is the essential pillar that supports being'. Because it figures as self-causing, being can be affirmed as an infinite 'power to exist and produce. All discussions of power, productivity, and causality in Deleuze, as in Spinoza, refer us back to this ontological foundation.'[10] There is no more general, generic or abstract condition behind creation, just as there is no more primordial sameness behind difference. Vital or creative difference itself is primary.

Readers who search through Deleuze's work for some more primordial concept beneath the creation of difference, some sort of enabling or transcendental condition of creation, will not find it. Deleuze's inaugural move is precisely to absolutise difference, to 'raise difference to the absolute', such that 'difference is behind everything, but behind difference there is nothing'.[11] As early as his first book, on Hume, Deleuze had realised that 'the fundamental principle of empiricism, the principle of difference', involves the indivisibility of our most elementary ideas. 'What is essential in an idea is not that it represents something but rather that it is indivisible', and for that very reason primary or unconditional (ES, 90). Since it is primary and indivisible, such an idea will allow us to think an 'eternally positive differential multiplicity' (DR, 288). The idea of difference, which is to say the idea of *differing* ideas, will allow us to think distinct creative trajectories, subtracted from the stability of any created or constituted identity and without reference to anything other than the being or creating of this trajectory itself. The production or creation of difference is what there is. It is precisely creation that, self-enabling or self-creative, itself enables everything it creates. The only condition for our understanding of creation, as we shall see, is thus its affirmation pure and simple. The absolutely primary principle, the ultimate ground of Deleuze's groundless metaphysics, is thus simply that 'power or "will" which engenders affirmation and the difference in affirmation' (DR, 55tm). From this perspective, being is not merely the object of affirmation nor affirmation a power of being, but rather 'affirmation itself is being, being is solely affirmation in all its power' – precisely because 'to affirm is to create, rather than to bear or to endure' (NP, 186tm).

This is what was at stake in the anti-Cartesian naturalism that Deleuze finds and applauds in Spinoza. By conceiving of nature in strictly mathematical and mechanical terms, Descartes had stripped it of 'any virtuality or potentiality, any immanent power, any inherent being'. Descartes invested genuine being 'outside Nature, in a subject which thinks it and a God who creates it' while remaining external to it (EP, 227); Descartes thereby prepared the way for Kant and the critical turn of modern philosophy. What Spinoza–Deleuze affirm, by contrast, is a power that differs, creates and thinks itself, immediately. Such power must operate in a purely immanent manner, to the exclusion of any transcendent separation of cause from effect or creator from creating (EP, 322). An immanent cause stands in relation to its effect as a creating stands to the creature it sustains. 'A cause is immanent [...] when its effect is "immanate" [*immané*] in the cause, rather than emanating from it. What defines an immanent cause is that its effect is in it – in it, of course, as in something else, but still being and remaining in it.'[12] In keeping with the univocity of being, though the created depends upon the creating as something that produces and thus exceeds it, both belong to one and the same order of self-causing creation.

This is also the crux of Deleuze's argument with Aristotle, which serves as the prelude to one of the most original and demanding of his books, *Difference and Repetition* (1968). By the Aristotelian criteria of representation, two terms differ when their difference depends on something else, i.e. on something that they have in common. A differing as such then ceases to be primary, ceases to proceed in itself; difference loses its immanence. Two terms can now only be said to differ if they can first be said to agree in something else; terms can differ in species only if they first belong to the same genus, and they can differ in number only if they belong to the same species. It is on the basis of their common being-human, for instance, that we can say that one person (or gender, culture, community...) differs from another. Different terms are different because they can be compared or related, i.e. because they share an underlying identity. Difference that is either too large or too small to be related can then be ruled out as incoherent. It is too large if it implies a comparison between incomparable orders of being (between the divine and the human, the astral and the sublunar); it is too small when it tries directly to distinguish indivisible objects. Aristotle's 'specific difference, therefore, in no way represents a universal [...] idea encompassing all the singularities and turnings of difference, but rather refers to a particular moment in which difference is merely reconciled with the concept in general'.[13] Against Aristotle and the whole Aristotelian legacy, Deleuze sets out to free the concept of difference from any external mediation, any subjection to the normalising channels of generality, identity, opposition, analogy and resemblance. In opposition to the Greeks, 'modern thought is born of the failure of representation, of the loss of stable identity and of the discovery of all forces that act under the representation of the identical' (DR, xix). In keeping with the general movement of such thought, Deleuze seeks 'an absolute concept of difference', one 'liberated from the condition which made difference a merely relative maximum' (DR, 33tm).. This absolute difference will be 'articulation and connection in itself; it must relate different to different *without any mediation whatsoever* by the identical, the similar, the analogous or the opposed [...]. Every object, every thing must see its own identity swallowed up in difference [...]. Difference must be shown *differing*', adequately and immediately (DR, 117, 56).

Along with Spinoza, it is above all Bergson who guides Deleuze's thinking of this point. Himself a trenchant critic of the categories of both representation and mechanism, Bergson updates an affirmative and vitalist conception of nature in suitably post-Kantian (and post-Hegelian) terms. From start to finish, Deleuze's philosophy is everywhere consistent with the point of departure he adapts from Bergson in opposition to Hegel: whereas according to Hegel any given 'thing differs with itself because it differs first with all that it is not', i.e. with all the objects to which it relates, Deleuze's Bergson affirms that a 'thing differs with itself first, immediately', on account of the 'internal explosive force' it carries within itself.[14] According to Bergson, this force, or life, is precisely the vehicle of a continuous creativity. Reality is ceaseless, indivisible movement and invention. Living creativity is self-generating and self-sustaining, driven always and everywhere by a common impulse that 'makes of the whole series of the living one single immense wave flowing over matter'.[15] Pure creativity is immaterial by definition, and so long as we 'understand by spirituality a progress to ever new creations', so then *living* should itself be understood as a purely spiritual force.[16]

Of the several things that Bergson adds to Deleuze's neo-Spinozist conception of things, the most important is a much more elaborate conception of time. Bergson's great question concerns the (ultimately paradoxical) temporality of creation as such. If Spinoza is oriented to the eternal or non-durational sufficiency of creation, Bergson is concerned with its development or evolution over time. ('An eternity that becomes' – as we'll see in Chapter 6, section IV, this is precisely what Deleuze will require of his own philosophy of time). To affirm the univocal equation of being and creation is to say that being is an enduring process or action rather than static substance or timeless thing.

> Everything is obscure in the idea of creation if we think of things which are created and a thing which creates, as we habitually do [… For] there *are* no things, there are only actions […]. God thus defined has nothing of the already made; He is unceasing life, action, freedom. Creation, so conceived, is not a mystery; we experience it in ourselves when we act freely.[17]

Again, 'everything is obscure if we confine ourselves to mere manifestations', for instance actual or organic manifestations of life. 'All becomes clear, on the contrary, if we start by a quest beyond these manifestations for Life itself', i.e. for the manifest*ing* as such.[18]

IV

The equation of being and unconditional creativity implies a univocal, adequate and immanent understanding of being. It also implies that being holds together as a sort of open whole, an 'Omnitudo' or 'unlimited One-All' (WP, 35, 38; cf. DR, 37). Once carried to the absolute, there is nothing that might qualify the activity of being or creation. There is nothing outside being in relation to which being might be. There is nothing outside reality – no second or further reality, no horizon to reality, no difference in kind between thought and thing… – that might limit what it does or is. Nothing mediates being. Difference itself doesn't apply to something other than itself, and a differing does not apply to something that would otherwise *be* the same. Being is itself differing, so Deleuzian reality is a process of immanent and infinite self-differentiation. 'Everything divides, but into itself' (AO, 76; cf. DI, 40–1).

Every dividing or creating is of course individual and distinct. Creatings are disparate, rather than totalising or integrative. Every creating is absolute, but must proceed as *an* indefinite 'local absolute'.[19] By the same token, however, every distinct creating is an aspect *of* an unlimited energy or force. 'Each thing, each being is the whole, the whole realised to a certain degree or another', or as Leibniz puts it, the infinitely differentiated 'universe is like a whole which God grasps in a single view'.[20] All existent individuals are simply so many divergent facets of one and the same creative force, variously termed desire or desiring-production, life, *élan vital*, power. Since nothing can transcend it, creative 'immanence is immanent only to itself and consequently captures everything, absorbs All-One, and leaves nothing remaining to which it could be immanent' (WP, 45).

Deleuze's whole account of differentiation thus takes as its starting point 'a unity, a simplicity [...], a virtual primordial totality' (B, 95; cf. DR, 185). It will rediscover an equally simple telos as its eventual end, when it posits the ultimate inclusion of all planes of reality within a single plane of immanence (what Deleuze and Guattari will call *the* plane of immanence), their coexistence within a single plane of consistency. As its name implies, a plane of consistency is 'a plane upon which everything is laid out, and which is like the intersection of all forms, [...] a single abstract Animal for all the assemblages that effectuate it'. Although this plane itself divides into a multiplicity of planes and processes of actualisation, nevertheless all these diverse 'planes make up only one, following the path that leads to the virtual' (or away from the actual).[21]

The assumption of unlimited creativity means, therefore, that the one must be immediately articulated with the all and vice versa. Deleuze does not displace the one in favour of the multiple so much as embrace the unity of the multiple and the internal multiplicity or differentiation of the one. 'The One expresses in a single meaning all of the multiple. Being expresses in a single sense [*sens*] all that differs' (TP, 254tm; cf. NP, 24). Creative difference is *immediately* intra- rather than inter-individual, and is powered by a force that articulates the all or whole with the instant or point. Once absolved of all extrinsic mediation, once withdrawn from any constituent relation to organic integrity or socio-psychological form, being is free to undertake creative sequences that (like Mandelbrot's self-replicating fractals) are indifferent to scale. The vital principle of Deleuze's philosophy of difference is always some version of 'a differenciator of difference which would relate, in their respective immediacy, the most universal and the most singular' (DR, 32). Within the one-all, within this singular field of absolute self-difference, merely relative differences cease to apply. Within the one-all there can be no fundamental difference between cosmic and molecular, far and near, moment and whole, instant and eternity.[22] Once they have been sufficiently uprooted from any actual constraints or territory that might contain them, the molecular and the cosmic merge in a single open movement which deploys space as such (TP, 347, 343, 327). A similar logic applies in the dimension of time. As we'll see when we come back to this point in Chapter 6, each distinct act or event of creation is adequate to the whole of creative time in its entirety and eternity; in their indivisible virtuality, they 'all form one and the same single event' (LS, 63–4). By the same token, an appropriately creative subject will 'consummate each of the states through which it passes [...] in the space of an instant'; at the limit he or she will 'consume all of universal history in a single moment [*en une fois*]' (AO, 41, 21tm). Being is, or changes, with the force of a power that creates the very medium of its changing, a power beyond all possible mediation.

So while multiplicity may sometimes appear to be the privileged if not exclusive dimension of Deleuze's ontology, we must not forget that multiplicity is always also 'the inseparable manifestation, essential transformation and constant symptom of unity. Multiplicity is the affirmation of unity' and 'the affirmation of multiplicity is itself one'.[23] What unifies difference or multiplicity is not a principle of internal sameness or order but rather the absoluteness of difference itself, its refusal of limitation or externality. Everything divides into itself, but the 'self' of infinite self-division is itself indivisible.

It is again Bergson who guides Deleuze's understanding of these things. The key to Bergson's philosophy is his insistence on the indivisible continuity of time. Bergson conceives of time as the dimension of uninterrupted creation, such that 'the duration of the universe must be one with the latitude of creation which can find place in it'.[24] As it evolved, however, indivisible living energy has given rise to forms of life – notably human beings – that themselves became capable of imposing artificial divisions upon time and life. Life is an indivisible flow, but we experience it *as if* it were divisible. In reality, time is continuous change but we tend, precisely in order to make the most of 'our' time, to divide it into measurable segments. Organisms and species are part of the same evolving surge of life, but we tend to think of them as isolated and distinct.

In this way Bergson further anticipates Deleuze's answer to the unavoidable question: if life or creation is indivisible, why then do we so stubbornly try to divide it into distinct moments, organisms or forms? Why do we tend to think of continuous actions as isolated things? Bergson answers: because it is in our own immediate interest to do so. It is useful, for the sake of our preservation or for the satisfaction of our needs, to approach the world as if it were made up of distinct moments and objects whose relationships can be measured and predicted and thus managed or controlled. Our intelligence (like our conception of utility) has evolved so as to serve our practical interests, rather than any quest for true knowledge. The way we ordinarily think is a function of how we have evolved, rather than a facet of universal evolution as such. Our evolution as conscious living beings, in other words, is precisely what encourages us to misunderstand the true nature of life. Reality is creation but the creatings that we are make us creatures of a particular kind, and precisely this creatural configuration discourages us from appreciating what we are.

Consider for a moment one of Bergson's simplest and most insistent examples, the case of physical movement. Like any aspect of reality, motion is indivisible, and though every movement is discrete, with its own beginning and end, its emergence is a facet of universal motion, an aspect of the movement of the whole. The impetus behind motion is the same as the impetus behind everything that lives: the course of any given movement 'is created in one stroke, although a certain time is required for it; and although we can divide at will the trajectory once created, we cannot divide its creation, which is an act in progress and not a thing'.[25] Properly understood, all of reality is precisely act rather than thing, production rather than product. Reality is the deployment of movings rather than a collection of moved things. What we choose to perceive and then represent of such a movement, however, is precisely a matter of our representation and not of reality itself. Movements through space *are* indivisible, but this doesn't stop us from representing them merely in terms of what they traverse, as if they were made up of discrete units of space. We tend to reduce a movement through space to the mere trajectory that it generates, since trajectories (or representations of movement) are divisible things that we can map, measure, and inflect.

Such reduction both helps us to satisfy our practical interests and frustrates our desire to understand the nature of reality. Our everyday experience, the usual data of our senses and consciousness, is well adapted to the urgencies of practical action. But if we try to ground our understanding of reality upon such data then we will only arrive at 'fictitious problems' and 'insoluble contradictions' – problems which arise, like Zeno's paradoxes, from treating something that is really indivisible as if it were composite and divisible.[26] What we conventionally call a 'fact' is not the real itself but 'an adaptation of the real to the interests of practice and to the exigencies of social life'.[27]

True philosophical insight must set out, then, not from facts or from rationalised versions of our ordinary understanding, but on the contrary, from those moments in which such understanding is suspended. Insight is never a matter of actual fact. It can begin when the pressures of practical action yield in favour of a disinterested and ultimately disembodied intuition – intuition of reality as it is in itself. Such intuition is available to anyone who literally opens their mind, by interrupting their habitual state of practical distraction. It is most dominant in those who live most creatively, those who realise that to live is simply to engage in the process of 'creating oneself endlessly'.[28] More, such self-creating is itself simply a facet of a more general, properly universal or cosmic creation. Those who realise this most profoundly – the dreamers, the artists, the philosophers, the mystics... – are precisely those people who most succeed in subordinating their personal or creatural interests to the impersonal imperatives of creation itself.

V

As this last point suggests, one thing that is emphatically *not* implied by our initial equation of being and creation is that everything is equally creative. On the contrary, all beings are indeed creative, but unequally so. 'Equal, univocal being is immediately present in everything, without mediation or intermediary [...but] things reside unequally in this equal being' (DR, 37). This inequality is determined by the proximity of any particular creating to the immeasurable maximum of pure creativity or intensity, i.e. the degree to which its creative velocity, so to speak, approaches the limit of a literally infinite or absolute speed. Every distinct creating corresponds to a certain degree of absolute creative intensity. Every given moment expresses the whole of time, but at variable degrees of compression or impoverishment. Every event or creating expresses the whole of creation, more or less inadequately. Univocity thus ensures an ultimately *quantitative* understanding of expressive difference. Every creating is more or less adequately expressive of that immanent whole in which 'everything coexists with itself, except for the differences of level' (B, 100). All existent individuals actualise varying degrees of a single virtual force or differing, a single abstract animal or machine (TP, 46). Or rather, since being is difference, since to be is to differ, so then each act of being is a differing degree of difference: strictly speaking 'there are no differences of degree in being, but only degrees of difference itself' (DI, 49tm).

In principle, therefore, apparent or qualitative differences between creatures should always be reducible to quantitative differences between creatings. As a general rule, 'quality is nothing but difference in quantity', 'quality is nothing other than contracted quantity'.[29] In any given field, it should be possible in principle to rank the various degrees of intensity that it contains. The field made up of living things, for instance, is stretched between maximally and minimally creative forms of life – between human forms distinguished by their capacity to experience and become virtually anything at all, and less complex organisms that remain confined to a tightly constrained set of functions. After von Uexküll, Deleuze and Guattari offer the example of a tick: deprived of hearing and sight, a tick apparently lives within the limits of just three capabilities or 'affects' – its ability to detect a passing mammal, to fall onto it, and to burrow into it.[30] To know an organism is thus to count out its affects, i.e. to enumerate the kinds of action and interaction it can sustain (TP, 257; EP, 94; NP, 62). In principle at least, the worlds associated with each organism or set of organisms should be quantifiable in the same way. This is why, far from embracing a sort of ontological anarchism, Deleuze accepts, with Nietzsche, that intensive 'hierarchy is the originary fact, the identity of difference and origin [...]. The origin is the difference in the origin, difference in the origin is hierarchy.'[31]

To stick to the most significant paradigm, according to Spinoza the essence of any given individual or mode depends on the amount of divine power or creativity that it is able to express. 'Individuation is, in Spinoza, neither qualitative nor extrinsic, but quantitative and intrinsic, intensive'. It is 'purely quantitative', and proceeds in keeping with a divinely determined degree of power. Any actual mode, human or otherwise, 'is, in its essence, always a certain degree, a certain quantity, of a [divine] quality' or attribute. All modal essences are defined as intensive degrees of power. A mode's material existence then simply follows from the attribution of extensive parts to this pre-determined degree. All modes 'are quantitatively distinguished by the quantity or capacity of their respective essences, which always participate directly in divine substance'.[32] The more of God it expresses and the more adequate its means of expression, the more creative or powerful the mode.

On this point, Deleuze will further agree with Leibniz that 'everything can be said to be the same at all times and places except in degrees of perfection'.[33] Or again, 'everything is always the same thing, there is only one and the same Basis; and: everything is distinguished by degree, everything differs by manner [...]. These are the two principles of principles' (LB, 58). In Leibnizian terms, every individual is individuated as a distinct perspective on the universe as a whole, and what distinguishes such

19

individuals is the comparative reach and clarity of their perspective. Every individual, or monad, expresses the whole of the infinite universe, but it does so more or less clearly, again according to a purely quantitative scale. Every given monad expresses the whole infinite world, but *clearly* expresses only one particular zone of the world, $1/n$, in keeping with a strictly quantitative or hierarchical scale: $1/2$, $1/3$, $1/4$... The value of n determines the position of the monad, on a scale running from a minimum value – the position of the damned – to a maximum value – the position of reason or reflection. The damned are darkened monads, with only one clear perception, their hatred of God. Reasonable monads, by contrast, are able to extend and intensify their zones of perception, to open up a 'clear zone so wide and so intense that they lend themselves to operations of reflection or deepening that makes them tend toward God' (LB, 130, 92, 113). The task of any particular creature is simply to give appropriate voice to that part of creative becoming that it is able to express.

Unfortunately, certain creatures are characterised by especially stubborn forms of resistance to such expression, i.e. by especially obstinate forms of attachment to their creatural delusions. Creative manifestings are alone real, but they may give rise to manifested things isolated from their manifesting, and thus reduced to 'things' pure and simple. Some facets of creative or immaterial spirit may identify with their material incarnation. This is the whole drama of the human condition (and it is why philosophy must adopt, as its essential task, the orientation of thought beyond this condition). But although it is a mistake and an illusion, this condition is a supremely well-founded illusion. Our tendency to misunderstand ourselves and the nature of reality, for instance to treat as divisible that which is in reality indivisible, is not the result of a simple oversight or laziness. This tendency is built into the way we have evolved, the way we habitually are, the way we have adapted to the material pressures of life. The way we live obscures the reality of life. We are a facet of reality that is organised in such a way as to be ignorant of what it is. And most philosophy is doomed to incoherence because it seeks to ground an understanding of reality upon this very ignorance, i.e. upon the conditions of our habitual experience. As Deleuze will conclude, 'all our false problems derive from the fact that we do not know how to go beyond experience toward the conditions of experience, toward the articulations of the real [*du réel*]' (B, 26).

Despite our ignorance, we nonetheless remain a facet of this reality, and we can always come to learn what we do not initially know. With sufficient effort, we can learn to become what we are. Such learning will proceed, negatively, through disruption or disorganisation of our experience, and positively, through an immediate intuition of the real. Philosophy has no other goal than to pursue this joint task. This means that philosophy is nothing less than a continuation and intensification of being itself, an operation applied to the immanent obstacle of creativity (its obstruction by the products it produces). Philosophy will thus complete the human adventure by escaping it, and in the process it will offer creative spirit a way out of its material exile. Philosophy will be the discipline that creativity requires, and invents, so as to continue along its most intensive (most creative, most spiritual or immaterial) path. Philosophy is the vehicle through which spirit can escape its necessary confinement in matter.

This is why the philosopher and the mystic occupy such a privileged place at the summit of Bergson's hierarchical cosmology. Material obstacles have forced the evolution of spiritual life into myriad divergent channels, and in most of these channels living creativity has eventually run dry. But if the story of evolution as Bergson tells it is the story of compromises life has been forced to make with and in matter, the climax of that story is precisely the moment when, with humanity, conscious life invents a form that is finally capable of bypassing all material, organic, social or intellectual obstruction – a form through which it might advance on a purely spiritual plane. 'Everywhere but in man, consciousness has had to come to a standstill; in man alone it has kept on its way. Man, then, continues the vital movement indefinitely.'[34] This movement not only continues but is intensified in those humans who transcend their creatural limitations for the sake of creation itself. Mysticism figures as the culmination of Bergson's system because

> the ultimate end of mysticism is the establishment of a contact, consequently of a partial coincidence, with the creative effort which life itself manifests. This effort is of God, if it is not God himself. The great mystic is to be conceived as an individual being, capable of transcending the limitations imposed on the species by its material nature, thus continuing and extending the divine action.[35]

The great mystics are people who become perfectly transparent vehicles for the singular creative force that surges through all living things. They incarnate a maximally expressive power or creativity. By leaping across all social and material boundaries, they achieve 'identification of the human will with the divine will'. They 'simply open their souls to the oncoming wave', such that 'it is God who is acting through the soul in the soul'.[36]

The description of such action is explicitly mystical in Bergson but only implicitly so in Deleuze. One of the aims of the present book is to demonstrate that this difference, at least, is largely insignificant.

VI

Every individual is thus more or less expressive of the whole. The whole as such, however, is not itself presentable. The whole can only be conceived as a virtual or non-actual, non-presentable category. Virtual and unpresentable are synonymous terms. This is a final and especially significant implication of Deleuze's ontology (and its further elaboration will absorb most of the following chapter).

For the time being, it is enough to note that while everything is given as a facet of the whole or one-all, this whole can never be given, or become giveable. Precisely since it is nothing other than ongoing creation, the whole is never presentable in any static or finished state. It *is* only as a process of endless transformation. 'If the whole is not giveable, it is because it is the Open, and because its nature is to change constantly, or to give rise to something new.'[37] Although any given moment compresses the whole of indivisible time in a passing instant or present, only the present itself is presentable, precisely because the present, or actual, *presents* itself as limited and divisible.

(Just like everything else, presence is an activity, not a state: presence is always a pre-senting, a making-present). Just as the monism of substance eliminates relations between actual objects so as to conceive them as virtual aspects of a single expanding universe, so too 'a single duration will pick up along its route the events of the totality of the material world.' Free from the filters of consciousness or psychology, a single intuition will grasp the 'impersonal time in which all things will flow'.[38] The singular time thus intuited, however, can never itself be measured or presented, let alone rep-resented. The indivisible time and intensive space of a creating bear no resemblance to the presentable, extensional, and measurable dimensions of created actuality. Or again, a creating can be thought but not presented: all that actually appears of a creating is the creature (the individual, the work, the sound, the image, the wound…) it creates.

Another virtue of Bergson's account of mysticism is that it suggests a first way of explaining the ineluctably virtual status of our all-inclusive whole (i.e. a first way of accounting for the deferral and disruption of presentation across the unpresentable con-tinuity of time). Bergson suggests that an uncompromised form of mystical intuition might have enabled an immediate presentation of creation or the whole as such, without passing through the mediation of time. Bergson's mystic is that person or rather that impersonal super-person who seeks 'to complete the creation of the human species and make of humanity what it would have straightaway become, had it been able to assume its final shape without the assistance of man itself'. To complete the creation of the human species is nothing other than to make it an adequate vehicle for creation *as such*, i.e. it is to participate in God's own 'undertaking to create creators'.[39]

Why then does this creation remain incomplete? Towards the end of his last book Bergson pauses to consider the counter-factual alternative, and the result is a passage full of resonance for Deleuze's own contribution to this creation of creators. If we posit, says Bergson, 'the existence of a creative energy which is love, and which desires to produce from itself beings worthy to be loved', then we can always imagine such creation as taking place in a world 'whose materiality, as the opposite of divine spiritu-ality, would simply express the distinction between being created and creating, between the multifarious notes, strung like pearls, of a symphony and the indivisible emotion from which they sprang'. In such a world, virtual or spiritual creatings and their actual or material incarnations would be free to coalesce as 'complementary aspects of creation'; life and matter might blend in a single animation, creating there, created here. Unfortunately, Bergson concludes, such happy 'interpenetration has not been possible on our planet'. In our world, life has been obliged to embody itself in matter that was poorly adapted to its vital *élan*. As a result of this inadaptation, what we know of creation has been deflected from its original and immediate goal. Matter's resistance to creative life forced it to split along the various and 'divergent lines of evolutionary progress, instead of remaining undivided to the end'. Even along the one line along which the *élan* eventually broke through, even here, this exceptional (human) line soon bent back against itself. 'The movement which started as straight ended as circular. In that circle humanity, the terminal point, revolves.'[40]

How are we to get out of this terminal revolution? Bergson concludes that our only option is to 'follow the lead of the mystic'.[41] Only mystics, or people who become like mystics, can live in a manner adequate to the living that lives through them.

By the same token, only such people, or similar people, can endure what Deleuze will call a virtual *event*. And as a philosopher capable of such endurance, Deleuze will then seek to show that our world, so long as it is suitably oriented towards its creative outside, may indeed become the very one that Bergson found missing.

VII

Before going any further, it may be worth looking briefly at a couple of representative samples of the sort of events or *outings* that Deleuze's ontology is designed to embrace. Since his work is packed with any number of suggestive examples, we might as well look at the first and the last entries in his collected essays – a posthumously published piece on desert islands, written in the early 1950s, and a final reflection on the impersonal singularity of life, which appeared just before his death in 1995. This haphazard combination of themes may already shed some light on the nature of that distinctively 'subtractive vitalism' which informs the whole body of his work.

The 1950s essay, 'Causes and Reasons of Desert Islands', is about the separateness that defines an island and that allows us to dream of *deserted* islands as a sort of island ideal. Because we can imagine it as separate from the rest of the world, an island can figure as a place invested with an uncontaminated potential. A truly deserted island, Deleuze suggests, is a place from which the world itself might be created anew. Unfortunately, actual islands rarely are deserted. Most islands are populated, and by owning and inhabiting them their human occupants thereby attach them to the mundane routine of the world as it is. The inhabitants of an island trap it in a static actuality. Robinson Crusoe is the very model of such an inhabitant, the anti-islander par excellence. A pure proprietor, Robinson turns his once deserted island into a comfortable version of home. The young Deleuze does not hide his scorn – 'one can hardly imagine a more boring novel' than *Robinson Crusoe*, and 'every healthy reader dreams of seeing Friday eat Robinson' (DI, 12).

The only way out of this situation, the only way to 'recover the mythological life of the deserted island', is to find some way of inspiring its inhabitants to become the vector of their own de-population, their own evacuation or subtraction. An island might be inhabited and yet become spiritually deserted, provided that its inhabitants become 'sufficiently, that is absolutely, separate, and provided they are sufficient, absolute creators'. Deleuze acknowledges that 'this is never the case in fact', but the possibility can be imagined as a virtual telos that will align both people and cosmos in the creation of a new earth. (As we shall see, this telos is what Deleuze and Guattari will later name 'deterritorialisation', and 'deterritorialisation is absolute when it brings about the creation of a new earth' [TP, 510]). If they can find some way of taking up and continuing the *élan* that produced the island as separate and deserted, then far from compromising it, humans bring the desertedness to its perfection and highest point. In certain conditions which attach them to the very movement of things, humans do not put an end to desertedness, they make it sacred. Those people who come to the island indeed occupy and populate it; but in reality, were they sufficiently separate, sufficiently creative, they would give the island only a dynamic image of itself, a consciousness of the movement which produced the island, such that through them the island would in the end become conscious of itself as deserted and unpeopled. The island would be only the dream of humans, and humans, the pure consciousness of the island. For this to be the case, there is again but one condition: humans would have to reduce themselves to the movement that brings them to the island, to the movement which prolongs and takes up the *élan* that produced the island. Then geography and imagination would be one. (DI, 10–11)

The island would thus be restored to its desertion, and at the same time would give rise to 'uncommon humans, absolutely separate, absolute creators, in short, an Idea of humanity, a prototype, a man who would almost be a god [...], a pure Artist, a consciousness of Earth and Ocean'. This would be nothing less than 'a human being who precedes itself. Such a creature on a deserted island would be the deserted island itself'. The creation of such creatures ensures 'the survival of a sacred place in a world that is slow to re-begin'.[42]

Despite obvious differences of context and theme, a version of this same creative separation or subtraction also informs the last essay that Deleuze published during his lifetime, 'Immanence: A Life...' (1995). The timing and topic of this essay encourages us to read it as a sort of philosophical testament; there are certainly few other essays that offer so clear and so compressed an overview of Deleuze's general orientation. Of the several literary allusions Deleuze makes in this brief essay, one is especially suggestive of its argument and of the logic of his philosophy as a whole. This is a reference to a minor episode in Dickens' late novel *Our Mutual Friend*. The unloved character Riderhood, who makes his living fishing corpses out of the Thames, himself almost drowns in that same river when his boat is run down by a steamer. Some onlookers then carry him, half-dead, up to Miss Abbey's pub, and a doctor is called in to revive him. 'No one', Dickens writes, 'has the least regard for the man; with them all, he has been an object of avoidance, suspicion, and aversion.' Nevertheless, the spectacle of this struggle between life and death solicits a response deeper than empathy:

> The spark of life within him is curiously separable from himself now, and they have a deep interest in it, probably because it IS life, and they are living and must die [...]. Neither Riderhood in this world, nor Riderhood in the other, could draw tears from them; but a striving human soul between the two can do it easily. He is struggling to come back. Now, he is almost here, now he is far away again. And yet – like us all, when we swoon – like us all, every day of our lives when we wake – he is instinctively unwilling to be restored to the consciousness of this existence, and would be left dormant, if he could.

Life and medicine soon win the day, and the patient recovers. But 'as he grows warm, the doctor and the four men cool. The spark of life was deeply interesting while it was in abeyance, but now that it has got established in Mr Riderhood, there appears to be a general desire that circumstances had admitted of its being developed in anybody else, rather than that gentleman.'[43]

The most important thing to retain from this exemplary episode, I think, is the crucial difference between the spark (the virtual 'creating') and the person (the actual 'creature') it animates. The person Riderhood is an object that has certain objective qualities; like any object, he is more or less appealing, more or less hateful or sympathetic. He is individuated by what he does and has done, by his origins and background, by the personality he has come to acquire, by the relations he sustains with other people, and so on. Such is the creatural dimension. The spark itself, however, subsists on a quite different plane. The spark is perfectly unique, perfectly singular – it is *this* spark, and no other – yet fully 'separable' from the object it sustains. This is the point that interests Deleuze:

> No one has described what a life is better than Charles Dickens [...]. Between [Riderhood's] life and his death, there is a moment that is only that of *a* life playing with death. The life of the individual gives way to an impersonal and yet singular life that releases a pure event freed from the accidents of internal and external life, that is, from the subjectivity and objectivity of what happens: a 'Homo tantum' with whom everyone empathises and who attains a sort of beatitude. It is [...] a life of pure immanence, neutral, beyond good and evil, for it was only the subject that incarnated it in the midst of things that made it good or bad. The life of such individuality fades away in favour of the singular life immanent to a man who no longer has a name, though he can be mistaken for no other.[44]

What befalls Riderhood here, moreover, is simply an extreme version of the sort of process that Deleuze identifies as characteristic of literary writing in general. Writing is a process that sweeps individual characters up in intensive movements that explode their constituted limits. It is a process that 'elevates them to a vision that carries them off into an indefinite [*un indéfini*], like a becoming that is too powerful for them' (CC, 3).

It is not I or you who lives: 'one' (*une vie*) lives in us. The indefinite ones that live and die in us 'in no way take the place of a subject, but instead do away with any subject in favour of an assemblage [...] that carries or brings out the event insofar as it is unformed and incapable of being effectuated' by actual or individuated persons. We access the one that lives in us through experiences that we can grasp only by abandoning our determination to speak as our*selves*, by 'letting go of [our] ability to say I'.[45]

A life, this spark of life, is the singular yet anonymous event or creating that sustains any given individual or being. What truly lives through such an individual is this pure affirmative potential alone.[46] Individuals *live* when, beyond the limits of what is lived, they minimise the constraints of their incarnation to the advantage of that spark of pure life that lives in them (but that is 'in' them at a distance greater than that of anything which stands actually outside them). They live the life of *this* singular spark that animates them.

The whole of Deleuze's philosophy is a sustained effort to devise a redemptive logic adequate to just such pure events or creatings, in keeping with the idea that 'a life is composed of one and the same Event, despite the variety of what might happen' (LS, 170). What is lived or thought can always be described within the coherence of a single destiny, so long as we remember that this coherence is that of *a* virtual creating and not that of *the* actual creature. The coherence of a creating can only be grasped by suspending and then eventually abandoning the coherence of the creature to which it gives rise.

This dependence of the actual upon the virtual is the topic of our next chapter; its suspension and abandonment will be taken up in Chapters 3 and 4.

2

Actual Creatures, Virtual Creatings

'The knowledge of things bears the same relation to
the knowledge of God as the things themselves to
God' (EP, 14).

We know that being is creation and that creation embraces all there is. Being is just as
essentially differential, however – this is just what it means to be *creative*, after all, rather
than static or chaotic. Since it is absolutely creative, being differentiates or distinguishes
itself in an infinitely multiple number of ways, such that the 'unit' or most basic element
of being is not an inconsistent or continuous flux but rather a distinct process or operation: *a* creating. A creating proceeds as the sufficient reason behind the actual entity or
state of affairs that it then establishes. Being is the inexhaustible proliferation of creatings or events of creation, 'forms of a thought-Nature that span or fly over [*survolent*]
every possible universe' (WP, 177–8).

In addition, every distinct event or creating gives rise to a certain kind of existent
creature – an organism, a personality, an object, an experience, etc. Creation is one but
it proceeds as two, through this distinction of creatings and creatures. *Creare* is one, we
might say, but it involves both the active *creans* and the passive *creaturum*. The creating is
'implied' or 'implicated' within its creator; the creature is an explication or unfolding of
the creating (EP, 16). Creatings present creatures, but are never themselves presentable.
The geometric examples that Deleuze retains from Spinoza are familiar: we actively
construct a plane through the movement of a line, a circle through the rotation of a line
segment, a sphere through the rotation of a semicircle, and so on. Deleuze's aim is very
concisely to apply a similar logic to the whole of creation, to 'construct the real itself,
rather than remain on the level of mathematical entities' (EP, 136).

Both creatings and creatures are facets of a single order of creation. They both are
in one and the same way. But the modality of their being is different. Differentiated
creatures are *actual*, extended and definite forms of being, and their existence depends
on the interactive constraints of their material situation. Differentiatings or creatings
are *virtual*, and are intensive rather than extensive. Creation is primordially and essentially self-differing, and its 'self-differentiation is the movement of a virtuality which
actualises itself' (DI, 40tm).

The crucial point is that all of the productive, differential or creative force in this dual configuration stems from the virtual creating alone, and not from the actual creature. This doesn't mean that the creating is transcendent of the creature. A creating doesn't operate upon the creature from a position external to it, like a transitive cause upon its effect. Creation is precisely the immanent combination of both creature and creating: the creating is more 'internal' to the creature than any actual inside. Nevertheless, as the verbal forms suggest, only one of these two terms is active. It is only the creating that differs or produces, and it is only the creating *as such* that can claim to be properly new. However novel or impressive an actual work of art, for instance, it bears no resemblance to the process that created it, to the power of its *working*. However novel it might be in respect to other existent creatures, a newly created individual is never itself new in the Deleuzian sense. However much we multiply the number, complexity and diversity of created individuals, we will never reach the power of the new as such.

This is perhaps the most important distinction in the whole of Deleuze's work. A virtual creating is not just new in relation to what already exists, or in relation to the old, or to the about to be old. A creating is new *in itself*, in its being, for its own time but also for the whole of time. A creating is new because it is creative, precisely – because it is invested with an inherent power to make-new, to transform, change, disrupt, differ, and so on. 'The new, with its power of beginning and beginning again, remains forever new, just as the established was always established from the outset, even if a certain amount of empirical time was necessary for this to be recognised.' The (soon to be) established, or created, can never itself be new or creative, regardless of how distinct it may be in relation to what has already been established. This is why 'Nietzsche's distinction between the creation of new values and the recognition of established values should not be understood in a historically relative manner, as though the new values were new in their time and the new values simply needed time to become established' (DR, 136). No, the essential difference is between (a) values that more or less quickly come to be established and thus recognised, represented, honoured, and so on (i.e. *valued* values), and (b) the pure process of valuing anew or revaluing (i.e. *valuing* values), a process that generates all discernible values but which itself evades discernment.

Any constituted or creatural identity is in reality only the simulation or semblance of an identity, a mere 'optical "effect" produced by the more profound game of difference' and the repeating of difference (DR, xix). So when Deleuze and Guattari declare that 'we are made of lines', what is most essential is the difference between lines that are *drawn* around established identities, shapes or territories, and the active *drawing* of pure lines of flight, drawings liberated from any relation to territory, identity or shape. As individuals we are made up of sequences of rigid, segmented or molar identities on the one hand, and of more supple, more molecular becomings or 'fluxes' on the other hand. But both of these dimensions are determined by a deeper, more dynamic, more indefinite and thus more unreservedly inventive movement – the pure movement of an abstract line of flight or deterritorialisation. This third kind of line is what 'carries us away' towards a destination that is neither foreseeable nor pre-existent. The line of flight is 'simple, abstract, and yet it is the most complex of all' because if it seems to emerge after the other two, in reality 'this line has always been there, although it is the opposite of a destiny: it does not have to detach itself from the others, rather it is the first, and the others are derived from it'.[1] In the dimension of actuality, the third, purely creative line will always appear to arise after the others, since we must begin with what is individuated or created. Creation only exists in the form of creatures, and only creatures can think the process from which they result. In reality, however, it remains the case that what is individuated – the actual person you have become – is indeed a *result*, the product of a producing that is itself primary. The lines that we are may appear to be alternately shaped or shaping, constituted or constituting, passively lined or actively lining, but there is ultimately only *the* line of continuous variation or creation: in the end, 'there is only one line, the primary line of light', which is only intermittently and temporarily 'relativised' or interrupted (TP, 194; D, 124, 147).

Deleuze regularly insists on this unilateral configuration. As a general rule, transformative 'becoming [*le devenir*], change, and mutation affect composing forces, not composed forms' (FC, 87tm). The destiny of the creature, as we shall see in the next couple of chapters, is simply to invent the means (appropriate to its material situation) of emptying or dissolving itself so as to impose the least possible limitation upon the creating that sustains it.

Deleuze will thereby concur, in his own way, with the most fundamental of theophanic convictions – that while everything is a manifestation of God, we can know God *qua* God 'only through God, and not through the creatural'.[2] To adapt Leibniz's way of putting it, God is the ocean of which we are only drops: while every creature is nothing other than an expression of God, nevertheless any given creature can no more express the plenitude of God than a single drop can express the depth and power of the sea.[3]

Though creation is one, it proceeds through the dualism of creating/creature in order eventually to express and intensify the monism that it is. Every apparent 'dualism is therefore only a moment, which must lead to the re-formation of a monism [...]. We employ a dualism of models only in order to arrive at a process that challenges all models' and that generates 'the magic formula we all seek – PLURALISM = MONISM' (B, 29; TP, 20–1).

At the same time, however, we know that this monism never sinks into mere undifferentiation. A creative ontology is distinct from a merely chaotic anarchy. Being is creation rather than chaos. Chaos creates nothing that endures (LB, 76–7). Chaotic determinations are characterised 'by the infinite speed with which they take shape and vanish'.[4] Chaotic determinations are ephemeral, whereas every creating generates a certain minimal consistency – the consistency of its own becoming or transformation, the line of its own development, however jagged or disruptive. *A* singular life will live as both indefinite and singular [*une*], just as an embryo (to cite one of Deleuze and Guattari's favourite examples) will undergo a dramatically violent process of transformation, but it will remain *an* embryo. In somewhat the same way, Deleuze and Guattari's first requirement of a work of art or literature will be that it stand up on its own, that it last. A creating *qua* creating retains a virtual or ideal self-sufficiency, but it will only be 'actually' creative if it is also incarnated in an existent creature which both expresses and obstructs it. The existence (and thus resistance) of the creature is itself an internal necessity of creation; creatural opacity is an immanent and unavoidable obstacle to the expression or development of being itself.

Much of Deleuze's philosophy is concerned with the development of adequate means of confronting this obstacle. 'There is nothing which does not lose its identity as this is constituted by concepts, and its similarity as this is constituted in representation, when the dynamic space and time of its actual constitution is discovered' (DR, 218). There is no creature that fails to become other than itself or that resists its re-orientation to the telos of the imperceptible, once it finds a way to think the principle of its own creating.

Since Deleuze himself first found a way to think such principles through Spinoza and Bergson, we'll begin this discussion of the virtual and the actual with them.

<h1 style="text-align:center">I</h1>

The virtual is no doubt the single most important and most elusive notion in Deleuze's philosophy. The recent evolution of the word's general meaning (in phrases like 'virtual reality') unhelpfully associates it with the artificial or merely apparent; readers would do better to retain something of the older, now archaic meaning of the word, which relates it to the possession of inherent virtues or powers.

It's this meaning of the word that infuses the whole Spinozist conception of reality, and while the conventional distinction of virtual and actual is foreign to Spinoza's philosophy, nevertheless it's again this philosophy that should orient our first interpretation of this aspect of Deleuze's work. Much of the essential difference between virtual and actual (along with the key to Deleuze's understanding of *essence* and its homophonic cognate *sens*, or sense) follows directly from Spinoza's celebrated distinction of an active or creative *naturans* from a passive or created *naturata*.[5]

As we saw in the previous chapter, Spinoza seeks to conceive of nature and of all the particular things it contains as the infinitely ramified expression, or naturing, of a single self-creating reality or substance. Every discernible individual is in reality an active individuating or modifying of this divine and univocal substance. 'Each idea of each body, or of each singular thing which actually exists, necessarily involves an eternal and infinite essence of God.'[6] We can think of these singular things or modifications of substance, however, in one of two ways. We can either 'conceive them to exist in relation to a certain time and place', and in particular in relation to ourselves, or we can 'conceive them to be contained in God and to follow from the necessity of the divine nature'. To conceive them in this second way, i.e. to conceive them as 'true or real', is to understand them as offering an adequate expression of an eternal and infinite essence of God.[7]

To consider individuals in the first way, as actual or existent, is to consider them as individuated in the world and thus as affected by what happens to them and by their myriad relations with all other constituted individuals. Considered in this way, the individuated are passive in relation to what creates or causes them. They rely upon the imagination, rather than the intellect, to make sense of the world. They tend to understand things in terms of fortune and contingency rather than of rational autonomy and necessity. They suffer the effects of their passions. They live in a state of incomprehension and 'bondage'. The individuated qua individuated have only a temporary and limited existence, and have only inadequate ideas of what they are or what they can do. 'So long as the human mind perceives things from the common order of nature, it does not have an adequate, but only a confused and mutilated knowledge of itself, of its own body, and of external bodies' (IIP29C).

The process whereby an individual may come to consider itself as 'true or real', by contrast, is simply the process through which it learns that it is nothing other a distinct facet of God's infinitely active and eternally creative power. Such an individual 'knows that it is in God and is conceived through God' (VP30). The more it conceives or is conceived in this way, the more 'perfect' and powerful it becomes. And since (for reasons we'll come back to in Chapter 4) an adequate idea is one that expresses its cause, the more such an individual understands itself and other individuals as *individuatings* of God the more its thinking proceeds through adequate ideas. Fully to understand ourselves in this way is our 'salvation, or blessedness, or freedom'.[8] Once we have understood ourselves as expressing an eternal essence of God, then we realise that the merely actual or creatural 'part of the mind which perishes with the body is of no moment in relation to what remains' (VP38S) – its perfect or immaculate part.

II

Deleuze's decision to use the adjective 'virtual' to describe such a part follows first and foremost from his reading of Bergson. As Deleuze understands it, Bergson's whole project affirms the primacy of the virtual, understood as 'an absolutely positive mode of existence', as 'something absolutely simple that realises itself', precisely by differing from itself.[9]

We saw in the previous chapter how, from a Bergsonian perspective, 'all our false problems derive from the fact that we do not know how to go beyond experience toward the conditions of experience, toward the articulations of the real' (B, 26). Our false problems arise precisely because we tend to confine our attention to the domain of our (actual) experience of reality, rather than to the (virtual) nature of reality itself.

Our actual experience, for instance our normal perception of an object or image, is governed by our ordinary interests and needs: the needs we have as beings endowed with organic and materially existent bodies. We normally only see what is useful or interesting to us at any given moment. When a cow sees grass, it sees food rather than photosynthesis. The domain of the actual is thus subordinated to the requirements of interest and to the actions required for the pursuit of interest.[10] The interests of action, for obvious reasons, focus concentration on the present moment. As the French meaning of the word makes clear, the actual [*l'actuel*] is first and foremost an aspect of the present. The present is that dimension of time in which things literally fall into their allocated place. The present is that moment in which time appears to be subordinate to space, in which the spatial concerns of my acting body momentarily (but routinely) dominate the passing flow of time. As Bergson understands it, my present experience simply consists in the awareness that I have of my body, i.e. of a certain combination of spatially specific sensations and movements. And since 'sensations and movements are localised at determined points of this extended body, there can only be, at a given moment, a single system of movements and sensations. That is why my present appears to me to be a thing absolutely determined', as the 'very materiality of my existence'.[11] The present subordinates the intensive passing of time to a specific extension in space, and because we are ordinarily and regularly interested in what we can do in the present, we assume that this subordination is itself lasting and determinant.

This is precisely where our false problems begin. For the actual moment of such determination, this ostensibly solid materiality, is also a moment of merely ephemeral duration. As everyone knows, the present does not last. To say that intensive time comes to be extensionally fixed or spatially determined in the moment of the present is tantamount, in fact, to saying that it is *never* so fixed or determined. The solidity of the actual is only apparent. The actual, i.e. the present or extensive, may seem solid and determinate, and insofar as we bend our knowledge of reality to the satisfaction of our interests then we have every interest in maintaining this semblance. But as Bergson argues in his most remarkable book, *Matter and Memory*, any psychological account of memory and of the mind more generally is doomed to incoherence if it tries to ground itself on the primacy of such actual perceptions. His targets include explanations of memory whereby the remembering of a perception would involve the mental storage of a discreet fragment of time, as if memory involved only the retention of progressively distant or weakened perceptions – as if the past was built up out of the accumulation, one after the other, of so many once-present moments. The details of this argument needn't detain us here, but it would be hard to exaggerate the importance, for Deleuze, of Bergson's alternative to such accounts.[12]

Rather than the illusory solidity of the actual, rather than the merely apparent sturdiness of extension, Bergson insists that the true fabric of reality is instead intensive and virtual, and that the lasting ground of our experience is not the present but the non-present, i.e. the whole continuum of time itself (or what Bergson calls the 'pure past'). The conventional, present-centred account tries to conceive of the past in aggregative terms, as built up through the accumulation of successive slices of the present. Bergson inverts this argument: in reality, all of past time exists together, all at once, as a single synthetic flow. The whole of the past is preserved in itself, complete in every detail, and what Bergson calls pure memory is simply this preservation as such. How could it be otherwise, if reality is a continuous and indivisible movement of creation?

Now if all of past time exists as an indivisible whole, if the whole of the past remains equally real or alive and if reality is nothing other than this whole, then what needs explanation is not what makes reality whole but rather what allows us to experience it, most of the time, as merely partial or limited. What limits it, what prevents this whole from ever being present, is precisely the imposition of the present itself. The whole can only 'be' as non-present, or non-actual. To be present is itself to isolate, according to the needs of the moment, according to the priorities of a creature that acts in keeping with its interests, only those few aspects of the whole that are relevant to these actions or needs. Although our every past experience is perfectly preserved in pure memory, 'to act is just to induce this memory to shrink, or rather to become thinned and sharpened, so that it presents nothing thicker than the edge of a blade to actual experience, into which it will thus be able to penetrate'.[13] The past isn't compiled together from so many present parts. It is rather the present that imposes, as it occurs, a drastic sharpening or limitation upon the past. The present performs a severe constriction of time, and the more pressing the imperatives of present action, the narrower this constriction will be. The more urgent or automated the action – the more action comes to act like a reflex or like a purely instinctual response to a stimulus – the more punctual the present compression of time. The reflexive present is just time reduced to an 'objective' actuality, and thus reduced to a minimum of indetermination, freedom, or creativity. It is reduced, in other words, to the minimal (most compressed, or actualised) degree of virtuality.[14]

Clearly, the past in this sense, the past as continuous whole or synthetic flow of indivisible time, can only exist in a virtual dimension. But there is nothing privative about this 'only' – on the contrary. The present is actual, the past is virtual. And for the same reason that the actual, despite its seeming solidity, is in reality ephemeral and illusory, so too is the virtual, despite (or rather on account of) its immateriality and non-presence, the only true and lasting dimension of reality. In reality it is the virtual, not the actual, that is creative or determinant. Or to put this another way: all that is 'actually' determined only seems so from the limited perspective of a particular organism, preoccupied with its interests and with its limited capacity for action. In reality, such determination is just a form of local adaptation. It is the result of entrenched habit, of 'a set of intelligently constructed mechanisms which ensure the appropriate reply to various possible demands'.[15] Real determination, on the other hand, is the creative dynamic of being as a whole. Distracted by its actions, an actual organism mistakes its local adaptation for its 'own' determination. It fails to grasp that any 'actual present is only the entire past in its most contracted state' (DR, 82tm), that it is nothing other than a more or less compressed, more or less de-virtualised facet of a virtual whole.

In other words, although the organism is indeed ordinarily condemned to act within the limits of its actual situation, it will only *understand* it if it manages to work its way back to what philosophy will identify as the 'real starting point'. This starting point, as Deleuze explains in his own short book on Bergson, is a simple unity, a virtual totality. If 'differentiation must always be understood as the actualisation of a virtuality that persists across its actual divergent lines', this is 'because it presupposes a unity, a virtual primordial totality' – the unpresentable totality of creation or creative time as such (B, 95). And why does this unity remain virtual or non-present, unpresentable? Because we can access it only by forms of insight or intuition that are indifferent to the logic and priorities of the present or of presentation, i.e. the very forms of thought that are obstructed by our normal creatural habits. Hence the lesson that Deleuze will develop, one way or another, in virtually all of his own works: access to the real, to the real conditions of determination or creation, requires the disruption of these habits and the dissolution of these obstructions. If the actual is sustained by the interests of action then virtual insight will require the paralysis of action and the dissolution of the actor. If the actual is sustained by the coordination of a body that links sensations and actions in an organic 'sensory-motor mechanism', then access to the virtual will require the dislocation of this mechanism. If the actual is a function of the organism, the virtual will entail a generalised dis-organisation – the institution of a disorganised body, a body stripped of its creatural integrity and coherence, or what Deleuze and Guattari will call, after Artaud, a 'body without organs'.

Of all the various influences on Deleuze's own conception of the virtual, Bergson's notion of the pure past (i.e. its continuous preservation in pure memory) must be the single most significant. Although they fly in the face of common sense, the general contours of this notion may already be apparent. As virtual, memory will have no relation to action, sensation, or extension. If actual perception proceeds as a form of sensation (in anticipation of a bodily action or reaction), memory will proceed, uncontaminated by the mediation of sensation, as a form of pure or immediate intuition. As opposed to a fragment of the past that is merely reactivated for the purposes of the present situation, a pure memory has no interest in either action or the present and instead throws us immediately in the midst of the past, just as it was. A pure recollection or 'virtual image', as Deleuze will explain, 'is not a psychological state or a consciousness: it exists outside of consciousness', literally in the midst of the things as they were or are. 'It is in the past as it is in itself, as it is preserved in itself, that we go to look for our dreams or our recollections…'.[16] The past is not something that we might regret or miss: time is the dimension of creation or production, not absence or nostalgia. In other words, this pure past is not at all 'past' in the normal sense so much as the intemporal being of time itself, i.e. being in its becoming or developing. The pure 'past does not represent something that has been, but simply something that is and that coexists with itself as present. The past does not have to preserve itself in anything but itself, because it is in itself, survives and preserves itself in itself.' This is why, when we truly remember something we do not retrieve or reactivate a moment that was once present and now exists only as a mental trace or representation of what it once was, but rather 'we place ourselves, directly, in the past itself' (PS, 58). We do not remember the past so much as *think* it, i.e. allow it to think through us.

Precisely because it is virtual, pure memory is of no use to present, actual or creatural concerns. 'Pure memory, being inextensive and powerless, does not in any degree share the nature of sensation' or feeling – in other words, it is of no direct interest to an organism.[17] But for this very reason, because of its indifference to the creatural, pure memory is an adequate vehicle for creation as such. Pure memory is the domain of artists and seers – people who, in keeping with the cliché of the dreaming artist or distracted genius, are minimally concerned with action and interest. (As we shall see, the great effort of art will involve the extraction and preservation of the virtual or creative as such, independently of any actual compression – for no sooner is such a memory actualised, according to the needs of action and the present, than it loses its virtual completion and with it its creative force. And to anticipate a related issue to which we'll return later in this chapter: one clue to understanding Deleuze's otherwise impenetrable 'logic of sense' is that it is patterned on precisely this notion of a pure or virtual past. What this 'past is to time, sense is to language and idea to thought. Sense as past of language is the form of its pre-existence, that which we place ourselves in at once' [C2, 99–100; cf. B, 57]).

We should perhaps come back to one last point before moving on. I've said that the actual, though we habitually treat it as solid or substantial, is in reality ephemeral and illusory. The virtual alone is real. A virtual creating is the reality that lives in any actual creature. If you forget this point, the philosophies of both Bergson and Deleuze will make no sense at all. On the other hand though, it's just as essential to remember that the illusions of actuality are unavoidable and well-founded. Virtual creatings immediately give rise to actual creatures, and to be an actual creature is necessarily to be concerned with creatural interests and actions.[18] The actual does not exist separately from the virtual, and the virtual does not transcend the actual in some higher plane.[19] Rather, the two dimensions are given as facets of one and the same creative process, two aspects of one and the same 'expression' (and it will be the redemptive task of thought to explore the possible means of extracting or subtracting the one from the other). In Bergson's compressed terms:

> our actual existence, whilst it is unrolled in time, duplicates itself all along with a virtual existence, a mirror-image. Every moment of our life presents two aspects, it is actual and virtual, perception on the one side and memory on the other. Each moment is split up as and when it is posited. Or rather, it consists in this very splitting, for the present moment, always going forward [...] would be a mere abstraction were it not the moving mirror which continually reflects perception as a memory.[20]

As it crystallises in the 'now', every passing moment tips momentarily into the actuality of the present (and the apparent solidity of extension) – but by the same token, every present moment passes continuously from this ephemeral 'now' into the virtual continuity of the past. Every present moment, as Deleuze is fond of reminding us, would never pass on if it were not in reality also already passing or past.[21] Every actual is sustained by the virtual which passes through it. But although actual and virtual must be thought together, although there can be no counter-actualisation that is not accompanied by forms of re-actualisation, nevertheless the creative telos itself will not change. The task of any actual creature is always to 'counter-actualise', i.e. to reverse the process of its creaturalisation. Although 'the eternal truth of the event is grasped only if the event is also inscribed in the flesh', the grasping of this painful actualisation must in turn be doubled by a 'counter-actualisation which limits, moves, and transfigures it', and which, by liberating us from the time and body of our actualisation, 'gives us the chance to go farther than we would have believed possible' (LS, 161).

Philosophy will be precisely this: a way of living and thinking that reverses the movement that created us, the movement that led from the virtually or indefinitely real to merely actual definition. Philosophy inverts the movement that leads from meta-physics to psychology.

<h1 style="text-align:center">III</h1>

In his own conception of creation, Deleuze retains most of the features that Bergson associates with the virtual – its sufficiency, its intensity, its unpresentable temporality. He also draws on the way the term has more recently been used in the fields of quantum mechanics, mathematics, genetics, and complexity theory. Description of the emer-gence of unpredictable self-ordering trajectories from complex material situations is certainly one of Deleuze's concerns. But it is not his most important or distinctive concern, and since it and related topics are well covered in other recent books on or around Deleuze I will pay little attention to them here.[22] Instead, the point I'd like to stress about Deleuze's approach is the one that he makes most concisely in his late, com-pressed article on 'The Actual and Virtual', first published in 1996. 'Actualisation belongs to the virtual. The actualisation of the virtual is singularity [*singularité*], whereas the actual itself is constituted individuality.' In keeping with the conditions of immanent creation that we looked at in the previous chapter, the virtual is what 'constitutes the plane of immanence, in which the actual object dissolves'. Or again, whereas the actual is the 'product or object of actualisation, actualisation has only the virtual as its subject' – and the real plane of immanence is nothing other than that which 'reconverts object into subject'.[23]

That something is *actual* means that it exists in the conventional sense of the word, that it can be experienced, perceived, measured, etc. An actual human being, to go back to our Dickensian example, is always a particular person like Riderhood, a person with objective qualities, a personality, a life-story, someone who is more or less likeable, happy, and so on. Such a person is precisely the *object* of actualisation.

That something is *virtual* will mean, then, that it doesn't share any of these character-istics: its qualities will not be objective in the normal sense, nor perceptible, measurable, and so on. Creatings make present but are not themselves present or presentable. No more than Deleuze and Guattari themselves, you will never 'see' their virtual schizos, nomads, or bodies without organs. The virtual life that lives in Riderhood, remember, is not the actual 'subject who incarnated it in the midst of things [and] who made it good or bad'; it is rather the anonymous spark of life within him, with whom everyone empathises in a sort of immediate intuition or sympathy.[24] Such a living is our only genuine *subject*, and the task of such a subject is to be equal to the events that befall it, i.e. to the creatings that transform it.

It is the implacable though utterly unpredictable force of such transformation that is central to Deleuze's conception of the virtual, and that accounts for its difference from the merely possible.[25] To realise a possibility is to bring something effectively pre-existent into existence, to the exclusion of other existences and in keeping with a given set of causes, preferences or goals. The realisation of a possibility will resemble the pre-existent possibility itself; realisation of the possible is thus simply an aspect of actuality.

Virtual differentiation, by contrast, *creates* the very thing that it actualises. Precisely because 'actual terms never resemble the singularities they incarnate […], actualisation or differentiation is always a genuine creation' (DR, 212). Creation refers to nothing pre-existent, ignores resemblance and proceeds through a sort of 'inclusive disjunction': creation will create both this and that, or rather, through indiscernment and constant variation, neither-this *and* neither-that. 'Differentiation or actualisation is always creative with respect to what it actualises, whereas realisation is always reproductive or limiting' (DI, 101).

In short, the actual is constituted, the virtual alone is constituent.[26] This is the key to Deleuze's whole ontology of creation: the one is creative, the other created; the one composes, the other is composed. As a rule, no creative or virtual 'power-quality should be confused with the state of things which it actualises' (C1, 98). The more such a power cuts its links with merely actual states of things the more powerful it becomes. There is thus no more powerful or creative a formula, in this sense, than Bartleby's uncompromising 'I would prefer not to' – a formula that everywhere 'disconnects words and things, words and actions' and thereby 'severs language from all reference, in accordance with Bartleby's absolute vocation, *to be a man without references*' (CC, 73–4).

More precisely, we might say that the process of creation or constitution as Deleuze understands it involves three distinct but inter-related aspects.

There is first of all the pure impulse or élan of creativity itself, the affirmation of being conceived as a sort of primordial energy or constituent power, the inexhaustible source of pure potential or transformation. Considered on its own, isolated from what it constitutes, this constituent power can only be imagined as an unthinkable abstraction or paradox, as a whole that can never be presented or given. It figures as an inconceivably compressed point of pure intensity, a point of absolute compression (the whole of time condensed to a single point) which at every moment passes through every other conceivable point, and generates every possible configuration of points. This would be a point travelling at infinite speed, never in any one place because it distributes every place. It is Deleuze's immanent alternative to Aristotle's prime mover. In different contexts, Deleuze calls it the aleatory point, the paradoxical element, the dark precursor, nonsense, or the unthought. It is the ultimate and self-determining source of determination, behind which there is nothing at all: it is an all-determining force, which must simply be posited or affirmed all at once. We might cautiously call it a sort of virtual 'creator', so long as we remember that it is thinkable precisely only as unthinkable, it *is* only as no-thing, as beyond all distinction or presentation (in other words, so long as we remember, with both Bergson and Eriugena, that the distinction between creatings and a thing which creates is always an illusion[27]). Immeasurably intense in its pure implication, it is conceivable only through its infinitely diverse explication, only through the distinct creatings that it distributes as vehicles for its manifestation or expression. These creatings – our second term – are determinate virtual configurations, constituent powers or essences (variously called modal essences, degrees of power, events, ideas, concepts…), which further determine the material existence of our third, actual term (constituted bodies, presentable states of affairs, articulated propositions…).

A philosophy of virtual creation, as opposed both to speculation about a transcendent creator or a positivist curiosity about actual creatures, will be primarily concerned with the second of these three terms, i.e. with creatings as such. There is no transcendent creator, and, for all its apparent solidity, the actual is never anything more than an illusory and ephemeral result. What accounts for an individual are not the presentable characteristics of what is thus individuated but the dynamic processes of individuating itself, for instance the process whereby an embryo develops into an organism, a liquid solution into a crystal, a bubble into a sphere. (What happens, for instance, when a child blows a soap bubble through a plastic tube? A liquid membrane stretches to form a hollow shape around the rim of the tube. As it detaches from the tube, the bubble *becomes* spherical not by spontaneously conforming to the ideal geometric properties of a sphere but, as DeLanda notes, by actively 'minimising surface tension'[28]). Only the virtual is constitutive. The virtual is more real than the actual, precisely because its reality is intensive rather than extensive, constituent rather than constituted, spiritual rather than material.

This difference between 'intensive' and 'extensive' quantities or multiplicities is another of the fundamental concepts that Deleuze adapts from Bergson.[29] What's at issue here is again the distinction between, on the one hand, a reality whose nature must be understood, through intuition, as a flowing, indivisible whole, and on the other hand, what can merely be represented of such a reality. An extensive quantity, like the length or width of an isolated object, can be measured and divided without changing what is thus divided. An extensive set or collection is assembled by compiling a certain number of units or individuals, each with their discrete qualities and identity – remove some of these units, and those that are left remain unaltered. The 10 centimetres of length that are left over when a 20 centimetre board is cut in half remain the same as before. An intensive assemblage, on the other hand, comprises elements that are in constant flux, whose own qualities depend on the development of the set of the whole. One of the most obvious analogies is with a weather system, comprising zones of high and low pressure, higher and lower temperature, and so on, all of which coexist in a constant and complex evolution. Change one of the zones or elements and you will affect them all. To measure the 'actual' weather at any given moment in time and space is like taking a static snapshot of a process that itself remains in a state of continuous interactive change. The weather is only ever actual in the passing instant of a present moment, but what determines every such actuality is the dynamic motion of atmospheric forces as a whole. This motion or force itself cannot be grasped simply by measuring a series of actual states of affairs to which it gives rise: as motion or energy, it exists in intensive rather than extensive form.

Before Bergson, it is once again Spinoza who takes the first decisive steps towards a science of virtual multiplicities, when he affirms that the two attributes of divine substance which the human intellect can discern — thought and extension — are distinct but parallel. Since 'attributes constitute one and the same substance, modes that differ in attribute form one and the same modification' of that substance.[30] A human modification of substance, for instance, is composed of a mind (a finite mode of divine thought) and a body (a finite mode of divine extension). That body and mind are distinct means that the one has no causal influence or pre-eminence over the other, such that what causes or creates a mind is simply its eternal essence or idea in God; that they are parallel means that the one exists in a strict correlation with the other, such that the object of the idea that constitutes a mind is the 'actually existing' body that corresponds to it.[31] Every thinking is thus doubled with an extending. To every idea there corresponds the drawing of a line or a moving of forces. Every idea has its flow. For example, the idea of a circle and the geometric tracing of a circle are one and the same thing, conceived according to different attributes.[32] As Deleuze reads him, T.E. Lawrence will dramatise much the same principle when he presents abstract ideas not as inert forms of mental representation but as extended forces 'exerted on space following certain directions of movement', as 'entities that inspire powerful spatial dynamisms' (CC, 115, 119).

The point is that any given modification of substance can be conceived as either virtual or actual, individuating or individuated, across *both* the attributes of thought and extension. Both the abstract idea and the geometric tracing of our circle are equally virtual, as distinct from any actually or materially drawn circle. Contrary to what you might expect, the attribute of extension, when considered as an individuating attribute of substance, involves an indivisible and purely intensive or non-actual spatiality. Actual 'extensity' fails the ontological test that Deleuze associates, after Nietzsche, with the eternal return, since in it 'difference, the condition of eternal return, is cancelled' (DR, 243). So when Spinoza says that 'extension is an attribute of God', he certainly isn't making the 'absurd' claim that God is an actual or corporeal thing.[33] On the contrary, the extending of substance is as irreducible to any merely existent incarnation or instance of it as is thinking to any individuated thought. Extended substance, as Roger Woolhouse explains, is 'a reality of a kind which underwrites the possibility of actual instantiations of extension, of actual extended things'.[34] Spinoza offers the example of water, which we can conceive either as an actually individuated entity or as a virtual individuating:

> We conceive that water is divided and its parts separated one from the other – insofar as it is water, but not insofar as it is extended substance. For insofar as it is substance, it is neither separated nor divided. Again, water, insofar as it is water, is generated and corrupted, but insofar as it is substance, it is neither generated nor corrupted [...]. All things, I say, are in God, and all things that happen, happen only through the laws of God's infinite nature and follow from the necessity of his essence (IP15S5).

In other words, water is *actually* water only insofar as it appears thus, inadequately, to our imagination. In reality, however, what makes it what it is is the particular way it explicates or makes manifest a facet of creative substance, perceived under the attribute of extension. Water is God expressing himself as water, a virtual watering.

The logic of extension in this Spinozist sense is what underlies the virtual materiality of the configurations that come to preoccupy so much of Deleuze's later work, in particular the work written with Guattari. The names of many of these configurations are now widely familiar – rhizome, haecceity, abstract machine, body without organs, nomadic distribution, smooth space, 'any-space-whatever', and so on. In each case, what matters are not presentable or actual modifications of extension so much as virtual *extendings*, processes or 'states of pure and raw intensity stripped of their shape and their form' (AO, 18). Given any actual form or territory, what is decisive is always the movement of de-actualisation or deterritorialisation that 'liberates a pure matter' and dissolves the pertinent forms of identity or stability by dispersing them along a line of flight (D, 72–3). A smooth space, for instance, is one 'filled by events or haecceities, far more than by formed and perceived things. It is a space of affects, more than one of properties [...]. Intense *Spatium* instead of *Extensio*. A body without organs instead of an organism' (TP, 479; cf. CC, 173).

For the sake of simplicity we can take the one term 'haecceity' as a representative instance of this more general nomenclature. An echo of the same scholastic disputes which pitted univocal against analogical conceptions of being, a haecceity is as its etymology suggests a configuration that is immediately individuated as *this* unique or singular situation, rather than individuated as an instance or copy of an ideal model, or as a variation on a more general pattern. (The scholastic paradigm would be: God creates an individual soul as this unique soul, all at once, and not as a variation of a more generic human form or type, let alone as the mediated product of various general factors – social, economic, historical, psychological, etc. From the point of view of absolute creation, 'everything is ordinary!' for the same reason and in the same way that 'everything is unique!' [LB, 91]). A haecceity is a fully determinate virtual configuration which coheres on the creative plane of immanence and which is made up solely of intensive 'speeds and affects, independently of forms and subjects, which belong to another plane'. Personalities, objects, definite or definable things, presentable identities – all these belong on the plane of actuality. A virtual haecceity contains nothing actual, it consists entirely of virtual movements and virtual capacities to affect and to be affected. Deleuze and Guattari offer a whole raft of 'singular yet indefinite' illustrations: a life, a season, a time, a degree of heat, an intensity of white, a swarm, a pack, the hours of the day in Lawrence, etc., all of which must be intuited in their unique yet ordinary *thisness*. Or in the case of Freud's Little Hans, 'it is the wolf itself, and the horse, and the child that cease to be subjects to become events, in assemblages that are inseparable from an hour, a season, an atmosphere, an air, a life' (TP, 261–5).

The evocation of such assemblages is a perfectly typical example of the constructivist logic that governs books like *A Thousand Plateaus* and *What is Philosophy?*, but this logic isn't likely to mean very much until we can grasp more exactly what Deleuze means by the crucial term *event*.

IV

In most familiar physical situations, including relatively complicated ones like the weather, the ways in which virtual or intensive quantities are actualised usually conform to such a narrow and predictable range of behaviour that we tend to pay attention only to their result. Simple material situations are governed by limited and highly consistent forms of actualisation and are thus minimally creative. All being is creative, we know, but it is unequally so. These material situations are governed by the lowest form of creativity, in which almost nothing happens – in other words, they are situations in which what happens tends to conform to predictable patterns of causation. As Deleuze and Guattari will eventually explain, the distinctive concern of science is with the actual rather than the virtual (see below Chapter 6, section I).

The real philosophical interest of the notion of the virtual, and of the notion of an event that Deleuze identifies with it, lies precisely with its difference from conventional causal explanation. Any genuine event is 'free of all normal and normative causality'.[35] Since a power of pure difference is primary, so then given any particular thing 'what explicates it is difference, and not its causes'.[36] For obvious reasons, logics of creation are incompatible with logics of predictable causation or determination. Causality figures here as a primarily inter-actual or inter-creatural relation: as in the tired philosophical example in which one billiard ball hits another billiard ball, causation is a way of interpreting the influence of one actual thing upon another equally actual thing. Creation, on the other hand, involves a degree of virtual indetermination, a degree of potential that is irreducible to any discernible cause or cluster of causes. A creating, we might say, will assemble a series of contingently autonomous effects. Like a decision or an affirmation, like any exercise of freedom, a creating is a sequence sustained by its effects rather than determined by its cause. *A creating is an effect that becomes irreducible to its cause.* (Alternatively, a properly creative or immanent cause will be nothing other than 'a cause which is realised, integrated and distinguished by its effect' [FC, 37]).

It's no accident, then, that in one of the first books in which he develops his own notion of an event (*The Logic of Sense*, 1968), Deleuze insistently separates it from the domain of causation. Deleuze's peculiar logic of sense only makes sense as a non-causal logic. He defines an event precisely as a virtual or 'incorporeal effect', one that operates at a constitutive distance from its bodily cause. An event – 'event or creation': the terms are essentially synonymous (WP, 211) – figures here as an autonomous effect endowed with the power to generate a sort of 'quasi-cause' that serves only to confirm this autonomy. 'The event, that is, sense, refer[s] to a paradoxical element […] operating as a quasi-cause assuring the full autonomy of the effect', such that the cause of an event is 'nothing outside of its effect'. Such a cause 'maintains with the effect an immanent relation which turns the product, the moment that it is produced, into something productive' (LS, 95). Every relation between virtual and actual is thus creative rather than causal, and an event is first and foremost 'the part that eludes its own actualisation in everything that happens'. An event is actualised in a body and in a state of affairs but it also has 'a shadowy and secret part that is continually subtracted from or added to its actualisation […]. It is a virtual that is real without being actual'.[37] Because it isn't actual, an event is a sort of dead time in which nothing present or presentable can happen. 'The event is immaterial, incorporeal, unlivable: pure reserve.' The time of an event is a pure 'meanwhile' in which 'nothing takes place' (WP, 156, 158).

Take one of Deleuze's most illuminating examples, the event of a battle. If 'the Event in its essence is the battle' this is because, although it is diversely and simultaneously actualised by each participant in the battle, the virtual battle itself can be grasped only by escaping the perspective of any actually battling individual. Again in line with Bergson's inspiration, to grasp the virtual involves the suspension or dissolution of the actual as such. An actual soldier who is engaged in the battle, who acts and reacts in the midst of the battle, will remain unable to grasp the battle as event. Such insight will be reserved for those who can no longer act or react. The virtual battle-event 'hovers over its own field' and is 'graspable only by the will of anonymity which it itself inspires. This will, which we must call will "of indifference", is present in the mortally wounded soldier who is no longer brave or cowardly, no longer victor or vanquished, but rather so much beyond, at the place where the Event is present, participating therefore in its terrible impassivity.'[38] Only those who are past the battle can grasp it as event or essence. For the same reason, Beckett's exemplary characters are adequate to the virtual because, themselves exhausted, they have exhausted the domain of what is possible. 'Only the exhausted person can exhaust the possible, because he has renounced all need, preference, goal, or signification. Only the exhausted person is sufficiently disinterested.' Only the exhausted person is certain never to 'get back up' (CC, 154–5).

An event thus falls upon the world as something that is not itself of this world. An event is an action considered in itself, independently of the way it is acted out. The time of such action is the time of pure 'abstraction' as such (LS, 166). An event is an action abstracted from its actors and circumstances. An event immediately 'happens to things' (LS, 24), and transforms them. The event of a wedding connects two individuals; the event of a divorcing separates them. In any given case, what matters is the conversion of a result or state of affairs (this marriage, his wound, that death, her life) into an active though indefinite becoming or process – a wedding, a wounding, a dying, a living. What matters is the liberation of this process from the inertia of its actualisation. Deleuze mentions the example of Berg's 'Concerto in Memory of an Angel', a piece occasioned by the death of the young Manon Gropius. Whereas words are so burdened with meanings and connotations that they almost invariably 'imprison and suffocate us' along with the thing they describe, Berg's 'music manages to transform the death of *this* young girl into *a young girl dies*'. The concerto converts a definite and demonstrable fact into an indefinite event, a dying; such 'music brings about an extreme determination of the indefinite as pure intensity that pierces the surface' of things, as the 'disconnected' intensity of a creating liberated from its creature (CC, 173).

What Deleuze calls sense [*sens*] is simply another synonym for event, so it should come as no surprise that 'the most general operation of sense is this: it brings that which expresses it into existence…' (LS, 166). For instance, whereas an actual tree may be brown or green, '"to green" indicates a singularity-event in the vicinity of which the tree is constituted. "To sin" indicates a singularity-event in the vicinity of which Adam is constituted' (LS, 112). If an event can be expressed as a verb it will be on the model of such pure infinitives which, independent of any particular or actual conjugation, act with a power that determines the course of their actualisation (i.e. both the state of affairs to which it gives rise, and the proposition which articulates it). 'The infinitive verb expresses the event of language […], without person, without present, without any diversity of voice' (LS, 185; cf. EP, 104–5). And as nouns and adjectives lose their constituted meaning or identity in favour of 'the infinite equivalence of an unlimited becoming', as they are 'carried away by the verbs of pure becoming and slide into the language of events, all identity disappears from the self, the world, and God' (LS, 3).

To grasp an event is thus to align yourself in keeping with its determination, to embrace it as your destiny, as 'yours' in a way that is both utterly intimate (because it concerns you more profoundly than your actual interests or identity) and yet utterly impersonal (because it is both disinterested and non-identical). Consider again the event of a wound, or wounding. Deleuze will embrace unreservedly the *amor fati* of Stoic ethics: 'my wound existed before me; I was born to embody it'. Understood as an event, the wound is not the result of inter-actual relations or causes. To accept my virtual wound is to disregard the process of its actual causation (and thus to forego any temptation of regret). As event, the wound hovers above me as both indefinite yet sufficient. Although non-actualised, it is fully determinate and complete in itself. An event 'lacks nothing'. The wound as event then 'incarnates itself or actualises itself in a state of things or a lived experience [*un vécu*], but it is itself a pure virtual on the plane of immanence which pulls us into a life', i.e. into the composition of an impersonal yet singular living (as distinct from the definite individuality of a personal or composed life). So if my wound existed before me, this *before* must be understood 'not as a transcendence of the wound, as higher actuality, but as immanence, virtuality always at the heart of a milieu (field or plane)'.[39] And if I was born to embody its actualisation, this is precisely insofar as 'I' am able to sustain its transformative counter-actualisation. 'I was born to embody it as event because I was able to disembody it as state of affairs or lived situation.' I was born actually to embody it only insofar as I am worthy of it *as virtual event*, precisely – only insofar, in other words, as I am capable of its 'counter-effectuation' (WP, 159–60). Again, to counter-actualise or counter-effectuate an event is to affirm 'that part which goes beyond [its actual] accomplishment, the immaculate part' (D, 65).

This last process, the process of counter-actualisation, is perhaps the key to Deleuze's whole conception of the event and to the difference between causal and creative logics. One of the most striking and initially perplexing moves that Deleuze makes in *Logic of Sense* is to distinguish, along Stoic lines, between a domain of 'bodily causes' on the one hand and a domain of 'incorporeal effects' on the other. According to the Stoic conception of things, as Ronald Bogue explains, all bodies are included in a single divine or cosmic body; rather than relate to each other as cause and effect they co-exist as so many facets of this exclusive causal force. 'The knife does not cause the effect of a gash in the flesh; rather, the knife and flesh intermingle in the self-causing development of the cosmic body of God.'[40] Bodies thus belong to the causal depths; effects, by contrast, belong to an entirely different plane, a surface upon which they hover as virtual or 'incorporeal' events. You might expect, then, an explanation of how the causal depths determine these surface effects. Deleuze duly accepts that every event does indeed emerge from the 'depth of corporeal causes' (LS, 147). However, the general effort of the book is to complicate if not disrupt the mechanics of this production. 'The event results from bodies [...], but it differs in nature from that of which it is the result [...]. It is attributed to bodies, but not at all as a physical quality.'[41] Though an event may be occasioned by the movement of bodies 'it is not itself of the order of bodies', but rather 'towers over its own accomplishment and dominates its effectuation' (D, 64). An 'event is coextensive with becoming' (LS, 8), and a creating or becoming is always irreducible to its object or cause.

Rather than seek to understand the mechanism of their causation or production, Deleuze emphasises instead the virtual sufficiency of the events thus 'caused'. In every case, 'the event itself, the affective, the effect, goes beyond its own causes, and only refers to other effects' (C1, 106). Rather than try to explain causation as such, Deleuze shifts attention to the way events of sense are produced or created, on the assumption that such production takes place solely on the incorporeal surface of things, at a fundamental distance from any depth or cause. In Deleuze's idiosyncratic account, virtual sense is 'produced by the circulation of the element = x', i.e. by the self-moving circulation of a paradoxical 'quasi-cause' that traverses the incorporeal surface at infinite speed (LS, 70). In keeping with the Stoic inspiration behind *Logic of Sense*, what matters here is less an understanding of causes than an insight which might allow us to attain 'the will that the event creates in us, of becoming the quasi-cause of what is produced within us [...], of producing surfaces and linings in which the event is reflected, finds itself again as incorporeal, and manifests in us the neutral splendour which it possesses in itself in its impersonal and pre-individual nature' (LS, 148). What matters is the discovery of ways of aligning yourself with the creative processes that work through you. Although it's an exceptionally and perhaps symptomatically complicated sequence in his work, it may be that Deleuze only evokes causality at all so as to drive it down into the chaotic and sterile obscurity of the depths (a place from which it will hardly re-emerge in his subsequent books).[42]

To anticipate a point I'll come back to in Chapter 6, the essential thing to remember here is the transformative power of counter-actualisation or counter-effectuation per se. If actualisation involves a 'deep' or 'chaotic' movement from a virtual event to an actual state of affairs, counter-actualisation involves something more than the mere reversal of this movement. 'Actualisation and counter-effectuation are not two segments of the same line but rather different lines', and the latter movement, the movement of extraction that leads from actual to virtual, performs a sort of renovation or purification of the virtual itself. Counter-actualisation accesses 'a virtuality that has become consistent', i.e. that has attained a purely creative (or conceptual) intensity within the plane of immanence (WP, 160, 159). It's this extractive isolation that is properly transformative. Counter-actualisation makes the event 'more distinct, trenchant and pure'. It retains from it 'only its contour and its splendour' (LS, 150) – it retains, in other words, its creative force alone, extracted from the obscure depths of worldly causality. What Deleuze and Guattari will call artistic percepts and affects can be conceived only as 'autonomous and sufficient beings that no longer owe anything to those who experience or have experienced them' (WP, 168).

Creation always involves an escape, a fleeing, a flight, an exit. The essential effort is always to extract a pure potentiality, a virtual creating from an actual creature, such that the former can be thought as wholly independent of the latter. It's because it serves to free a creating from its creatures that real 'metamorphosis is the liberation of the non-existent entity for each state of affairs, and of the infinitive for each body and quality' (LS, 221). Jorge Iven's film *Rain*, for example, presents pure rain as it never actually exists or existed, 'rain as it is in itself, pure power or quality which combines without abstraction all possible rains and makes up the corresponding any-space-whatever' (C1, 111). The invention of just such forms of transformative subtraction or purification will be the primary task of all art and philosophy, and it already inspires what Deleuze describes in *Logic of Sense* as the work of the actor or mime:

> To be the mime of what effectively occurs, to double the actualisation with a counter-actu-alisation, the identification with a distance, like the true actor and the dancer, is to give the truth of the event the only chance of not being confused with its inevitable actualisation […]. To the extent that the pure event is each time imprisoned forever in its actualisation, counter-actualisation liberates it, always for other times (LS, 161).

V

Thus abstracted from the actual complications of causality, virtual events figure as aspects of that one-all which we already know to be the true dimension of reality itself. Still in keeping with Bergson's conception of virtual time, each individual event occurs as a singular aspect of an indivisible and un-presentable whole. If (in keeping with Stoic terminology) *Chronos* names the time of actuality and the present, 'the time of measure that situates things and persons, develops a form, and determines a subject', then *Aion* is the name of virtual, indivisible and thus un-presentable time. Non-actual, 'always already passed and eternally yet to come, Aion is the eternal truth of time: pure empty form of time, which has freed itself of its present corporeal content'. Aion is 'the indef-inite time of the event', the 'locus of incorporeal events' (TP, 262; LS, 164–5). And because virtual creation is ultimately (though unpresentably) one or indivisible, so then 'each event is adequate to the Aion in its entirety' (LS, 64). As we've seen, the singular-ity of Bergsonian time is perfectly explicit: 'not only do virtual multiplicities imply a single time, but duration as virtual multiplicity is this single and same Time' (B, 83). The configuration of Deleuzian creation is no less singular. All creative events 'commu-nicate in one and the same Event. They have therefore an eternal truth, and their time is never the present which realises them and makes them exist. Rather, it is the unlim-ited Aion, the Infinitive in which they subsist and insist' (LS, 53).

We are now in a position to anticipate how a philosophy of virtual creation, one that concerns itself primarily with the individuation of virtual creatings, is also one that *orients* these creatings back towards that singular creator which we identified, earlier in this chapter, as the first of creation's three aspects. Here this aspect takes the form of an aleatory point or purely paradoxical instance. 'The paradoxical instance is the Event in which all events communicate and are distributed. It is the Unique event, and all other events are its bits and pieces' (LS, 56). Since they are paradoxical, precisely, the examples (Blituri, Snark, etc.) that Deleuze provides in his *Logic of Sense* do not themselves have any discernible sense; themselves non-sense, they are supposed to distribute the terms of sense across the whole field of creation.[43]

It's the singular or non-relational configuration of such distribution that aligns it with more conventionally theophanic conceptions of creation and the apparent ethical problems such conceptions seem to involve. If God is good and everything is an expression of God, how to explain the existence of evil? of suffering? of ignorance and sin? If compared to Spinoza or Leibniz Deleuze rarely couches such questions in these terms, the way he deals with them is much the same. Every creating is a facet of creation, and since creation is an indivisible (and thus unpresentable) whole, all creatings are perfectly compatible amongst themselves. Every aspect of real duration can 'coexist together without difficulty' (B, 77). The spark of life that animates even an objectionable character like Dickens' Riderhood is itself a force with which everyone can empathise. As a rule, 'all events, even contraries, are compatible [...]. Incompatibility is born only with individuals, persons and worlds in which events are actualised, but not between events themselves or between their a-cosmic, impersonal and pre-individual singularities.' Every virtual event is a facet of the one creative surge, and the 'essential point is the simultaneity and contemporaneity of all the divergent series, the fact that all coexist' (LS, 177; DR, 124).

Spinoza had already paved the way for this conclusion. Since every distinct attribute is an attribute of one and the same substance they are all 'necessarily compatible' (EP, 79–80), and since every mode is in turn the mode of one of these attributes their compatibility is given as a matter of course. The order of modal essences is 'characterised by a total conformity' (EP, 211), and if all modal 'essences agree, this is just because they are not causes of one another, but all have God as their cause' (EP, 194). And Leibniz? Although his affirmation of an infinite multiplicity of distinct substances or monads may make the demonstration of such compatibility seem less obvious, his counterbalancing insistence that creation is subject to the rule of pre-established harmony ensures a comparable result:

> It is precisely because all absolute forms are incapable of being contradicted that they can belong to a same Being, and, in being able to, they effectively belong to it. Since they are forms, their real distinction is formal and carries no ontological difference among beings to which each might be attributed: they are all attributed to a single and same Being that is both ontologically one and formally diverse.[44]

Along the same lines, what Deleuze calls ideas are 'complexes of coexistence', in keeping with the assumption that in a certain way, 'all the Ideas coexist' (DR, 186). If Deleuze has become famous for his emphasis on disjunction and non-resemblance (the non-resemblance between virtual and actual, i.e. between creating and creature), the essential thing to remember is that these 'disjunctions are inclusive' rather than exclusive. Among his innumerable artistic examples, consider the exemplary case of Proust's *In Search of Lost Time*. At first glance it may seem that its 'parts are produced as asymmetrical sections' or 'hermetically sealed boxes'; after all, Proust 'maintained that the

Whole itself is a product, produced as nothing more than a part alongside other parts, which it neither unifies nor totalises' (AO, 42–3). But this actual disunity depends in turn upon the virtual unity of the inspiration that sustains it. The dissolution of the actual whole or world is itself compatible with that unpresentable unity which encompasses and affirms all possible worlds. The whole of the *Search* is thus 'one and the same story with infinite variations'. It involves the myriad refraction of one and the same virtual reality, in which every actual object comes apart, on the model of Albertine's face as it shatters into 'molecular partial objects' (AO, 70).

In other words, at the same time and for the same reason that it orients these creatings towards their unthinkable creator, such a philosophy plays down the creatures in which they may actually be confined. Incompatibility or exclusion can only begin with the illusion of distinct actualities or specific subjects. The synthesis of virtual inscription on what Deleuze and Guattari will call the body without organs, for instance, does not 'involve any exclusion, since exclusions can arise only as a function of inhibiters and repressors that eventually determine the support and firmly define a specific, personal subject' (AO, 38–9). Such exclusion will be avoided if the formation and definition of specific actualities is itself undone, so as to prepare the way for an intuition of that virtual plane of immanence or Aion in which 'nothing other than the Event subsists, the Event alone, Eventum tantum for all contraries' (LS, 176).

VI

What emerges from this general schema is the unqualified dependence of the actual upon the virtual. The virtual process of individuation creates not only individuals but also, in a sense, the raw materials of its own process. 'Individuation properly precedes matter and form, species and parts, and every other element of the constituted individual' (DR, 38). Whatever the field, Deleuze always seeks to reassert the 'primacy of individuation over actualisation'. Everywhere he looks he finds evidence to prove that virtual or differential 'individuation always governs actualisation'. In the field of living beings, for instance, purely differential 'intensity is primary in relation to organic extensions' and actual 'types [are] determined in their species only by virtue of the individuating intensity' (DR, 250–1). In the case of an idea, what matters are the 'internal differences which dramatise an Idea before representing an object'. What matters are the aspects of an unconditional differing that 'unfolds as pure movement, creative of a dynamic space and time which correspond to the Idea' (DR, 26, 24). An idea always 'differentiates itself [...]. The Idea is fully differential in itself, even before it differenciates itself in the actual.' The determination or differentiation of the virtual is prior to and independent of its actualisation or differenciation.[45] Needless to say, whenever an Idea is actualised its actualisation proceeds according to its own rules and its own time and space, and the empirical peculiarities of this space and time deserve consideration as such. Nevertheless, with respect to the virtual that it actualises the actual is characterised by its essential redundancy, in much the same way that 'the world he produces adds nothing to God's essence'.[46]

47

The crucial thing is that relations *between* the actuals as such, one actual to another, are deprived of any productive or creative force. As a rule, in any given series the positions of actual terms 'in relation to one another depend on their "absolute" position in relation to [...] the paradoxical element or aleatory point' that distributes the actual series in the first place.[47] In each case the creative 'movement goes, not from one actual term to another, nor from the general to the particular, but from the virtual to its actualisation – through the intermediary of a determining individuation' (DR, 251tm). The process that generates continuous variation, for instance, operates with a strictly unilateral and unidirectional force. Continuous variation is

> constituted not from one present to another, but between the two coexistent series that these presents form in function of the virtual object (object = x). It is because this object constantly circulates, always displaced in relation to itself, that it determines transformations of terms and modifications of imaginary relations within the two real series in which it appears [...]. The displacement of the virtual object is not, therefore, one disguise among others, but the principle from which, in reality, repetition follows in the form of disguised repetition.[48]

It is this virtual displacement that distributes if not generates its actual terms. Creative determination belongs to the circulating as such, and never to the series thus circulated.

Artaud's exemplary theatre of cruelty, for instance, is 'defined only in terms of an extreme "determinism," that of spatio-temporal determination in so far as it incarnates an Idea or nature [...], a pure staging without author, without actors and without subjects' (DR, 219). Artaud stages a 'sequence of spiritual states which are deduced from one another as thought is deduced from thought'.[49] This is theatre which acts without representation or intermediary, with an immediate, overwhelming intensity. The pure or creative difference that it deploys is the 'only extreme, the only moment of presence and precision. Difference is the state in which one can speak of determination as such'. In short, pure 'difference is this state in which determination takes the form of unilateral distinction' (DR, 28).

Deleuze will insist on much the same power of virtual determination when he tries to identify the fundamental operation at work in the structuralist projects of his contemporaries Lacan, Althusser and Levi-Strauss.[50] In the case of these and other comparable projects or 'problems', merely actual 'solutions are engendered at precisely the same time that the problem determines *itself*' (LS, 121). The virtual problem is what 'orientates, conditions and engenders' its set of actual solutions (DR, 212). The decisive role in this engendering will be played by a virtual differenciator or *precursor*. 'Given two heterogeneous series, two series of differences, the precursor plays the part of the differenciator of these differences. In this manner, but in virtue of its own power, it puts them into immediate relation to one another; it is the in-itself of difference or the "differently different"'. Such a precursor is the 'the self-different which relates different to different by itself'. It alone has the power to differentiate or determine. Considered in itself (i.e. independently of what it differs), the precursor 'has no place other than that from which it is "missing", no identity other than that which it lacks'. It is a sort of indefinitely self-varying object = x. In other words, although it is itself a force of pure differing, this virtual object or precursor conceals itself and its functioning in the actual field or series that it differs. Its own invisible path 'becomes visible only in reverse, to the extent that it is travelled over and covered by the phenomena it induces within the system' (DR, 119–20). What Deleuze applauds in the Althusserian reading of *Capital*, for instance, is precisely its insistence upon a virtual (and thus unpresentable) power of determination in the last instance. The economic dimension is virtually determining, and its determinations are then actualised or 'incarnated in the concrete differenciated labours which characterise a determinate society'. The virtual determining or structuring never acts transitively or in keeping with chronological progression of historical time. It is not mediated by the cumulative pressure of actual constraint. Rather, it simply 'acts by incarnating its varieties in diverse societies and by accounting for the simultaneity of all the relations and terms which, each time and in each case, constitute the present: that is why "the economic" is never given properly speaking, but rather designates a differential virtuality to be interpreted, always covered over by its forms of actualisation' (DR, 186).

Every virtual or determining quality thus enjoys what Deleuze and Guattari will later call a sort of creative autonomy or 'self-movement' (TP, 317). In his reading of Foucault's work, Deleuze will again go to considerable trouble to preserve the autonomy of determining (composing) forces from merely determined (composed) forms on the other. Everything springs from 'the *spontaneity* of power's ability to affect', paired with the wholly passive 'receptivity of the power to be affected', to be made visible, to be articulated or stated (FC, 77). Deleuze assumes that 'the question of primacy is essential' and if the *statement* [*énoncé*] is primary it is because it enjoys an effectively absolute power to constitute or individuate the actuality to which it applies. The virtual statements that define delinquency, for instance, apply immediately to actual individuals (prisoners) and actual spaces (prisons) in a unilateral determination that 'does not refer back to any Cogito or transcendental subject that might render it possible [...], or to any Spirit of the Age that could conserve, propagate and recuperate it'. Instead, 'like Bergsonian memory, a statement preserves itself within its own space', unrelated to those people or places to which they apply (FC, 4). A virtual statement isn't defined by what it denotes or signifies, so much as sustained by its own inherent spontaneity (79). Whereas a merely actual 'proposition is supposed to have a referent', the discursive object of a virtual statement 'does not in any sense derive from a particular state of things, but stems from the statement itself. It is a derived object, defined precisely by the lines of variation of the statement existing as a *primitive function*' (8–9). The rules governing such a statement 'are to be found on the same level as itself', defined 'by certain inherent lines of variation', as a bundle of 'intrinsic positions' (5–6). The upshot, once again, is an absolute self-determining power: 'by virtue of their spontaneity, [statements] exert an infinite determination' over the constituted domains of the visible or actually presentable (67).

The only effective relation between actuals, in other words, is determined by the differentiation of the virtual or virtuals that they actualise. Individuation does not proceed through the distinction of 'qualities and extensities, forms and matters, species and parts', but generates all these things as secondary phenomena of its own action (DR, 247); 'every individuating factor is already difference and difference of difference', a differing that stems from a 'full, positive power' of pure disparity (DR, 257–8). The error that Deleuze never tires of correcting, after Bergson, is that which mistakes a creative movement for 'a relation between actual terms instead of seeing in it the actualisation of something virtual'.[51] In any given field of individuation, 'virtuals communicate, immediately, above the actual that separates them'.[52] Leibniz's monads, for example, express the entire world but have no windows or doors and thus no actual relations with each other. Since 'the world does not exist outside of the monads that express it, the latter are not in contact and have no horizontal relations among them, no intraworldly connections, but only an indirect harmonic contact to the extent they share the same expression' (LB, 81). The individuality of an actual body or state of affairs, its bundle of intrinsic modalities, is thus delegated from without, in advance (DR, 36–7; 250–1). 'Actualisation comes about through differentiation' of the virtual but it is the virtual that remains the exclusive subject of this differentiation, such that 'actualisation belongs to the virtual' alone.[53]

Although it can never be given or presented, since the virtual (idea, problem, event, statement, concept…) is what accounts for the individuation of a given entity or situation, adequately to *know* this entity or situation is to know it in its virtual dimension alone. The actual per se just gets in the way of such knowledge. To know reality is thus to see through actuality. To know reality is to intuit what cannot be given, presented or represented. Although a creating is not representable, nevertheless Deleuze always assumes (again no less than Spinoza or Leibniz) that we can attain a perfectly adequate intuition of what creatings are. The domain of creatings is a domain of immediate certainty and sufficiency. Error and illusion are peculiar to the domain of representation. Illusion arises only within the domain of constituted actuality. Our perception of resemblances among actuals, and in particular of our own resemblance to ourselves (my sense of being properly 'myself', being true to myself, and so on) is pure delusion. Such 'resemblance is an effect, an external result – an illusion which appears once the agent arrogates to itself an identity that it lacked' (DR, 120).

When pressed on this point, Deleuze is quite happy to accept the essentialist or Platonic implications of his position (so long as we remember that this Plato doesn't think essences as identity-bound or created forms, but as dynamic creations or multiplicities). This is the position he adopts, for instance, in a 1967 debate with a specialist in German Idealism, Alexis Philonenko:

> Deleuze: It seems to me we have the means to penetrate the subrepresentational, to reach all the way to the roots of spatio-temporal dynamisms, and all the way to the Ideas actualised in them: the elements and ideal events, the relations and singularities are perfectly determinable. Illusion only comes afterward, from the direction of constituted extensions and the qualities that fill out these extensions.

Philonenko: So illusion appears only in what is constituted.

Deleuze: That's right [...].

Philonenko: [...] If you push illusion over to the side of what is constituted, without accepting illusion in genesis, in constitution, are you not in the end just coming back to Plato (when in fact you would like to avoid such a thing), for whom precisely constitution, understood as proceeding from the Idea, in as much as it can be understood, is always veracious, truthful?

Deleuze: Yes, perhaps (DI, 115–16tm).

Deleuze finds what may be his most promising (albeit most obscure) vehicle for this kind of exact but virtual or subrepresentational determination in a relatively arcane field of mathematics. Drawing on a number of episodes in the 'esoteric history of differential philosophy', Deleuze's evocation of the differential ratios (dx/dy) that were employed in early versions of infinitesimal calculus is surely the most challenging section of *Difference and Repetition*. Deleuze appears to agree with Bergson's enthusiastic appreciation of infinitesimal calculus as 'the most powerful method of investigation known to the mind', precisely because it allows us to grasp motion 'no longer from outside and in its manifest result, but from within and in its tendency to change'.[54] Although non-expert readers (like the present author) are in no position to assess the finer points of this argument, it is well worth trying to convey the gist of the sequence.[55]

What Deleuze is looking for is an account of mathematical functions or ratios which ensures, first, that the components of a ratio of the type dx/dy are 'reciprocally determinate', i.e. that the virtual differing expressed as dx is fully and exclusively determinate in relation to dy and vice versa (while remaining utterly indeterminate in relation to an actual or differed quantity x itself), and second, that they are then fully determinant of any actual calculation or numerical presentation, for instance the actual set of their solutions. In the first case, differential relations determine their own components in such a way that they 'allow no independence whatsoever to subsist' (DR, 183). The differential dx only *is* in relation to dy: this 'relation' is not then *between* two distinct entities so much as the process that determines these entities themselves. This sort of 'individuation does not presuppose any differenciation; it gives rise to it' (DR, 247). In the second case, differential relations immediately establish the actual, individual or differentiated values that might be attributed to these elements, precisely because they themselves remain pre-individual or non-actual. 'It is not the differential quantities which are cancelled in dy/dx or 0/0 but rather the individual and the individual relations within the function' (DR, 171). The moment when dx/dy becomes *actually* indistinguishable from 0/0 is the moment in which, since all measurable or 'created' values have been annulled, it is possible to glimpse the mathematical equivalent of a pure creating as such (since in this as in every case, the creating as such endures when its creature is annulled). By the same token, a differential function tends to disappear behind the production of its actual result, just as a virtual problem disappears in the actual solutions that it generates (or a creating disappears in the thing it creates). A virtual problem is both 'transcendent in relation to the solutions that it engenders on the basis of its own determinate conditions' and 'immanent in the solutions which cover it' – solutions which simply follow directly on from the process whereby the problem determines *itself* (DR, 177–9; LS, 121).

While the precise kinds of algebraic relations that Deleuze has in mind are too technical to summarise here, the example of a very basic function might at least convey the basic idea. Given a simple function like $x = 2y$, for instance, it is very easy to calculate what x must be for any *actual* y. If y is 1 then x is 2, if y is 3 then x will be 6, etc. So long as y is a finite or measurable quantity, however large or small, such calulation remains perfectly automatic. The solution is simplest of all, of course, when y is just set to zero: twice zero is again zero. Strictly speaking though, as far as the function $x = 2y$ itself is concerned, $0 = 2(0)$ is as valid a result as any other actual solution: this twice zero would indeed still be *virtually* twice the size of zero itself, even though this 'being-twice' now has no actual or measurable meaning. The virtual ratio, in other words, is independent of any actual value we might assign to it. Something similar happens when one of our variables is made to tend towards zero, i.e. when it comes immeasurably close to zero but isn't quite yet equal to zero. Immediately before it reaches zero, so to speak, there would be a moment when the variable would be only virtually or 'infinitesimally' larger than zero. In our example, the rate at which x will approach zero will still be half that of y, and it will remain so even at the very moment when both variables come to be equal to zero itself (and thus become actually indistinguishable: 0/0).

In other words, when the actual or measurable dimensions of such a relationship have been evacuated (or brought indiscernibly close to zero), the virtual relationship can then be grasped for its own sake, as absolutely determinate of any actual value. Considered in themselves, differentials are thus forms of a purely 'ideal difference'. 'Differentials certainly do not correspond to any engendered quantity, but rather constitute an unconditioned rule for the production of knowledge or quantity, and for the construction of series or the generation of discontinuities which constitute its material […]. The differential is pure power, just as the differential relation is a pure element of potentiality' (DR, 175). There is no more an interactive relation between this virtual or composing power and its actual or composed result than there is *between* a given set of genes and the organism that incarnates them.

Along the lines of this last analogy, it might be worth briefly cementing this point with one final illustration, the case of biological evolution. As Deleuze and Guattari understand it, biological evolution proceeds neither through the relations of struggle, competition or support that may exist between actual organisms, nor through the dialectical interaction between actual organisms and their actual environment. As opposed to an 'orthodox Darwinism with its focus on discrete units of selection', they maintain that 'evolution takes place from the virtual to actuals. Evolution is actualisation, actualisation is creation'.[56] As Mark Hansen has recently demonstrated in convincing detail, because they dismiss the actual 'organism as a molar form that negatively limits life', Deleuze and

Guattari's approach to biological individuation remains profoundly 'alien to the conceptual terrain of current biology and complexity theory'.[57]

Rather than recent versions of complexity theory or post-Darwinian biology, the real models for Deleuzian individuation are again the theophanic philosophies of Spinoza and Leibniz. Spinoza's account couldn't be simpler. A human being, like any finite being, 'has no power of its own except insofar as it is part of a whole [...]. We are a part of the power of God' (EP, 91–2). Every individual is a mode or facet of God, and every mode has two aspects, one virtual, one actual. The virtual aspect of a mode is its essence, which is what accounts for it or causes it to be what it is. A mode's essence is directly determined or created by God, and is nothing other than an intensive degree of God's own power. Like any virtual event, a modal essence *is* for all eternity and its being is entirely independent of its actual existence. Such existence, by contrast, is of course temporary and contingent. 'A mode exists, if it actually possesses a very great number of extensive parts corresponding to its essence or degree of power' (EP, 202). The ongoing existence of the mode will depend upon the stability of a certain relation of 'movement and rest' among its composite parts; 'a given mode will continue to exist as long as the same relation subsists in the infinite whole of its parts'.[58] A mode ceases to exist when, for example as a result of harmful encounters with other existent modes, this relation weakens or comes to an end. Neither the birth nor death of a mode, however, has any effect upon its virtual essence as such.

Leibniz maintains an equally unilateral configuration. 'The individuality of the body or the thing comes from elsewhere. And in effect, what is individual and what individuates the alterable body is only the soul that is inseparable from it' (LB, 65). What individuates such a virtual soul or monad are the singular qualities it is made to possess. Each individual is predicated to have or to enfold all that it contains. 'The organism is defined by its ability to fold its own parts and to unfold them, not to infinity, but to a degree of development assigned to each species' (LB, 110, 8). This degree is fixed, determined by God. To every particular monad thus corresponds a body made up of the quantity of components whose own monads fall within this monad's power or dominance. An actual or 'specific body belongs to my monad, but [only] as long as my monad dominates the monads that belong to the parts of my body'. As we have seen, the whole, infinitely complex arrangement holds together in a hierarchical pyramid of monadic inclusion, ranging from the damned, or absolutely dominated, to the reasonable, or absolutely dominant (LB, 110, 113).

The relative position of a monad within this pyramid or scale is further determined by its ability to be worthy of the qualities it contains, i.e. to provide them with an adequate expression. For example, the monad Julius Caesar 'condenses a certain number of unique, incorporeal, ideal events that do not yet put bodies in play, although they can only be stated in the form, "Caesar crosses the Rubicon, he is assassinated by Brutus..."'. Such are the primary predicates that God has assigned to Caesar. If a monad then has an actual body, it is because such a body may be required for the complete expression of these predicate-events: Caesar must have a body capable of crossing a river, and capable of being assassinated, because he *is* this crossing and this being-assassinated. In line with the Stoic ethic of the *Logic of Sense*, Caesar's only real task is to become worthy of the events he has been created to embody. *Amor fati*. What Caesar actually does adds nothing to what he virtually is. When Caesar actually crosses the Rubicon this involves no deliberation or choice since it is simply part of the entire, immediate expression of Caesarness, it simply unrolls or 'unfolds something that was encompassed for all times in the notion of Caesar'[59] – and a world in which Caesar did not cross the Rubicon would thus have to be an entirely different world.

Such unabashedly 'pre-critical' notions might seem far removed from the concerns of a contemporary philosopher who so often reminds us that the virtual coherence of sense 'excludes merely, and yet supremely, the coherence of the self, world and God' (LS, 176). But does the fact that Deleuze applauds the death of God mean that he is also willing to bury the classical idea of an infinitely perfect essence or all-powerful creative force? Not at all: as Deleuze understands it, the death of God simply means the death of transcendence, i.e. the death of an uncreative or finitely creative God, a God that remains at a distance from creation. The death of God signals 'the abolition of the cosmological distinction between two worlds, the metaphysical distinction between essence and appearance' (DI, 74). Needless to say, Deleuze adamantly rejects any notion of God linked to the static stability of the world, to the consolidation of personal or organic identity, to the transcendence of ideal forms – in short to notions incompatible with the affirmation of a properly unlimited creative power.[60] But when it comes to explaining the individuation of virtual creatings he relies, no less than Spinoza and Leibniz, upon an intensive form of power whose primary medium is spiritual and whose paradigmatic vehicle is divine.

Deleuze makes no effort to conceal what is ultimately at issue here. We know that actual 'individuals suppose nothing other than Ideas' (DR, 252), that 'we are always patients where Ideas are concerned' (DR, 219). The next question is inevitable: 'Where do Ideas come from, the variations of their relations [*rapports*] and their distributions of singularities? Here, again, we follow the path to the bend at which "reason" plunges into a beyond. The ultimate [*radicale*] origin was always assimilated to a divine and solitary game' (DR, 282; cf. LS, 64) – that is, the game of unqualified creation as such, behind which there lies only the pure potential of absolute constituent power or play. This is a power which, escaping this world, will eventually call for the 'creation of a new people' and the 'creation of a new earth' (WP, 108–9).

3

Creatural Confinement

'To move beyond the human condition, such is
the meaning and direction [sens] of philosophy'
(FC, 124–5tm).

From a Deleuzian perspective, the one real philosophical problem is simply this: although there *are* only creatings, these can give rise to creatures which then get in the way of creation. There are only creatings, but some of these creatings give rise to the unavoidable illusion of creatural independence. Creation thereby generates an interminable series of internal obstacles to its own intensification or development. Creative intensity is necessarily 'explicated in systems in which it tends to be cancelled', i.e. in systems of actual, measurable extension. Spatial extension is itself 'precisely the process by which intensive difference is turned inside out and distributed in such a way as to be dispelled, compensated, equalised and suppressed in the extensity which it creates' (DR, 228, 233). Again, life is nothing other than creative movement, yet 'life as movement alienates itself in the material form that it creates; by actualising itself, by differentiating itself, it loses "contact with the rest of itself". Every species is thus an arrest of movement', and homo sapiens is no exception to this rule (B, 104; cf. EP, 214–15).

Our only problem, in other words – but there is no greater problem – is that we generally live in ignorance or denial of what we are. Although only the virtual determines the real, we assume instead that the actual offers the most reliable basis for reality. In reality, active becoming or transformation is a matter of composing forces and not composed forms, but unfortunately *we* begin precisely as composed forms, as actual creatures, trapped in ignorance, impotence and slavery.[1] We are born to inherit delusions of ontological equivocity or dualism – in particular, the belief that we are subjects as distinct from objects, and thus subjects who must represent and interpret objects. All creatures capable of thought need to escape their ignorance and *become* thoughtful. A creature will actively express creation only by becoming, in the most active and literal sense, creative.

Unfortunately, despite (if not because of) their apparently unique capacity for thought, human beings have a particular affinity for thoughtlessness. We have a special knack for transforming our active, open or creative dimension into reactive closure and inertia. Creative force is active, it creates the very objects of its perception, but becoming anti-active or 'becoming-reactive is constitutive of man. *Ressentiment*, bad conscience and nihilism are not psychological traits but the foundation of the humanity in man. They are the principle of the human being as such' (NP, 64). The whole human drama stems precisely from the fact that, as Nietzsche understood with particular clarity, in humanity '*creature* and *creator* are united' – and that the prevailing human response is one of pity for the 'creature in man', i.e. pity for precisely that aspect of our being that should instead be broken and 'purified', made to become 'incandescent'.[2] Or as Eriugena might put it: whatever we call 'hell' is not a place, it is the psychological state to which we commit ourselves insofar as we refuse to abandon the circumstances that sustain our specifically creatural delusions.[3]

Essential to any philosophy of creation, then, is an account of how it might be led thus to limit or work against itself. The versions Deleuze offers of such an account come in a characteristically dizzying variety of forms – the constitution of 'man' and in particular of moral man in *Nietzsche and Philosophy*; the mediation and representation of difference in *Difference and Repetition*; the institution of worldliness, of *mondanité* and romantic love, in *Proust and Signs*; the castration of desire and the limitation of schizophrenia to a merely medical condition in *Anti-Oedipus*, and so on. There's no need to go through all these sequences here. In each case, what Deleuze is looking for is an account of the human and of the creatural more generally that both acknowledges its unreal or illusory status and yet doesn't fall back into the well-worn patterns of transcendence, i.e. that doesn't simply condemn, from a higher or more eminent perspective, the creatural as fundamentally inferior or unsalvageable. Deleuze's philosophy is redemptive, not pessimistic. In other words, Deleuze needs an account of how creative desire might be led to desire its own repression – an account of why people 'fight for their servitude as stubbornly as though it were their salvation'. This remains 'the fundamental problem of political philosophy', if not of philosophy altogether, and the basis for its properly clinical or symptomalogical function.[4] Such an account must remain consistent with the imperative of creative univocity, to the exclusion of any judgemental equivocity or transcendence.

After all, the production of actual creatures is a fundamental aspect of what creation *is*. The creatural is itself an aspect of creation, rather than its falsification or debasement, or a lower reality that must be transcended. Intensive difference isn't simply cancelled in the system of extension, it also 'creates this system by explicating itself'. Intensity itself creates the system that annuls it in explicated actuality, that draws it outside itself (even as it endures, at the same time, in its virtual, intensive and differential form, since its every explication also allows it to remain 'implicated' within itself [DR, 228]). The things God creates do not in any sense lessen or exhaust God, and an infinitely creative substance 'has an absolutely infinite power of existence only by exercising in an infinity of things, in an infinity of ways or modes, the capacity to be affected corresponding to that power' (EP, 95). While creatural opacity is a necessary and immanent obstacle to creation, nevertheless ordinary creatural concerns can themselves be transformed to become a vehicle of insight.

This is enough sharply to distinguish Deleuze from any philosophy that flees or despises ordinary life for the sake of something better or higher outside it. Philosophers as different as Plotinus and Kant both assume that genuine metaphysical insight must be insight of a dramatically special kind, something very different from the knowledge offered by our ordinary senses, consciousness and life (and it's precisely for this reason that Kant, unlike Plotinus, concludes we are not capable of metaphysical insight). Deleuze, by contrast, agrees with Bergson that our ordinary experience of time may allow us directly to grasp real being and movement. Properly understood, such experience can become an adequate vehicle for an intuition of real movement. All the same, this 'properly understood' is itself crucial and transformative. Creatural concerns can only become the vehicle for insight if properly oriented, precisely *away* from the creatural and *towards* the creating. The philosophical project is one of developing, with and within the materials generated by actualisation, a mechanism of counter-actualisation. Philosophy will lead from actual to virtual; from the world, it must lead out of the world. Does this mean a return to transcendence, a leap into an otherworldly beyond? Not at all: 'out' doesn't mean 'beyond'. Extra-worldly doesn't mean other-worldly. To move virtually out – to *out* – involves neither actual externality nor a transcendent ideal; the *outing* that is a line of flight or deterritorialisation need not move through actual space. All that will ever actually be presented along the path from actual to virtual will be actual as a matter of course; all the same, it must serve to orient those who are exposed to it outside itself, towards the virtual that is alone creative of the world.

To put this in more explicitly theophanic terms: God expresses himself in the creatural, the creatural is nothing other than God, and the creatural offers an adequate path that leads to God. Yet to perceive God it is nonetheless necessary to *follow* this path, i.e. to move out past the creatural as such. What lives in the creature is not *in* the creature, precisely. What lives in the creature is not the creature itself, but the God who creates or expresses himself through it. God's divinity or creativity can be grasped only via God, not the creatural, even though the creatural remains our only basis for this grasping. Our grasping is one that begins within limits that it must strive more or less immediately to exceed. As Deleuze's contemporary Henry Corbin explains, absolute creativity (or God) 'cannot be an object (an objective given). He can only be known through himself as absolute Subject, that is, as absolved from all unreal objectivity', from all merely 'creatural' mediation.[5] Via Spinoza, Deleuze sets out from much the same point of departure. 'God produces an infinity of things because his essence is infinite', but the production of these actual things is itself secondary rather than primary, derivative of God's own infinite creativity. 'God expresses himself in himself "before" expressing himself in his effects: expresses himself by in himself constituting *natura naturans*, before expressing himself through producing within himself *natura naturata*' (EP, 14). The expressive or 'explicative' determination that links the implicated *naturans* (the virtual creating) and the explicated *naturata* (the actual creature) is strictly unilateral and irreversible.

We might note in passing that, adjusted for different contexts, this principle could be extended to much of the most inventive work undertaken in contemporary French philosophy more generally, including the work undertaken by figures as disparate as Bergson and Sartre, Lacan and Foucault, Levinas and Baudrillard, Badiou and Rosset. Each in their own way, the priority for all these thinkers is less to dissolve the subject (the subject of freedom, or creation, or speech…) than to dissolve everything that *objectifies* or normalises this subject. The most general goal has been to evacuate all that serves to reduce an essentially creative being to the mere creature of objective forces.[6] The same Bergson who insists that our ordinary intuition of time may allow us to grasp creative movement, for instance, also acknowledges that our equally ordinary tendency to understand ourselves not in terms of movement and time but in terms of 'objective' stability and space is what leads us astray. As we have seen, by 'following the usual data of our senses and consciousness we arrive in the speculative order at insoluble contradictions'.[7] The real task, although never simply to leap beyond the creatural into some other realm, is thus nonetheless to reverse the inner movement of our creation or actualisation, i.e. to dissipate the creatural and thus re-establish our links with the continuous whole of virtual reality. The goal is to escape confinement within the creatural without yielding to the temptation of an abrupt transcendence of the creatural. The goal is to build or find that force within ourselves, within the world, that opens a route out of both self and world.

In other words, the goal is to trace a sustainable 'line of flight' – a flight out of your place, out of your body, out of your self, out of our world. A 'line of flight or deterritorialisation' is Deleuze and Guattari's term for 'an abstract line of creative or specific causality' (TP, 194; D, 124, 147). Every creating, every virtual or 'abstract' machine, is oriented by such lines of flight, i.e. forms of flight that do not respond to some external threat, that are not forms of flight *from* something, so much as the vectors of a pure escape, a pure movement *out* of something. Flight is here solely a matter of *taking* flight. As creatings, lines of flight are themselves primary and constituent; they are 'not phenomena of resistance or counterattack in an assemblage, but cutting edges of creation and deterritorialisation' (TP, 531n.39; cf. K, 41).

Each such taking-flight has to pull away from several successive forms of detention. Living creatures are held down, in the first place, by what they take to be the unalterable constraints of their actual organic form. Creatural forms issue directly from the process of their actualisation, and are sustained by cumulative layers of stratification or territorialisation. Creatural consolidation then proceeds around transcendent 'molar' poles that vary with each situation – for instance around '"the" Sovereign or "the" Law, in the case of the State; the Father in the case of the family; Money, Gold or the Dollar in the case of the market; God in the case of religion; Sex in the case of the sexual institution', etc. (FC, 76). Mechanisms of transcendence make creatures 'resonate together' in stable patterns and administrable, manageable relations (TP, 433). Creatural stasis is further reinforced by a belief, based on our investment in such transcendent forms, in the primacy of merely derivative or specific differences, in 'the long error of representation', in the presumptions of metric measurement, of what Deleuze and Guattari deride as 'royal' or 'major' science.

As far as human beings are concerned, the consolidation of our creatural condition, and of the illusions that will accompany it, is the result of a number of mutually reinforcing features. Of the various strata that actualise and bind us, Deleuze and Guattari identify the 'organism, signification, and subjectivation' as the most fundamental. 'You will be organised, you will be an organism, you will articulate your body – otherwise you're just depraved. You will be signifier and signified, interpreter and inter-preted – otherwise you're just a deviant. You will be a subject, nailed down as one […] – otherwise you're just a tramp' (TP, 159).

If creation is to become all that it can be then each of these forms and strata will have to be systematically dismantled, but each throws up its own particular kinds of defence. In the domain of philosophy, the most stubborn such defence is the investment that we typically make in the processes of representation and the metaphysical premises that accompany it. Our commitment to representation and the pseudo-philosophical super-vision of appropriate means of representation only serves to strengthen all that isolates and distinguishes us as particular beings. We thereby identify with our inherited organic limits, rather than align ourselves with that intense anorganic life which lives on the impersonal plane of the cosmos. Rather than think at a level of coherence which is indis-tinguishable from a being-thought, we restrict thought to the mere supervision of those forms of mental behaviour (recognition, classification, consumption…) which preserve our bio-cultural distinction at the price of creative sterility. This is why an affirmative philosophy always seeks to surpass the human condition. Deleuze's critique of what will emerge as perhaps the most significant antagonists of his project – psychoanalysis and Kantian critical philosophy – should be seen as an aspect of his rejection of representa-tion and the creatural illusions it sustains. Deleuze will replace these and other logics of representation with his creative logic of sense.

This chapter will go through each of these points in turn, beginning with the limits imposed by organic form.

I

It is again Bergson who anticipates the initial move at work in Deleuze's subtractive vitalism. If being simply is creation, then we know that creation itself requires no expla-nation other than its affirmation or acknowledgement. Creation is what there is. The real problem is rather the opposite: how is it that so many creatings are stifled, blocked, or at least come to be channelled along predictable and thus minimally creative paths? Since 'life as a whole is movement itself', why is that 'the particular manifestations of life accept this movement unwillingly, and constantly lag behind?' Real life moves ever forward whereas these manifestations seem only 'to mark time'. Bergson's analogy frames the problem very nicely: 'like eddies of dust raised by the passing wind, living things turn back upon themselves, borne up by the great current of Life'.[8] They resist this current even though it alone moves them, even though they are nothing but it – even though this same current is what powers their very turning back.

In terms of the dynamic of memory and perception that Bergson develops in *Matter and Memory*, likewise, what calls for explanation is not the preservation of the virtual past but its compression in the ephemeral present. The pure past is reality itself, which 'preserves itself automatically'. Reality requires no faculty or mechanism to sustain it, or preserve it, or organise it in some rationally respectable way. Reality is sufficient, and memory, as a vehicle for the intuition of reality, is sufficient as well. What needs explanation isn't the process of remembering, but of forgetting.[9]

Bergson explains our capacity to forget or impoverish the past, to filter the past according to the mere interests of a present action, in terms of the very structure of the brain. The brain is precisely the mechanism which evolved, in order to advance our creatural interests, so as to ensure that the way we receive and respond to objects in the world is adapted to the pursuit of those interests. In Bergson's compressed phrase, the discontinuous or 'cinematographical character of our knowledge of things is due to the kaleidoscopic character of our adaptation to them'.[10] Needless to say, the evolution of the brain is hardly an extrinsic aspect of human development. What obscures our understanding of reality isn't a mere failure of knowledge. The obscurity stems, instead, from the mechanism which presides over the very core of our organic constitution. More, the obscurity stems from the same mechanism that, properly used, will allow for its dissipation. The brain is the source of metaphysical confusion insofar as we rely on intelligence to serve our practical needs, but it is also the source of illumination insofar as we allow 'impractical' intuition to suspend these needs and expose the true reality of things.

If then life as movement alienates itself in the material form that it creates, this alienation is nonetheless fully immanent to life or movement itself. Our tendency to remain ignorant of the real is 'to be explained simply by the necessity of living, that is, of acting'. No sooner than I become aware of having an actual body than I begin conceiving of it and other bodies as 'distinct material zones'. My

> body itself, as soon as it is constituted and distinguished, is led by its various needs to distinguish and constitute other bodies [...]. Our needs are, then, so many search-lights which, directed upon the continuity of sensible qualities, single out in it distinct bodies. They cannot satisfy themselves except upon the condition that they carve out, within this continuity, a body which is to be their own, and then delimit other bodies with which the first can enter into relation, as if with persons. To establish these special relations among portions thus carved out from sensible reality is just what we call *living*.[11]

If Bergson subsequently turns so much of his attention, after *Matter and Memory*, to the mechanics and evolution of life, he does so precisely in order to find, within life, the means of dissolving the limits that living itself throws up. Our needs confine us within life, but 'by unmaking that which these needs have made, we may restore to intuition its original purity and so recover contact with the real'. To reverse in this way our creatural passage from 'the immediate to the useful' would allow us to go back to 'the dawn of our human experience'.[12] This dawn – the dawn of the world, of '*the world before man, before our own dawn*' – is a moment to which Deleuze will never cease to return. It is a moment in which movement remains freely creative, the moment of a 'primary regime of variation, in its heat and its light, while it is still untroubled' by any form of organic mediation.[13]

The actual or lived organism is thus itself the first and deepest obstacle to the virtual power of living, to the 'powerful, non-organic Life which grips the world' (C2, 81). Pure vital energy is 'inorganic, germinal, and intensive', and its creation coheres on a plane that excludes the organism (TP, 499). A creative body is not an actual body but a wholly virtual one: a body without organs (BwO). Such a body is not a merely undifferentiated non-body. It is not literally deprived of organs. It is deprived, rather, of any *actual* organisation of its organs, i.e. of their integration within an actual organism along lines shaped by its needs and interests, by its ability to act and react, by its sensory-motor coordination. For such a body, 'the organs are not the enemies. The enemy is the organism [...] as a phenomenon of accumulation, coagulation, and sedimentation that, in order to extract useful labour from the BwO, imposes upon it forms, functions, bonds, dominant and hierarchised organisations, organised transcendences' (TP, 159). Beneath the actual organism and the constituted or molar identity that it radiates as a force of anti-creation there are innumerable micro or molecular sub-identities, which make up the real or non-organic substance of the organism. These machinic or larval selves operate at a level inaccessible to the organism itself. 'Underneath the self which acts are little selves which contemplate and which render possible both the action and the active subject. We speak of our "self" only in virtue of these thousands of little witnesses which contemplate within us: it is always a third party who says "me"' (DR, 75; cf. 219). Every organism, every actual individual, is in reality a disparate multiplicity or 'groupuscule, and must live as such' (AO, 362).

Such living is precisely the achievement of what Deleuze and Guattari call a 'becoming-animal'. To become-animal is not to identify with or acquire the form of an organism. It is not to imitate an actually existing animal. On the contrary: to become animal is 'to cross a threshold of pure intensities that are valuable only in themselves, where all forms come undone, as do all the significations, signifiers, and signifieds, to the benefit of an unformed matter of deterritorialised flux'.[14] To become-wolf, for instance, is to enter into the virtual creating of a wolf and not merely to have some sort of relation with actual wolves, let alone to represent yourself as a wolf. To become wolf is to begin to configure a wolfish creating on a body subtracted from its actual, creatural or organic configuration. It isn't a matter of the wolf as actual animal so much as the event of a virtual *wolfing*, 'the instantaneous apprehension of a multiplicity in a given region [...]. I feel myself becoming a wolf'. To become part of a *pack* or swarm is to loosen the grip of those great molar identities which otherwise define and confine you, from the inside-out: self, family, state, career... (TP, 31–2, 233; cf. K, 7). The exemplary form of such a becoming-animal, then, is not this or that actual animal but rather the generic egg or embryo of any-animal-whatever. Embryonic transformation is a good example of a composing as opposed to a composed force. 'The destiny and achievement of the embryo is to live the unlivable, to sustain forced movements of a scope which would break any skeleton' (DR, 215). Such is the heroism of the 'first beings', the embryos and larvae of thought, which live and think on the edge of the liveable.

A pure spatio-temporal dynamism [...] can be experienced only at the borders of the liveable, under conditions beyond which it would entail the death of any well-constituted subject endowed with independence and activity [...]. There are systematic vital movements, torsions, and drifts, that only the embryo can sustain: an adult would be torn apart by them. There are movements for which one can only be a patient, but the patient in turn can only be a larva [...]. Thought is one of those terrible movements which can be sustained only under the conditions of a larval subject [...]. The philosopher is a larval subject of his own system (DR, 118–19).

Deleuze and Guattari will never stop inventing new mechanisms to undo or dis-organise the organism, to evacuate worlds, environments, territories, species, and individuals of their actual or molar identity. The general goal is always a variation of the same effort – to make Nature operate in the only way it should: 'against itself' (TP, 242).

II

Of all the natural forms that thus work against themselves, there seems to be none more extravagant or obstinate than our own human form. What is it that distinguishes the human being from within the order of general organic being? Here it is Hume and Nietzsche who act as Deleuze's most important guides. Nietzsche offers a cosmomythical genesis of the human, while Hume tracks its emergence out from the dis-organised mechanics of cognition.

What Deleuze finds in Hume is an account of how the human subject comes to be constituted within the flux of experience. The essential thing is already implied by his insistence that the emergence of such a subject is precisely that, i.e. the *result* of a process, and not a transcendental necessity or norm. 'The mind is not subject, it is subjected' (ES, 31). Conceived as emergence or result, the subject is then a form that can subsequently be undone.

According to Hume, what is primary is not the subject but mind's immediate experience of indivisible atoms of existence or perception. What is primary is the flux of the sensible, the set of perceptions that we experience as 'distinct and independent'. True empiricism has for its foundation 'an animated succession of distinct perceptions' (ES, 87). Here as everywhere in Deleuze, the point of departure depends on the affirmation of difference as primary: the experience of difference or of the separable is '*the* experience. It does not presuppose anything else and nothing else precedes it.'[15] What is primary, or given, is simply a mass of different perceptions, immediately registered by the mind as a series of distinct impressions or ideas. The question is then: how, out of this primary flux of differences, can something like a coherent, organised human subject develop? The subject is not itself given and the 'given is not given to a subject; rather, the subject constitutes itself in the given'. The subject is constituted in the given as something that transcends it, and 'in this formulation of the problem, we discover the absolute essence of empiricism' (87).

Hume's approach to the problem is well known. The subject is not a necessary and constant condition of our experience of reality. The subject emerges within this experience as a result of the way experience comes to take shape over time. The subject emerges through repetition and anticipation – in short, through the consolidation of *habit*. 'Habit is the constitutive root of the subject, and the subject, at root, is the synthesis of time' (ES, 92–3). More specifically, the mind that registers the primary flux of experience is transformed into a subject through two sets of principles, 'principles of association and principles of the passions', both of which are governed by the more general principle of utility. Rather as in Bergson's account of the actual or lived organism, Hume's genesis of the subject within the flux of experience subordinates it to the demands of actual interest and need. 'The subject is the entity which, under the influence of the principle of utility, pursues a goal or an intention; it organises means in view of an end and, under the influence of the principles of association, establishes relations among ideas. Thus, the collection becomes a system.'[16] In other words, the mind, itself indistinguishable from what it perceives, is subjected when, animated by its passions and needs, the principles of association (contiguity, resemblance, and causality) come to order its otherwise disparate experience of impressions or ideas. These principles of association 'fix and naturalise the mind' in the form of a subject (ES, 24).

To this extent, at least, Deleuze's early book on Hume sets much of the agenda for his subsequent work. In order to liberate (i.e. unfix and de-naturalise) the mind, it will be necessary to disrupt or reverse the process whereby it comes to be subjected. It will be necessary to develop a 'cogito for a dissolved self' – the *cogitor* of an inhuman nature or mind. And if the subject constitutes itself in the mind by transcending mind, if it emerges within experience by mediating experience, if 'the only content that we can give to the idea of subjectivity is that of mediation and transcendence' (ES, 85), then two of the most consistent priorities of Deleuze's philosophy will be to refuse both mediation and transcendence. After Hume, Deleuze will set out to break the 'shackles of mediation' and 'hunt transcendence down in all its forms' (DR, 29; WP, 48). More, if 'subjectivity appears as soon as there is a gap between a received and an executed movement' (C2, 47), as soon as a gap opens between sensation and the actual subject of that sensation – i.e. as soon as it is possible to transcend and thus mediate the real – then before it does anything else a philosophy of creation must devote itself to closing this gap.

III

Nietzsche lends this project an inimitable urgency and intensity. No modern philosopher has done more to 'expose the "subject" as a fiction' (NP, 123). Nietzsche allows Deleuze to supplement his empiricist account of the cognitive emergence of the human subject with a quasi-cosmological account of the human as an especially virulent form of anti-creation. Humanity is the form that creation takes when it denies or turns against itself.

The point of departure here is thus the difference between creation and anti-creation, or between what Nietzsche calls active forces as opposed to reactive forces. 'In

63

the beginning, at the origin, there is the difference between active and reactive forces.' Active forces are transformative or inventive, and 'energy which is capable of transforming itself is called "noble". The power of transformation, the Dionysian power, is the primary definition of activity.' Active willing is itself creation: 'to will = to create'. Active forces alone are primary, they are the exclusive source of action or energy. As the name implies, reactive forces are not themselves an original kind of force so much as the form that active force (which alone acts) takes on when it is interiorised or reflected back against itself.[17] As a rule, 'only active force asserts itself, it affirms its difference' or its singularity immediately, without reference to anything either (objectively) external or (subjectively) internal to itself (NP, 57).

Active forces are thus absorbed in what they do, in the acting as such, whereas reactive forces allow for the separation of an actor from the action. Reaction isolates a doer from the doing. Active forces do what they are, non-reflexively, whereas a reactive force reflects upon what is done by or to it. Far from being the vehicle of insight, human 'consciousness is essentially reactive [...]. In Nietzsche consciousness is always the consciousness of an inferior in relation to a superior to which he is subordinated' (NP, 41, 39). In other words, whereas active forces appropriate and dominate whatever they act upon, reactive forces begin with a subjective response to their subordination. An active force creates, consumes or destroys; the bearer of a reactive force asks why it is being destroyed, resents its destroyer and attributes malice to it. The human being, then, is simply that being which has taken on such resentment as its organising principle. 'Far from being a psychological trait the spirit of revenge is the principle on which our whole psychology depends... [T]he whole of our psychology, without knowing it, is part of *ressentiment*' (NP, 34). An envious, belittling negativity or nihilism is constitutive of the human, and with the human 'the whole world sinks and sickens, the whole of life is depreciated, everything known slides towards its own nothingness'. Conversely, since humanity is indistinguishable from ressentiment, 'to move beyond ressentiment is to attain the "end of history as history of man"'.[18] If life is to live it will require the death of man. Genuine or creative affirmation will only proceed 'above man, outside man, in the overman [*Übermensch*] which it produces and in the unknown that it brings with it' (NP, 177). Creation must always find some way of returning to the dawn of the world, to a time before or after man.

And yet, though the human is an obstacle to life, though the creature obstructs its creating, there is no other vehicle for the dissipation of this obstacle than the creature itself. The creating alone creates but it creates *through* the creature – there is no other plane of creation, there is no higher reality than that of the human and the world. Again, the movement out from the world is not a movement into a reality beyond the world. The overman is only 'above' man insofar as this above is itself produced by man. Only man can reach the dawn of man. Redemption from the human is the task of the human alone. Only man offers the resources of undoing man (precisely by 'becoming-woman', and then animal, then inorganic, then molecular, then imperceptible...[19]). As Deleuze's Bergson will subsequently show, although man is that animal whose actual organic constitution makes it ignorant of creative life, nevertheless it is only on the line of Man that the *élan vital* successfully 'gets through'; man in this sense is 'the purpose of the entire process of evolution'. It could be said that in man, and only in man, the actual becomes adequate to the virtual. It could be said that man is capable of rediscovering all the levels, all the degrees of expansion and contraction that coexist in the virtual Whole. As if he were capable of all the frenzies and brought about in himself successively everything that, elsewhere, can only be embodied in different species [...]. Man therefore creates a differentiation that is valid for the Whole, and he alone traces out an open direction that is able to express a whole that is itself open. Whereas the other directions are closed and go around in circles, whereas a distinct 'plane' of nature corresponds to each one, man is capable of scrambling the planes, of going beyond his own plane as his own condition, in order finally to express naturing Nature.[20]

Nietzsche offers a somewhat more forceful route to much the same outcome. The will to power is nothing other than 'giving' or 'creating' as such (NP, xii). But as the human is consolidated it increasingly infects active power. Over time, nihilism or the becoming-reactive of forces comes to bend the whole will to power against itself. Negation prevails. The question is then: 'how can nihilism be defeated? How can the element of values itself be changed, how can affirmation be substituted for negation?' The answer is simply to allow negation to run its full course, to consume itself and thereby flip back into its opposite. The return of affirmation will proceed via the consummation of negation. 'The transmutation which defeats nihilism is itself the only complete and finished form of nihilism. In fact nihilism is defeated, but defeated by itself', once it assumes a completed or totalising form (NP, 171–2). It remains the case that only affirmation can create new values, and in the end 'affirmation takes the place of all negations' – but affirmation can only replace negation if there is nothing left of negation. Negation must first negate itself. Negation must exhaust itself and vanish, leaving not so much as its empty place. Negation must leave nothing of its place other than the possibility of a wholly different place: the place itself must change, until 'there is no longer any place for another world'. Once this has been achieved then 'the whole of the negative has become a power of affirming, it is now only the mode of being of affirmation as such' (NP, 173–9).

The best way to understand this conversion sequence is as a variant of our more general logic of counter-actualisation.[21] It is in and through the reversal of the actual that we return to the virtual, to an intensified, transformed, redeemed or converted virtual, one restored to its full creative potential. This would be a virtual that is once again nothing other than its own renewal, its own creating anew. If actual 'man imprisoned life, the overman is what frees life within man himself, to the benefit of another form' (FC, 130). Our 'finest creating', as Nietzsche himself puts it, is thus to turn ourselves into the 'forefathers of the overman' by actively sacrificing all that sustains the merely human – or, to anticipate the argument that we will take up in our last chapter, by setting the stage for the drama of eternal return. Return is precisely that which 'releases, indeed it creates, the purely active and pure affirmation'.[22]

In the work of his friend and fellow Nietzschean, Michel Foucault, Deleuze finds the basis for a more contemporary account of the constitution and eventual death of man. Foucault situates this death at the culmination of the historical development of the human sciences that he traces in his book *The Order of Things*; the way Deleuze re-describes several of the moments of this development says a great deal about his own conception of the 'man-form'.

In a first, classical, or early modern stage, reality is directly identified with the infinite, i.e. with God as infinite power of understanding, infinite power of creation, and so on (FC, 88). 'So long as God exists [...] then man does not yet exist' (FC, 130). This of course is the stage that Deleuze (rather more than Foucault) associates with the exemplary insights of Spinoza and Leibniz. The objects of science here include only those things which can in principle be extended to infinity, built up in indefinite series on the basis of a single principle, e.g. money or wealth in the science of economics, specific differences in biology, and so on. To know or explain something is to extend or unfold its principle to infinity. But less than an active participant in the creation of reality, the human itself is identified with a mere limitation placed upon such an infinity – for example, the human power of understanding is conceived as a limited form or finite mode of an infinite power of understanding. The great effort of knowledge in the classical age thus remains the effort to *locate* itself or its limits within the infinite.[23]

In a second, specifically modern stage, the limits of human finitude become (with Kant) 'positively' constituent rather than merely privative. Rather than construct general series on the basis of infinitely productive principles, each element in a series now takes on an actual energy and local autonomy of its own. Organisms are caught up in the ongoing evolution of living beings (Lamarck, Darwin); languages no longer figure as variations of a universal grammar or general power of speaking but as dynamic elements of the historical constitution of 'collective wills' (Bopp, Schlegel); the force of work becomes constituent of wealth, and 'work itself falls back on capital (Ricardo) before the reverse takes place, in which capital falls back on the work extorted (Marx)' (FC, 128). Specific historical tendencies and developments thus come to replace a general deductive order, and the agent that coordinates these various histories is of course 'man' himself, *man in his actuality*, understood as an actually living, working, and speaking being. Man is now subject and object of his own knowledge.

The third, contemporary stage, our stage, the stage that anticipates the *overman*, is then the stage that counter-actualises this human finitude. The goal is not simply to return to the infinity of the first stage (with its attendant 'limitation'). The goal is to affirm an 'unlimited finity', to make of finitude itself the new basis of an active or creative infinity. Knowledge now seeks to affirm the disjunctive forces of life, labour and language in themselves, in their creative trajectories, liberated from the coordinating influence of man. The infinite can now work directly through the finite, so to speak. Unlike the first stage, the finite (the actual) no longer figures as a limitation upon the infinite. It is within or rather *through* a finite living organism that there lives an infinite power of Life. It is directly within and through a finite speaking being that there speaks an infinite power of Language, and so on; through the finite literary mechanisms invented by Mallarmé, Péguy, Artaud and others, contemporary language 'turns back on itself in an endless reflexivity' (FC, 131).

Compared with the first stage, this third stage is more absolute rather than less. Though singular and finite, *a* creating will proceed with the whole power of infinite creation itself. Although the infinite now passes through the human, it is no longer mediated or located. It explodes all possibility of historical or territorial location. In the end, classical philosophy was governed by its rational convergence *with* God. Our third stage, by contrast, puts the human 'in charge of the animals', 'of the very rocks', 'in charge of the being of language (that formless, "mute, unsignifying region where language can find its freedom" even from whatever it has to say)'.[24] In other words, only our third stage effects a kind of becoming-God *of* the human, a becoming infinite of the finite.

V

Among the various other ways in which Deleuze seeks to explain the constitution of the human, the most important and certainly the most notorious is tied to the name of Oedipus. From the moment that Deleuze starts to collaborate with the psychoanalyst Félix Guattari, in the late 1960s, actual 'man' and 'Oedipal man' become increasingly interchangeable terms. As I mentioned briefly in the previous chapter, this reactive valorisation of Oedipus is one of several symptoms of a significant (though far from fundamental) shift in Deleuze's work. In the *Logic of Sense* (1969), 'it is with Oedipus that the event is disengaged from its causes in depth, spreads itself at the surface and connects itself with its quasi-cause from the point of view of a dynamic genesis'. It is thus largely thanks to Oedipus that psychoanalysis can still figure there as 'the science of events' and the 'art of counter-actualisations' (LS, 211–12). In 1969, Deleuze (again like Foucault) can still yoke psychoanalysis to what we identified in the preceding section as our third, contemporary form of knowledge. Three years later, however, in *Anti-Oedipus*, psychoanalysis in general and Oedipus in particular come to play very much the opposite role. The logic of counter-actualisation itself doesn't change, neither here nor in the remainder of Deleuze's work, but the value he attributes to these all too human mechanisms changes dramatically.

In *Anti-Oedipus*, 'Oedipus' is the name that Deleuze and Guattari give to the specifically subjective form of transcendence, i.e. to the psychological equivalent of the organism. Oedipus unites transcendence and organism in a single repressive form: it is Oedipus that enables desire to desire its own repression. Oedipus achieves this by combining personal and collective forms of transcendence (AO, 79).

In the sphere that is constituted as private or personal, Oedipus serves to supervise and normalise the consequences of what psychoanalysis calls castration. Whereas virtual or creative desire is immediately productive of its object and thus lacks nothing, desire is castrated when it is configured as desire *for* an object and *of* a subject. At the same time that desire is detached from its object, its subject becomes the subject of this lack. The literal gap between sensation and action that is characteristic of all subjectivity becomes the definitive feature of the sexualised subject, and the traumatically elusive object of incestuous or Oedipalised desire is the missing object par excellence. The more Oedipalised a subject's desire, the more firmly it is caught in the confines of negation and lack. In this sense 'Oedipus is always colonisation pursued by other means, it is the interior colony' (AO, 170).

Over the course of human history, the consolidation of this private castration-transcendence has been doubled and reinforced by the public transcendence of the state. As Deleuze and Guattari explain at some length, in the political sphere anti-creation takes the form of the state. While only immediate or uncastrated (and hence aberrant or 'monstrous') desire is productive, the state emerges as an apparatus that transcends and captures the flow of production. The state figures in *Anti-Oedipus* as a kind of collective super-ego, keeping watch over the field of social action that it helps to normalise and coordinate. Supervised by the state, the subject can now be harnessed to the alienation of *work*, i.e. to labour motivated by its endless pursuit of the ever missing object of castrated desire. The capitalist organisation of labour, the transcendent organisation of the state, the metaphorical distribution of familial roles across the social field, the psychoanalytic interpretation of desire, all figure here as aspects of one and the same mechanism for the repressive mediation of the real. Oedipus is the device through which these various forms of transcendence hold together as a single, over-determined 'apparatus of capture'. Oedipus is what relates a psychological interiority to external social authority. The individual is doubly subjected through the castration of desire and the transcendent over-coding of the state.[25]

Moreover, Oedipus is what protects anti-creation from creative counter-attack. Oedipus offers a defence against both the psychological reversal of transcendence (namely the raw, immediate experience of immanent creation: schizophrenia) and the socio-economic evacuation of transcendence (namely capitalism's abstraction, de-coding, de-actualisation or de-territorialisation of all values in the indifferent medium of exchange value). Both capitalism's relative de-actualisation and schizophrenia's absolute de-actualisation are controlled and managed by Oedipus. If 'what all societies dread absolutely as their most profound negative [are] the decoded flows of desire', i.e. the de-actualised flows of virtual creation, then Oedipus guards against this limit of social coherence (AO, 177). 'Oedipus displaces the limit, it internalises the limit. Rather a society of [labouring] neurotics than one successful schizophrenic who has not been made autistic' (AO, 102). Confronted with the risk of capitalism's anarchic commodification and detoxification, i.e. with the abstraction of all values, Oedipus manages to shift the danger of an uncontrollable political or 'public' de-actualisation onto an eminently controllable, 'private' re-stabilisation of the actual or the molar. Oedipus reinforces the political work of exploitation or surplus extraction by internalising it (via the metaphorical mediation of the family) in the very configuration of consciousness and identity. The politics of exploitation and security plays out in a world populated by 'Mister Capital, Madame Earth and their child the Worker' (AO, 264). The first and most fundamental modern form of surplus extraction is simply the reproduction of the subject as such, the subject as dutiful worker and son, as docile labour.

As you might expect, recovery of the real must therefore begin with the dissolution of both the private and public forms of transcendent subjection, and the subsequent elaboration of a desire without person or state. Recovery proceeds through the dissolution of the psychoanalytic theatre of interpretation (the theatre in which desire is staged or 'represented' [*représenté*] at a distance from itself) in favour of the workshop or factory of immediate and thus automatic or mechanical desire. Recovery involves dismantling the theatrical representation of desire in terms of restricted family roles and metaphors and the restoration of their intensive social and political investments.[26] Whereas the concern of the subject, of the state, and of the organism, is always to conserve itself in its transcendent coherence (TP, 357), 'the whole task of schizoanalysis [is...] to substitute, for the private subject of castration [...] the collective agents of enunciation that for their part refer to machinic arrangements. To overturn the theatre of representation into the order of desiring-production' (AO, 271).

VI

Like all the various mechanisms that sustain a human actuality or anti-creativity, Oedipus thus bears an intimate relation to what Deleuze so insistently attacks as the 'long error of representation'.[27] Thanks to Oedipus, 'the whole of desiring-production is crushed, subjected to the requirements of representation'. This is indeed the 'essential thing: the reproduction of desire gives way to a simple representation [...]. Every time that production, rather than being apprehended in its originality, in its reality, becomes reduced in this manner to a representational space, it can no longer have value except by its own absence, and it appears as a lack within this space' (AO, 54, 306). Filtered through representation, desire ceases to be immediate or productive so as to become merely figurative or symbolic, a matter for interpretation, an illusion made up only of language, dream, or myth. True creative experimentation, by contrast, replaces the work of interpretation and operates as 'nonfigurative and nonsymbolic' (TP, 284).

An unqualified refusal of representation is one of the great constants of Deleuze's work, and it is common to all of his own philosophical ancestors. The whole of 'Hume's philosophy is a sharp critique of representation' (ES, 30). Nietzsche reduces representation to a component of 'slave' psychology (NP, 10). Bergson finds in representation the root of our misunderstanding of memory, if not of all our metaphysical confusion (DI, 29). Spinoza sharply distinguishes an idea of something from a representation of something, and associates the equivocal representation of God (as opposed to a direct participation in univocal being) with the misleading distractions of scripture (EP, 56–7). To create or to represent: in the Deleuzian universe this is a stark alternative.

To affirm a creative univocity is to deny in advance the gap that representation posits between reality and the way we interpret that reality, between a reality and the concept that we have *of* that reality, between the thing and the mere image that we retain of that thing. From the perspective of creation, there is only a difference of degree between a thing and the image or representation that we might substitute for the thing. As Bergson realised with particular clarity, it is 'necessary, at any cost, to overcome this duality of image and movement, of consciousness and thing'. Image is never the image *of* movement, it simply is the movement as such. 'IMAGE = MOVEMENT' (C1, 56, 58). More, an 'image is not a representation of an object but a movement in the world of the mind'; simply, 'the image is the spiritual life', all by itself (CC, 169). And for the same reason, if consciousness has any reality at all it is not, as phenomenology would have us believe, as the consciousness *of* something. Rather, if consciousness exists it is simply insofar as consciousness *is* something, insofar as it is indistinguishable from its thing and thus fully immanent to reality.[28] Our perception of a thing is nothing other than a selective 'prehension' of that same thing (C1, 64). Properly understood, then, 'there's no difference at all between images, things and motion' (N, 42) for these are *all* motions or things, or rather thing-*ings*: processes that actualise themselves through things. As far as Deleuze is concerned, Pasolini speaks for cinema as a whole when 'he refuses to talk of an "impression of reality" given by cinema. Cinema simply is reality, "cinema represents reality through reality".'[29]

In other words, perception or representation does not shed light on things that would otherwise remain opaque and obscure. Our consciousness does not make images from or of things. On the contrary, things are already images, 'things are luminous by themselves without anything illuminating them'. The real 'plane of the immanence is entirely made up of Light', and we ourselves are nothing but images, refractions or prisms of this one light (C1, 59–60). Our seeing eye is not directed *at* objects. Rather 'the eye is in things, in luminous images in themselves. "Photography, if there is photography, is already snapped, already shot, in the very interior of things and for all the points of space."'[30] Just as creative desire lacks nothing and is indistinguishable from the object it creates, so too does real perception participate directly in the creation of what it perceives. Like any adequate knowledge, suitably immediate 'perception puts us at once into matter, is impersonal and coincides with the perceived object'.[31] For example, whereas a traditional realism supposes the relative independence of its object, Deleuze affirms with Robbe-Grillet an immanent description which '*replaces* its own object'. Such a creation-description first 'erases or *destroys* its reality which passes into the imaginary, on the one hand, but on the other hand, powerfully brings out all the reality which the imaginary or the mental *create*'. The result is a vehicle through which 'the imaginary and the real become indiscernible'.[32]

According to Deleuze, one of the most telling symptoms of representation's failure to provide such a vehicle is its inability to grasp the real nature of repetition. As far as representation is concerned, repetition simply involves the production of similar if not identical sequences. What can be represented of repetition is only the *resemblance* of one actual sequence to another, for instance the features that turn a series of experiences (a game, a job, a process…) into an ordinary routine. Representation cannot adequately distinguish between repetition and a merely law-like generality or equivalence. Repetition becomes synonymous with substitution. Representation, in short, can conceive of repetition only as repetition of the same (DR, 270–1). But for reasons we'll come back to in Chapter 6, section IV, the affirmation of absolute difference simultaneously involves the affirmation of absolute repetition (and the two combine in the redemptive idea of eternal return). Creative repetition can only be thought as the repetition of difference itself. Repetition will have to be divorced from any mediation through resemblance and generality. True repetition must involve the intuition of fully singular occurrences, of differences that cannot be exchanged or substituted. Although we're not yet in a position to make proper sense of this, Bergson's indivisible conception of time may already point us in the right direction. If we think of time along Bergsonian lines as that which 'develops itself for itself', then if there is such a thing as repetition it cannot simply involve the duplication of discrete actual sequences (since in reality there are no such sequences). Instead, if each passing moment is nothing other the whole of time in its maximally contracted state, then each moment must be nothing less than a 'total and totalising' repetition of virtual time as a whole (DR, 287). In other words, if time is just the dimension of creation as such, we might say that every new creating repeats one and the same act of creation, precisely by creating something different or new. Or as Deleuze puts it in his most economical formula: 'if repetition is possible, it is due to miracle rather than to law' (DR, 2).

The problem with representation, then, is not simply that it tends to get things wrong. Representation doesn't just falsify what it represents. The error that is representation applies just as much to 'truthful' representation or correct representation – that is to say, to the conventional notion of truth itself. As Nietzsche keeps trying to tell us, 'thought is creation, not will to truth [...]. Philosophy does not consist in knowing and is not inspired by truth. Rather, it is categories like Interesting, Remarkable, or Important that determine success or failure' (WP, 55, 82). As conventionally understood, truth simply characterises the relationship between a given thing and whatever is taken to be an accurate representation of that thing. The real error, however, lies in the presumption that such a relationship could have any sort of validity at all. Rather than truth as correspondence, a philosophy of creation will prefer to valorise the 'power of the false' if, by doing violence to representation, it helps get us out of representation and into the domain of the interesting or remarkable. This is what motivates the various polemics that Deleuze and Guattari mount, especially in *A Thousand Plateaus*, against 'royal' or 'major' science – science understood as the measurement, analysis and manipulation of merely actual forms of being. Truth understood in terms of relative correctness is by definition judgemental and restrictive, i.e. anti-creative.[33] As a rule, thinking can only 'produce something interesting when it accedes to the infinite movement that frees it from truth as supposed paradigm and reconquers an immanent power of creation' (WP, 140). It is no accident that creative film-makers like Resnais 'deliberately broke with the form of the true, to replace it by the powers of life' (C2, 135).

For exactly the same reason that it refuses the conventional notion of truth, a univocal ontology also refuses conventional notions of metaphorical or ironic figuration. A plane of immanence comes to consist to the exclusion of all metaphor or analogy (TP, 69; K, 24). Spinozist univocity implies that one and the same individuating is expressed by corresponding modes in extension and thought, and the only notion of expression or sense that is compatible with this univocal realism is a literal and immediate one. Deleuze is characteristically insistent about this. 'All images are literal, and must be taken literally', just as all creative writing must proceed 'literally, without metaphor, to bring forth the thing in itself'.[34] Through genuine art, 'what disappears is all metaphor or figure [...]. One must speak and show literally, or else not show and speak at all' (C2, 183). Creative 'metamorphosis is the contrary of all metaphor' and like Spinoza and Artaud, Deleuze and Guattari's 'Kafka deliberately kills all metaphor'.[35] Again, in the direct or literal cinema of the time-image 'there is no room for metaphor, there is not even any metonymy, because the necessity which belongs to relations of thought in the image has replaced the contiguity of relations of images'. To create in the medium of cinema is 'to carry the image to the point where it becomes deductive and automatic, to substitute the formal linkages of thought for sensory-motor representative or figurative linkages', and thereby 'to make thought immanent to the image'.[36] Whenever we succeed in suspending or jamming our actual organic limits we make it possible to create an exclusively optical-sound image, an image without metaphor. Such an image 'brings out the thing in itself, literally, in its excess of horror or beauty, in its radical or unjustifiable character, because it no longer has to be "justified", for better or for worse' (C2, 20).

A univocal ontology thus breaks irrevocably with the whole tradition, from Aristotle through to Husserl and beyond, that conceives of knowledge and our being in the world in terms of the (critical or judgemental) *relation* between ourselves and the world. In a creative reality there can be no such relation, indeed there is neither self nor actual world – categories which serve only to inhibit an adequate intuition of creation. As a matter of course, representation fails to capture the immediate intensity of difference. Representation brings everything back to a fixed and immobile centre, to its subject. Representation can never keep up with creative movement or difference, which 'implies a plurality of centres, a superposition of perspectives, a tangle of points of view, a coexistence of moments which essentially distort representation'. Even representation taken to the infinite, representation as deployed by Leibniz or Hegel, still remains caught within the confines of identity.

> Infinite representation includes precisely an infinity of representations – either by ensuring the convergence of all points of view on the same object or the same world [Leibniz], or by making all moments properties of the same Self [Hegel]. In either case it maintains a unique centre which gathers and represents all the others, like the unity of a series which governs or organises its terms and their relations once and for all [...]. The immediate, defined as sub-representative, is therefore not attained by multiplying representations and points of view. On the contrary, each composing representation must be distorted, diverted and torn from its centre. Each point of view must itself be the object, or the object must belong to the point of view (DR, 56).

VII

If even Leibniz and Hegel fail to think the immediate production or creation of reality, if even they remain trapped within the illusory gap of representation, then perhaps the most anti-creative of all modern philosophers is the one who made of this gap the very principle of his critique of metaphysical intuition – Immanuel Kant. Kant is the philosopher of representation par excellence. Unlike the books Deleuze wrote on his allies Hume, Bergson, Nietzsche and Spinoza, when Deleuze came to write his short book on Kant he wrote it as the analysis of an 'enemy', as an attempt to 'show how his system works, its various cogs – the tribunal of Reason, measured use of the faculties (our subjection to these made all the more hypocritical by our being called legislators)'.[37] Kant offers Deleuze 'the perfect incarnation of false critique; that's why he fascinates me' (DI, 139).

It would be much too simple, nevertheless, to treat Kant exclusively as Deleuze's adversary. Deleuze himself is not a primarily critical thinker, and he is quite happy to embrace those aspects of Kant's work that he finds compatible with his own priorities. He affirms the implications of Kant's project that can be harnessed to the disruption of the subject and the de-regulation of our faculties.[38] The most important such aspect is probably Kant's famous critique of Descartes' cogito, his recognition that the thinking 'I' cannot directly determine its own being. The thinking subject does not itself provide the ground for its own being or activity, the cogito is not the author of what it does. Kant replaces Descartes' allegedly self-grounding subject with a passive subject, a subject through whom thought thinks. This was an important breakthrough (though surely less important than Spinoza's own anti-Cartesian *cogitor*). Kant realises that 'the activity of thought applies to a receptive being, to a passive subject which represents that activity to itself rather than enacts it'. Conscious thinking thinks only on the basis of an unconscious that eludes it.[39] And unlike Descartes' contemporary Spinoza, Kant takes the specifically modern step of realising that what thus separates what a subject is from what a subject does is nothing other than *time*. The aspect of post-Kantian philosophy which Deleuze affirms is the one that acknowledges that 'it is we who are internal to time, not the other way round […]. Subjectivity is never ours, it is time's, that is, soul, spirit, the virtual.'[40] Such was the great opportunity that Deleuze associates with Kant:

> The subject can henceforth represent its own spontaneity only as that of an Other, and in so doing invoke a mysterious coherence in the last instance which excludes his own […]. For a brief moment we enter into that schizophrenia in principle which characterises the highest power of thought, and opens Being directly on to difference, despite all the mediations, all the reconciliations, of the concept (DR, 58).

This moment of opportunity, however, was to prove brief indeed. Kant's whole project is subsequently designed to inoculate philosophy from the risk of precisely this kind of schizophrenia, and in particular from the delirium of intellectual intuition.[41] No sooner has Kant anticipated that 'I is an other' than he restores the unity of the self in the transcendental syntheses of apperception. No sooner has he approached the 'highest power of thought' than he retreats back into the systematic regulation of the faculties, organised precisely around the functional stability of the transcendental subject (and subsequently, of the moral subject). If the critique of pure reason led the subject to the brink of its theoretical dissolution, this was only to pave the way for the restoration of its integrity through the orderly exercise of representation and the abstract imperatives of practical reason. The Kantian project thus 'amounts to a supreme effort to save the world of representation' (DR, 87). Insofar as Deleuze acknowledges a 'true critique' he attributes it to Nietzsche, precisely against Kant. The Nietzschean critique of representation and reactive forces 'is of great importance for the history of philosophy, for it runs counter not only to Kantianism, with which it competes, but to the whole Kantian inheritance, to which it is violently opposed'.[42] After its momentary anticipation of the schizophrenic liberation of thought, the 'great operation of the Kantian "critique" served only to consolidate the actual operations of our common sense, and such common sense, the unity of all the faculties at the centre constituted by the Cogito, is the state consensus raised to the absolute' (TP, 376).

Kant, in short, invents the specifically modern way of preserving transcendence, by investing it *within* the immanent horizon of the subject's reflexive or reactive representation.

> Kant objects to any transcendent use of the synthesis, but he ascribes immanence to the subject of the synthesis as new, subjective unity. He may even allow himself the luxury of denouncing transcendent Ideas, so as to make them the 'horizon' of the field immanent to the subject. But, in so doing, Kant discovers the modern way of saving transcendence: this is no longer the transcendence of Something, or of a One higher than everything, but that of a Subject to which the field of immanence is only attributed by belonging to a self that necessarily represents such a subject to itself (WP, 46).

This is why Deleuze so consistently presents himself as a non- or even pre- rather than neo-Kantian thinker. He aligns himself with Leibniz or Spinoza precisely because their affirmative naturalism undoes, in advance, Kant's critical attribution of immanence to a subject which then transcends it. In defiance of the rules of Kantian perception, the great rationalists hurl us immediately into the raw intensity of nature's own creativity. They rather than Kant are the true ancestors of Artaud's schizophrenic, it is they who inspire us to 'experience pure forces, dynamic lines in space that act without intermediary upon the spirit and link it directly with nature and history' (DR, 10). Leibniz, for instance, offers a version of 'transcendental philosophy that bears on the event rather than the phenomenon' and that thus replaces 'Kantian conditioning by means of a double operation of transcendental actualisation and realisation'.[43] True perception is never conditioned by mechanisms peculiar to the subject; by escaping the mediation of the subject it becomes 'total, objective and diffuse' (C1, 64).

Whenever Deleuze himself uses the term 'transcendental', consequently, it doesn't refer to what Kant described as those conditions of possibility which shape our subjective experience, the conditions that guarantee the reliability of our representations of objects in the world. It simply refers to the way we intuit or *think* (rather than represent) the very being or creation of the world as such, and of ourselves along with it. When Deleuze uses the term transcendental it is to describe creativity as such, creativity subtracted from the constraints of the actual or individual. 'Transcendental' is then just a description of pre-individual reality as it is in itself, in the immanence of its creation and 'underneath' its consolidation in the creature. For the same reason, 'the transcendental field defines itself as a pure plane of immanence, since it escapes all transcendence of subject and object. Absolute immanence is in itself, it is not in something, for something, it does not depend on an object nor belong to a subject.' The (post-Sartrean) consciousness that corresponds to such a field is not that of a subject, especially not the subject of synthesis or representation. It can only be a strictly 'asubjective consciousness, a pre-reflexive impersonal consciousness [...], pure immediate consciousness without object or self', a 'consciousness traversing the transcendental field at infinite speed and everywhere diffuse'.[44] (Such a consciousness, we might note in passing, would clearly and very literally be un-analysable. If Kant is the philosopher of representation in its modern, *reactive* or reflexive form, what is the psychoanalysis that Deleuze and Guattari denounce in *Anti-Oedipus* if not another variation of this same reaction, i.e. of representation turned back against itself, representation become the internal mechanism for the transcendent subject's own self-supervision and self-normalisation?)

To a diffuse and asubjective transcendental consciousness corresponds a similarly disparate and an-objective 'transcendental empiricism'. Since there is no relation between subject and object, since the consciousness of something simply is that thing, Deleuze's transcendental field will not distinguish between mind and empirical reality. The term 'empirical' applies not to a collection of indifferent objects that might then be conceived or intended by a subject. There is only one plane of production-knowledge, consistent with the principle that 'the knowledge of things bears the same relation to the knowledge of God as the things themselves to God' (EP, 14). The concern of a transcendental empiricism is not with objects or creatures but with creatings, and its motivation is again a variation on Spinoza's theophanic logic: 'the more we understand singular things, the more we understand God'.[45]

The transcendental empiricism that Deleuze embraces after Artaud is thus designed to foreclose (transcendent) interpretation of what something *means* in favour of an (immanent) intuition of or participation in the process whereby something is produced (DR, 147; cf. AO, 109). To define something is not to explain what it means but to explicate what it *is*, i.e. to make or produce it in actuality. A properly adequate definition always involves the 'veritable generation of the object defined'. To formulate an adequate idea of something is to 'express its cause' (EP, 79, 133). Much the same ambition will motivate the constructivism that Deleuze and Guattari embrace in *Capitalism and Schizophrenia* – as when, for example, they seek to develop a mechanics adequate to express the behaviour of what they call desiring machines, in lieu of any self-bound, self-interpreting subject of desire, representation or lack. Unlike such a subject, desiring machines 'represent nothing, signify nothing, mean nothing, and are exactly what one makes of them, what is made with them, what they make in themselves' (AO, 288).

<h1 style="text-align:center">VIII</h1>

We can come back now to the point reached at the end of the previous chapter. Instead of a logic of representation Deleuze proposes a logic of creative expression or sense. As anyone who has read *Logic of Sense* is likely to admit, Deleuze's logic of sense doesn't initially seem to make a great deal of sense in the normal sense of the word. Sense here certainly isn't bound up with questions of meaning or signification. 'Sense is not to be confused with signification; it is rather what is attributed in such a way that it determines both the signifier and the signified as such' (LS, 50–1; cf. NP, 31). We already know that signification is merely a category of representation, or anti-creation. Signification is one of the mechanisms through which we remain trapped in our actuality. Along with the organism and the subject, it is one of our fundamental forms of stratification or territorialisation. To ask what something means, even to accept such a question as worthy of interest, is already to assume our lack of adequate knowledge. To ask what God means by this or that is to assume that we are not ourselves an aspect of God and that we are more or less removed from the making of this or that.

Deleuze's logic of sense refuses this distance and all its implications. This logic of sense begins when 'sense brings that which expresses it into existence', or indeed when, 'as pure inherence, it brings itself to exist within that which expresses it' (LS, 166). Sense is again a facet of creation pure and simple, and the logic of sense is just another variation of the logic of virtual events that we encountered in the previous chapter. As early as his 1954 review of Jean Hyppolite's book *Logic and Existence*, Deleuze had decided that 'philosophy, if it means anything, can only be ontology and an ontology of sense [*sens*]' and that the 'absolute identity of being and difference is called sense'.[46] The whole of *Logic of Sense* depends, in fact, on this equation: 'the event is sense itself'.[47] What further distinguishes an event of sense from an event of desire or art, for instance, is just that it occurs in the medium of verbal *expression* as such: propositional sense is actualised through language (and through the situations articulated by language), rather than through, say, sexuality or sensation. Sense is the primary and determining aspect of expression. Sense is 'something unconditioned, capable of assuring a real genesis of denotation and of the other dimensions of the proposition' (LS, 19). Just as an incorporeal event falls immediately upon the bodies it transforms, so too does sense fall immediately upon whatever it denotes or evokes. Whereas 'everything capable of denotation is, in principle, consumable and penetrable', virtual sense itself is the 'impenetrable' and 'cutting' force of creative expression (LS, 26–8).

The essential thing to remember here is again that Deleuze adapts this term 'expression' from Spinoza as a synonym for creation in general – creation in both its physical and spiritual dimensions. If 'what is expressed is sense', if modes are 'most *expressive* when they find their "sense"', their sufficient reason, this is because expression is nothing other than the adequate, literal and necessary manifestation of God. The expression of sense involves an immediate and sufficient determination that is 'deeper than the relation of causality or representation' (EP, 335). Such expression has nothing to do with mere representation or figuration. Instead, sense is a virtual express*ing*, a pure act of creation.

If sense itself is a virtual expressing, what is thereby expressed is an actual proposition on the one hand and an actual state of affairs on the other.

> What is expressed has no existence outside its expressions; each expression is the existence of what is expressed [...]. What is expressed must thus be referred to an understanding that grasps it objectively, that is, ideally. But it is predicated of the thing, and not of the expression itself; understanding relates it to the object designated, as the essence of that object.[48]

Representation or approximation has no role to play in such understanding. Our intuition of essential sense, as of any virtual determination, is perfectly adequate or exact. 'Sense is the genesis or the production of the truth, and truth is only the empirical result of sense' (DR, 154). There is thus little to stop Deleuze from embracing the Stoics' admirably counter-intuitive conception of speech: as Chrysippus maintains, 'if you say something, it passes through your lips; so, if you say "chariot", a chariot passes through your lips' (LS, 8).

Understood in this way as the actualisation of sense, words do not refer to things but *are* things in verbal form. Propositions do not describe things, they are the verbal actualisation of those same things. 'The event occurring in a state of affairs and the sense inhering in the proposition are the same entity.'[49] Sense is thus 'doubly generative: not only does it engender the logical proposition with its determinate dimensions (denotation, manifestation, signification); it engenders also the objective correlates of this proposition [...] (the denoted, the manifested, and the signified)' (LS, 120; cf. D, 63). It's the insistence on this univocity, to the exclusion of all resemblance or representation, that makes Deleuze's logic of sense both so extraordinarily *simple* yet so difficult to grasp.

There is nothing accidental about this difficulty. Our initial incomprehension of sense is another unavoidable consequence of our actual limitations. Since sense is virtual 'we can never formulate simultaneously both a proposition and its sense; we can never say what is the sense of what we say' (DR, 155). All that can *actually* be presented of virtual sense as such is mere non-sense.[50] All that we ever actually see or hear of a creating is its creature. Moreover, although sense has nothing to do with signification, as actual beings we are literally born and bound to confuse the one with the other. Deleuze insists that 'the essential thing is to separate the domain of signs, which are always equivocal, from that of expressions whose absolute rule must be univocity' (EP, 330tm), but in our metaphysical ignorance we are generally incapable of maintaining this separation. The configuration of our actual condition encourages us to treat reality as equivocal rather than univocal, as a matter of representation rather than expression.

As Spinoza observed with such uncompromising and subversive intransigence, nothing bears this out more dramatically (in the domain of theology) than our misplaced reliance on scripture and liturgy. As Spinoza reads it, most of scripture is just a collection of signs rather than expressions. God expresses himself through reality itself; the Bible is only a book *about* God, a collection of stories and teachings that seek to represent or signify God. Rather than express (or create) something, a sign serves only to indicate recognisable properties of the thing it signifies (EP, 49). Signs operate on the basis of analogy and representation – to signify God as a father, for instance, is merely to devise an image of him as having a power and authority on the familiar model of actual paternal authority. Sense or expressions, on the other hand, immediately create what they express: to express God is simply to be thought by God, to be a vehicle for God's ongoing creation, and thereby to grasp the whole of reality as an aspect of this same expressing. In the realm of genuine expression, 'the sign and the sense [*sens*], the essence and the transmuted matter blend and unite in a perfect adequation' (PS, 50tm). In other words, biblical representations or signs of God are not divine 'expression, but notions impressed in the imagination to make us obey and serve a God of whose nature we are ignorant' (EP, 51). The fact that we need God's nature to be 'revealed' to us through a naive dramatisation of his properties is only a symptom of our creatural needs and constraints. If we already understood that God simply is reality we would obviously have no need for any supplementary and illusory process of revelation (EP, 56).

The next question we need to address, then, is clear enough: how are we best to move from our initial ignorance to an eventual understanding?

4

Creative Subtraction

'Man will rise above earthly things only if a powerful equipment supplies him with the requisite fulcrum. He must use matter as a support if he wants to get away from matter. In other words, the mystical summons up the mechanical.'[1]

With this chapter we pass through the mid-point of this book and of Deleuze's own philosophical trajectory. Since this trajectory is rigorously consistent, the steps that remain to be taken will follow smoothly on from those that have brought us this far. We have traced the route of creation from the virtual to the actual; now we begin the process of counter-actualisation. We have considered the mechanisms that shape us and identify us; now we can engage in the invention of counter-mechanisms that will allow us to answer the question, 'How can we rid ourselves of ourselves, how can we demolish ourselves?' (C1, 66tm; cf. CC, 23–6).

The general sequence of this demolition is straightforward enough. We know that being is creation but that creation itself generates internal obstacles to its own continuation. Virtual creatings are obstructed by the actual creatures they produce. Like any actual being or creature, human beings tend to live as one such obstacle. The first task then, and the concern of the present chapter, is to develop the means, from *within* our actual or creatural constraints, of overcoming these same constraints. The next task (the concern of Chapters 5 and 6) will be to liberate and intensify the power of creatings as such.

The main mistake to avoid here is again the assumption that the virtual and the actual enjoy equal powers of determination, that creating and creature reinforce one another in some sort of mutual co-implication. No: the creating literally does what the word says, it *creates* the creature, which itself creates nothing at all. The *creans* determines the *creaturum*. There is no place here for something resembling dialectical feedback or progression. Even if a creative intensification accompanies every counter-actualisation, this intensification applies to the virtual (event or sense) alone. Even if the virtual is incarnated in the actual, the resulting incarnation is not 'equally' virtual and actual. When a virtual wounding is embodied in the person who is born to bear it, it is the wound and not the person who is primary and determinant. Or again, if you are individuated both as virtual haecceity and as actual person or organism, there can be no doubting the priority of the one over the other. As Deleuze and Guattari are careful to insist, 'we must avoid an oversimplified conciliation, as though there were on the one hand formed subjects, of the thing or person type, and on the other hand spatiotemporal coordinates of the haecceity type. For you will yield nothing to haecceities unless you realise that that is what you are, and that you are nothing but that.'[2]

We need, in other words, to find a way of reinterpreting creatural or organic life as facets of anorganic or creative life, the life that lives with the power and intensity of the cosmos itself. Perhaps the most important model for such reinterpretation is the development of Bergson's understanding of duration (*la durée*): initially approached in the psychological terms of internal time consciousness, as a personal experience of time as an indivisible flow, Bergson soon came to realise that duration can only be truly grasped once it is woven into the very fabric of things. Properly understood, 'psychological duration should be only a clearly determined case, an opening onto ontological duration'. Only at the level of ontology or cosmology can we understand, in keeping with the equation of being and creation, that 'duration means invention, the creation of forms, the continual elaboration of the absolutely new'.[3]

As for whatever is restricted to the creatural alone, whatever cannot be re-interpreted in terms of the creating that produces it, this must be purely and simply abandoned as a barrier to creation. The creatural qua creatural is unredeemable: while a virtual creating remains implicated in itself, 'the hard law of explication is that what is explicated is *explicated once and for all*', and thereby forever abandoned to its actuality (DR, 244). There is nothing properly creative to be salvaged from the actual or creatural *per se*, other than the energy released by its own dissipation. (As Deleuze reminds us, Nietzsche reserves 'only a light punishment for those who do not "believe" in eternal return: they will have, and be aware of, only an ephemeral life! They will be aware of themselves and know themselves for what they are: epiphenomena' [DR, 55]).

The only positive or affirmative thing that a creatural force can do is to dissolve itself. The only creative way of responding to reaction is to overcome it.[4] For any actual individual, what is essential is 'finally to acquire the power to disappear' (C2, 190; cf. N, 5). Like Foucault, Deleuze is looking for forms of experience or experimentation that will tear 'the subject from itself in such a way that it is no longer the subject as such, or that it is completely "other" than itself so that it may arrive at its annihilation, its dissociation'.[5] What Deleuze says of the German expressionists, artists of Kant's dynamic sublime, thus applies nicely to his own redemptive paradigm: they present an

> intensity which is raised to such a power that it dazzles or annihilates our organic being, strikes terror into it, but arouses a thinking faculty by which we feel superior to that which annihilates us, to discover in us a supra-organic spirit which dominates the whole inorganic life of things; then we lose our fear, knowing that our spiritual 'destination' is truly invincible (C1, 53).

In his essay 'One Manifesto Less', Deleuze provides a sketch of what is involved in such arousing annihilation, based on the example of Carmelo Bene's re-creation of Shakespeare's *Richard III*. 'You begin by subtracting, by cutting out everything that determines an element of power, in language and in gestures, in representation and in the represented.' You then further subtract all 'constants, stable or stabilised elements, because they belong to a major usage' and consolidate fixed or molar identities. Along with such constants, you should eliminate structure (since it maintains 'relations between invariants'), dialogue (since it codifies rule-bound relations of speech), history (since it lends figures of power their stability over time) and even the text itself, insofar as it confines the virtual creativity of language to actual configurations of speech. In a theatre thus purged of all actuality and representation, only creation as such will act. 'Everything remains, but under a new light.' Anything can emerge, but only as the 'sudden emergence of a creative variation, unexpected, sub-representational' (CB, 103–4, 122).

Guided as we have seen by the 'three virtues – imperceptibility, indiscernibility, and impersonality' (TP, 279), Deleuze's project is thus fundamentally austere or *subtractive*. It is subtractive, however, in a quite particular way. This particularity becomes immediately apparent through comparison with perhaps the only fully subtractive ontology in contemporary philosophy, the ontology developed by Deleuze's contemporary Alain Badiou.[6] According to Badiou, being that is conceived solely in terms of its pure being isn't something that we might intuit, translate, or know. If philosophy begins with Plato rather than with the pre-Socratics, this is because Plato approaches being through a strictly conceptual rather than a poetic or mythological apparatus; unlike the poet, the philosopher seeks to situate the precise theoretical point at which the conception of being becomes indiscernible from that which is beyond or other than being (the point which Plato names the Good, and which Badiou himself names pure or 'inconsistent' multiplicity). As opposed to a poetics of being, every ontology thus encounters, at the limit of its efforts to discern the being of being, a point that remains inaccessible to the work of this discernment: it enables a conceptual encounter with the indiscernible as such.

Unlike Badiou, of course, Deleuze equates being with a positive or vital intensity. Unlike Deleuze, Badiou is perfectly happy to accept that being itself is sterile rather than creative (precisely so as to clear the way for a still more emphatic and disruptive notion of creation or 'truth', reserved for sequences that begin with something other than being). Despite this fundamental difference, I think Deleuze is best read along comparably though unequally subtractive lines. Given any actual or positively presented situation, Deleuze will develop a mechanism of extraction that serves to isolate the indefinite virtual event or force that determines it; he will then orient every such event back towards a purely indeterminate, purely intensive power that exceeds any possible presentation or discernment. Precisely because they both seek to think forms of pure multiplicity or absolute difference, both Badiou and Deleuze privilege forms of indiscernment over the multiplication of discernible differences or distinctions. Less than the multiplication of distinct ways of being or behaving, Deleuze like Badiou is oriented towards the production of indistinct or generic modes of being. To *become* in the Deleuzian sense is not at all to attain a distinctive form or identity. On the contrary, it involves finding 'the zone of proximity, indiscernibility or indifferentiation where one can no longer be distinguished from a woman, an animal, or a molecule…'. To engage in the becoming that is a literary work, for example, is to 'open up a zone of indetermination or indiscernibility in which neither words nor characters can be distinguished'.

Eventually, the human form itself must dissolve through the work in favour of a 'new, unknown element, the mystery of a formless, nonhuman life [...], as if the traits of expression escaped form, like the abstract lines of an unknown writing'.[7] For the same reason, if what Deleuze calls an abstract line is 'the most alive, the most creative' form of line this is because it doesn't divide or encircle any discernible space. It doesn't trace a presentable boundary or shape. It simply passes through and between things, unpredictably, unlimited by either boundaries or shapes (RF, 164; cf. TP, 498).

Nevertheless, if Deleuze's philosophy is perhaps more usefully considered subtractive than multiplicative, its orientation is only subtractive *because* its foundation is creative. The actual is not creative but its dissolving can be. Counter-actualisation mustn't be confused with mere de-individuation or extinction. In keeping with Nietzsche's critique of Schopenhauer, although actual or creatural forms like the 'I and the Self must be replaced', such replacement should proceed in and by creative individuation as such, through the power of those 'individuating factors which consume them and constitute the fluid world of Dionysus. What cannot be replaced is individuation itself'.[8] The productive or dynamic work of individuation is not mediated by any form of identity or resemblance, but there is nothing incomplete or insufficient in this work. Individuatings lack nothing, 'they express the full, positive power of the individuals as such' (DR, 258). To refuse to recognise this point is to risk returning to a version of the distortion that informs Hegel's reading of Spinoza as a philosopher for whom all finite differentiation dissolves in the 'abyss' of infinite identity.[9] Deleuze's philosophy is subtractive but not ascetic. It is guided by sobriety, not renunciation.

I

We know that the essential dualism in this philosophy of creation is that between actual and virtual, or between created and creating (or again: between *naturata* and *naturans*, composed and composing, individuated and individuating, reactive and active, definite and indefinite, molar and molecular, striated and smooth, etc.). We must begin, however, with another and more immediately pressing dualism – the distinction between two general kinds of actuality, two orientations of the creature. This is the difference between (a) those forms of actuality that are oriented towards their consolidation and preservation (e.g. through personal fulfilment, social interaction, political integration, responsible communication, ethical concern, etc.), on the one hand, and (b) those forms which, oriented towards their dissipation, can set out to become adequate to the virtual events which sustain or inspire them. Noble vs. base, minor vs. major, rhizomatic vs. arborescent, nomad vs. sedentary, deterritorialised vs. territorialised – as Deleuze understands them, these and other related dualisms apply in the first place to a difference within actuality itself, i.e. to a difference between configurations that tend to consolidate or to break up actuality. Such is the difference between forms oriented towards a way of being *in* the world and forms oriented towards a way of being *out* of the world. The tendency to conflate these two opposing forms is responsible for much of the confusion that continues to surround the reception of Deleuze's work.[10]

Of course, actuals that are oriented towards their dissipation or counter-actualisation will thereby *become* indistinguishable from the virtual that they express. To become-nomad is precisely a version of the process whereby you realign your way of being in a smooth space shaped by active or molecular forces. Nomads, as Deleuze and Guattari describe them (in keeping with an argument to which we'll return later on), are 'in' actual history only as an exception from that history. The rhizome that Deleuze and Guattari evoke in the first of their *Thousand Plateaus*, likewise, is an organic form that incarnates an evasion of the limits of organic form. What a rhizome embodies is precisely its tendential disembodiment. The same could be said of the other counter-actualising forms of actuality that populate Deleuze's books – the schizophrenics ('no we have never seen one'), the artists, the seers, the minorities, the philosophers... (N, 12; AO, 380). In each case, what these forms become is the vehicle of a purely virtual creative force. But equally, in each case, it is these particular forms that endure and accomplish the work of this becoming. The actual is not simply the enclosure of the virtual; what is decisive is its tendency or *orientation*, precisely, either towards or away from such closure.

Before going any further it may be worth drawing briefly on the resources of a philosophical tradition geared around this question of orientation in the strict sense, not least because it will offer a parallel route to a further and equally essential difference that Deleuze will need to maintain, between creative subtraction or extraction on the one hand and mere extinction on the other. This is the Persian Islamic tradition known as Ishraq (literally: the philosophy of 'oriental illumination') which has been made available to francophone readers through the remarkable labours of Henry Corbin and Christian Jambet.[11] The things that separate Deleuze from the major Ishraqi thinker Shihab al-Din Yahya al-Suhrawardi (1154–91) are obvious enough. Al-Suhrawardi writes in an overtly theological and broadly neo-Platonic context, one governed by an uncompromising logic of transcendence. That there might nevertheless be some useful grounds for comparison is signalled by Jambet's recurrent and convincing comparison between al-Suhrawardi and Spinoza – an echo, perhaps, of the way Hegel picked up on the latter's 'oriental intuition'.[12] More to the point, what al-Suhrawardi seeks is precisely a form of spiritual redemption or counter-actualisation, the conversion of actual or objective opacity into singular forms of luminous virtuality. Even more emphatically than Deleuze himself, al-Suhrawardi elaborates a 'plane of the immanence [which] is entirely made up of Light', in which 'things are luminous by themselves without anything illuminating them', in which we and everything else are nothing but reflections and refractions of one creative light.[13]

Like all visions of the Islamic deity, al-Suhrawardi's 'Light of Lights' is radically singular and sufficient. God is 'that which subsists through itself'.[14] The original divine One is itself wholly unpresentable or unknowable, a *blinding* light. The One is not an accessible whole but that which, inaccessible, expresses itself in the multiple. The multiple is invariably expressive of the One but it is so to variable degrees, degrees determined by their absolute proximity to God. The aim of any given being is to return, to the full extent of its assigned degree, back towards the one light from which it springs.

Since 'to turn entirely towards God is liberation', so 'everything which erects an obstacle on the spiritual path' is evil or 'impiety'.[15] An initial struggle with such obstacles is unavoidable. Our own point of departure is not a homely place within the temple of light but an inherited 'exile' within that temple's earthly crypt. To gain access to the light from 'this dark lump that is our earth', the seeing subject must pull away from the material world and attain an exclusively spiritual existence.[16] When I move toward God, 'I separate myself from this world and join myself with the world above.'[17] At the same time, I separate myself from my*self*, so as to become a transparent vessel of light. Light alone is the medium of sight, and God alone has the power to see. Illuminated, the redeemed subject is no longer a 'subject opposed to an object'; rather, 'through the soul that knows, the real knows itself, becomes conscious of itself. Knowledge is illumination of the real in reality itself, it is Light reflecting on light.'[18] It is no longer a matter of 'I think' but of 'I am thought.'[19]

The great question that confronts al-Suhrawardi at this point (and the question that will confront Spinoza, Bergson and Deleuze when they reach much the same point) is simply this: what kind of individuality survives this illumination or dematerialisation? As the Sufi mystic al-Hujwiri notes, there is a crucial 'difference between one who is burned by His Majesty in the fire of love, and one who is illuminated by this Beauty in the light of contemplation'.[20]

The first path, the path of mystical extinction, the path exemplified by the ascetic al-Hallaj, leads to emptiness pure and simple. Here the essential process, as Jambet summarises it, is 'a universal and entire renunciation of the world', embraced as the price to be paid for a definitive spiritual redemption. The 'cut between creature and Creator' is preserved all the way through the redemptive effort, so as to be all the more entirely overcome at its end. 'It is by making within oneself the void of self that we experience God as this very void.' The final or redemptive revelation is then 'nothing other than the void itself, in which the mystic burns'.[21] In some of the more uncompromising formulations of his practice of spiritual detachment, Meister Eckhart appears to arrive at a similar conclusion.[22] In relation to God, all creatures, including angels, 'are a pure nothing. I do not say that they are a trifle, or that they are anything; they are pure nothing [...]. All creatures have no being, for their being consists in the presence of God. If God turned away for an instance from the creatures, they would perish.'[23] If creatures are not only the site of illusion and error but also lack any potential for insight, any potential for overcoming or undoing themselves, then the mystic is forced back to a position of passivity and dependence. If the creatural is nothing other than corruption, helplessness and sin then redemption must depend entirely on the abrupt and absolute mystery of divine grace. The mystic must choose: *either* darkness *or* light, either the creatural or the divine. 'Light [and] darkness cannot co-exist, or God and creatures: if God shall enter, the creatures must simultaneously go out.'[24] Understood in this way, the creatural could never itself construct the means of escaping itself.

Deleuze is firmly opposed to any such neo-Augustinian conception of things. Creation would cease to be creative if it collapsed into extinction. The alternative path, the path that both al-Suhrawardi and Deleuze will affirm, is the path of subtractive individuation or differentiation. Al-Suhrawardi's version has the virtue of foregrounding its explicitly spiritual dimension. The pure light is itself blinding and invisible; the dimension of vision and insight, then, consists as the multiple refraction of this light in an infinite proliferation of lightings. Al-Suhrawardi calls this plane of consistency the 'imaginal world' (the *'alam al-mithal'*, which Corbin usually translates as *mundus imaginalis*). Imaginal forms are virtual but fully individual refractings of light, or individual souls conceived as immaterial but distinct 'imaginings' of God. We can access the imaginal domain through the cultivation and exercise of our spiritual imagination; access to the one light is always refracted through the prism of a particular soul.[25] After Bergson, Deleuze likewise insists that 'instead of diluting his thought in the general, the philosopher should concentrate it on the individual [...]. The object of metaphysics is to recapture in individual existences, and to follow to the source from which it emanates, the particular ray that, conferring upon each of them its own nuance, reattaches it thereby to the universal light.'[26] After Spinoza, Deleuze will define essences precisely as 'pure figures of light produced by a substantial Luminosity' and no longer, as with Descartes, as abstract 'geometrical figures revealed by light' that remains external to them (CC, 148). Like what Spinoza will call the third or highest kind of knowledge, like what Bergson will describe as mystical intuition, Ishraqi illumination allows us to see ourselves as an immediate and singular facet of God – or rather it allows God to know himself by creating himself through us. As Corbin explains, what the Ishraqi seeks is thus an intuition of the singular or of the subject 'which is neither the product of an abstraction, nor a re-presentation of the object through an intermediary form or species, but a knowing which is identical to the soul itself [...] and which is essentially, as a result, life, light, and epiphany'.[27] Understood along these lines, Corbin argues, spiritual redemption has nothing to do with annihilation of the self through mystical fusion with the divine. It is rather through the realisation of that which is most individual and 'most profound in man that man fulfils his essential function, which is theophanic: to express God, to be a *theophore*, a vehicle of God'.[28] Or as Henry will put it: 'I myself am this singular Self engendered in the self-engendering of absolute Life, and only that. Life self-engenders itself as me.'[29]

The path embraced by al-Hallaj and Eckhart, the path of radical detachment and extinction, is one that Deleuze associates with the Schopenhauer who believes that we are 'at best beings who suppress themselves'. Against Schopenhauer's renunciation of the will, Deleuze always embraces a Nietzschean affirmation of power and will. In Nietzschean terms, 'the will is essentially creative', and an active or masterful force is one that creates values rather than extinguishes them.[30] Even Beckett-style exhaustion does not condemn us to an undifferentiated passivity: 'one remains active, but for nothing' (CC, 153). Deleuze privileges the figural art of Francis Bacon over a sterile geometric abstraction for much the same reason. In Deleuze's eyes, Bacon's painting is more powerful than modernist minimalism precisely because it avoids the painterly equivalent of nirvana. Rather than jump directly into the void of pure form (Mondrian) or fuse with the incoherent vitality of pure chaos (Pollock), Bacon assembles singular figures from the ruins of figurative representation so as to animate compositions that 'work immediately upon the nervous system', that 'extract directly the presences beneath and beyond representation' (FB, 51–2). Deleuze's Proust accomplishes a similar trick, insofar as he distils 'from every finite thing a being of sensation that is constantly preserved, but by vanishing on a plane of composition of Being: "beings of flight"' (WP, 189).

A version of much the same distinction should be enough to differentiate Deleuzian subtraction from the openly theological variations on this theme embraced by, for instance, Simone Weil and the early Walter Benjamin. Convinced that redemption only begins where history ends, Benjamin pursues forms of critical 'mortification' as part of the necessary expiation of our natural or creatural guilt. Such guilt arises from the simple (post-Edenic) fact of worldly existence or 'mere life'.[31] Only once they have been reduced to ruins stripped of all ephemeral beauty can creatural forms provide an occasion for a redemptive break in the worldly continuum of catastrophe, the basis for a 'faithless leap forward to the idea of resurrection'.[32] Weil arrives at a somewhat similar conclusion. Like any theophanic thinker, she knows that 'God alone is capable of loving God', and that as a result our first task is to minimise the obstacles that get in the way of this love.[33] The more the creature withdraws and renounces itself, the more we 'undo the creature in us', the more our creator shines through this *decreated* void: 'we participate in the creation of the world by decreating ourselves'.[34] Up to this point, at least, Deleuze's project has more in common with Weil's mystical asceticism than you might expect. Weil affirms a sort of spiritual deterritorialisation, a radical 'uprooting' from self and world, that warrants some comparison with their Deleuzian counterparts. But apart from an occasional acknowledgement of the 'shame at being human' (N, 172), Deleuze shares none of Weil's pathos. He shares none of her emphasis on misery, suffering and affliction. Deleuze is indifferent to the passion of the sinful creature. This is because, unlike Weil, he does not see creation as 'deifugal'. For Weil, creation involves a flight out and away from God. 'God could only create by hiding himself' for 'otherwise there would be nothing but himself'. Divine creation here diminishes rather than enhances or intensifies its creator, and its creatures must atone for this diminishing through detachment and self-renunciation along broadly Eckhartian lines. 'Insofar as I become nothing, God loves himself through me.'[35] Ascetic and negative in Weil, this process is positive and affirmative (though no less ascetic) in Deleuze.

We need, therefore, to bear these two general points in mind as we describe the subtractive orientation of Deleuze's work. In the first place, it is essential to acknowledge this orientation for what it is, i.e. to remember that it is geared to the indiscernible and the imperceptible, that its telos is more a spiritual sobriety than a material exuberance. Deleuze is no more a thinker of this world than are al-Suhrawardi or Bergson. This is the aspect of Deleuze's work that is distorted even in Alain Badiou's concise and illuminating account: because he is determined to drive a wedge between his own still more subtractive ontology (one based on the literal indistinction of being and void) and Deleuze's vitalist ontology, Badiou tends to present Deleuze as his mirror opposite and hence as a philosopher of nature, of the animal, and of the world. Badiou presents Deleuze as the poet of a living cosmos, the pre-Socratic alternative to his own post-Platonic austerity.[36] Badiou associates Deleuze's philosophy with a 'natural phenomenology', with 'a description in thought of the life of the world'.[37]

In the second place, however, it is no less essential to acknowledge the difference between subtraction and extinction. Only the actual can counter-actualise, and this counter-actualisation is itself (like everything that is) creative. Precisely because all finite creatures begin in ignorance of their degree of creative power, so then the process of actively *becoming* creative is essential and irreducible. We only learn what we can do by testing how we enter into composition with other beings, other bodies, other doings, by inventing new ways of affecting or of being affected. A large part of Deleuze's work is preoccupied with the work of such composition and invention. This is the aspect of Deleuze's project that is obscured by Slavoj Žižek's recent interpretation, a reading that effectively turns Badiou's approach on its head. Žižek is keenly sensitive to the ascetic dimension of Deleuze's early work in particular. He does his best to harness Deleuze to an effectively nihilist agenda, a vision of reality as 'the infinitely divisible, substanceless void within a void.'[38] But to preserve this vision, Žižek is obliged to posit among other things a radical break between the apparent emptiness of *Logic of Sense* and the apparent abundance of *Anti-Oedipus*.[39] In reality, however, there is no such break. The gap that Deleuzian difference immediately opens within itself (at every stage in his work) is never substanceless nor negative but always active and positive, the consequence of a primordial movement of self-differing or self-creating. For Deleuze, 'being is not an undifferentiated abyss' and already in *Logic of Sense* what differenciates being is a 'Dionysian sense-producing machine' whose 'subject is this free, anonymous, and nomadic singularity which traverses men as well as plants and animals independently of the matter of their individuation and the forms of their personality...' (LS, 107). What you are is a virtual movement which exceeds yet nevertheless traverses every actual location. Each distinct line of flight or creation races through the universe all at once, connecting each moment of intensity as so many unextended points, linking 'man and woman and the cosmos'. As virtual creatings we are the drawing of these lines as such, rather than any particular cluster of points. 'Each one of us has his own line of the universe to discover, but it is only discovered through tracing it' (C1, 195).

II

Of all the many ways that Deleuze's reading of Spinoza conditions his philosophy, none is more important than the account he derives of such *becoming*-creative, conceived precisely as a movement that skirts these twin dangers (of positive absorption within organic actuality or natural existence, and of mere extinction in the abyss of non-being).

We are already familiar with the single principle that animates the Spinozist universe. What there is is substance or God, such that everything that there is or that happens is a manifesting of God's action. 'God acts and directs everything by the necessity of his own nature and perfection alone.'[40] All individual beings or actions are simply modes or actualisations of this divine power to various degrees, and Spinoza's whole effort is to provide a rigorous, rational demonstration of the ancient intuition that 'God, God's intellect, and the things understood by him are one and the same.'[41] The great question is how *we* might come adequately to understand things in this one way. As Spinoza explains, an adequate definition should explain the 'inmost essence' of a thing, rather than its mere properties. An adequate definition or idea is an idea that expresses the cause of an object and accounts for its properties.[42] Adequately to define a circle as the rotation of a line segment around one of its end points, for instance, is itself to produce a circle, a figure which then necessarily includes among its actual properties the self-evident consequence that its every radius is equal.[43] An adequate idea does not represent or provide a merely mental image or sign of something; instead it enables 'the thing itself' to explicate itself'.[44] Unlike an ordinary, intuitive or imaginary idea of a circle (a vague notion of its 'roundness') which provides only an approximate description of how it appears, the mathematician's idea of a circle is adequate because it allows for the certain derivation of its various properties. Whether we seek to know circles or ourselves, the crucial distinction is this difference between adequate or inadequate knowledge: in the first case, we are actively aligned with what causes or accounts for what we know, whereas in the latter case we are just passively exposed to or impressed by an object that we cannot properly master or grasp. And when it comes to knowing ourselves, what we must learn is that our

> essence is constituted by certain modes of God's attributes [...]. Therefore, when we say that the human mind perceives this or that, we are saying nothing but that God, not insofar as he is infinite, but insofar as he is explained through the nature of the human mind, or insofar as he constitutes the essence of the human mind, has this or that idea.[45]

Again, since 'an adequate idea is just an idea that expresses its cause', so then 'the adequate idea for all things will express the cause of all things', i.e. God.[46] The derivation of adequate ideas thus finds in God its sufficient reason and orientation. 'Starting from the idea of God we deduce all other ideas, one from another, in "due order"', in keeping with the presumption that this deduction is itself parallel to the production of everything that exists in nature (EP, 138).

This idea of God, however, is one that we must first *acquire*. 'That one cannot begin from the idea of God, that one cannot from the outset install oneself in God, is a constant of Spinozism.'[47] Immediate or divine intuition will emerge as the only adequate way of thinking reality, but we must arrive at such intuition. 'Thinking is not innate, but must be engendered in thought' (DR, 147). This engendering takes place in three stages.

The initial stage or point of departure is dominated by a childlike ignorance and importance. Such is our creatural condition: 'we are born cut off from our power of action or understanding' (EP, 307; cf. 262–3). Our beginning is abject. If there is any truth in the story of Adam's original sin, for instance, it is not that our human weakness is to be explained as the result of this inaugural sin: on the contrary, Adam sins simply *because* he is childlike and weak. Our initial ideas are approximate representations or delusions. Our initial actions are driven by more or less thoughtless passions, appetites and needs. Our initial encounters with other individuals are generally mired in dependence and conflict. All ideas which are mediated by the way we perceive, imagine, experience or interact with other things are inadequate, i.e. 'confused and mutilated'.[48]

When we first see a circle, we see only something that looks round. Although such knowledge is necessary and useful, we have 'only an entirely inadequate knowledge' both of our bodies as they actually exist over time, and of the myriad objects that affect us or that we are conscious of.[49]

Over the course of the second stage we slowly construct the means of acquiring more adequate ideas and less passive ways of acting. As we gradually find out what a body can do, as we discover what we are capable of, we cultivate more fruitful encounters with other individuals. Such encounters enhance our power and understanding. As we become more active and less ignorant, the less these encounters will depend on blind passion and chance. Likewise, the more we come to understand the nature of other singular individuals the more we are able to develop 'common notions' that express something of the essence of these individuals – for example, the more familiar we become with material bodies, the more we are able to understand them in terms of common notions like movement and rest. Now we can understand our circle, any circle, in terms of abstract geometric principles. The behaviour of natural objects becomes less mysterious or hostile, more subject to the intelligible order of what we begin to fathom as the 'eternal truths' or 'norms of composition' which guide God's own actions. The intelligible 'order of Nature expresses God as its source, and the more we know things according to this order, the more our ideas themselves express God's essence'. While the cultivation of such common notions and active encounters does not by itself allow for the intuition of God, these notions and encounters can thus 'lead us to the idea of God' (EP, 291, 296–7).

The third and highest stage is reached via the direct expression of this idea. Here we attain sufficient 'knowledge of God's essence, of particular essences as they are in God, and as conceived by God [...]. From the third kind of knowledge we form ideas and active feelings that are in us as they are immediately and eternally in God. We think as God thinks, we experience the very feelings of God.'[50] Knowledge of this third kind is not based on an induction from individual things but on the contrary is one with the real (i.e. divine) process that gives rise to those things. We now know things in their unique thisness or haecceity, as participants in their production. Our adequate knowledge is no longer limited to abstract scientific or mathematical principles, but includes a perfect and immediate intuition, as if 'in one glance', of the essence of singular particularities as well.[51] We are now capable of thinking, so to speak, not just the production of any circle, but of *this* circle. Adequate knowledge of any given entity is not acquired through an experience or description, however accurate, of its creatural particularity, but through an intuitive grasp of its cause or creating.

How do we arrive at such ultimate knowledge? We reach it via nothing other than the idea of God itself. It is this idea that 'determines us, precisely, to "form" the third kind of knowledge, to enter into a direct vision' (EP, 301). The idea determines this because it is God's 'own' idea: only God can produce the idea *of* God. To think this idea is simply to allow it to think through us. In doing so we realise that what we ourselves are is nothing other than an aspect of this idea. In reaching the idea of God we only become what we already were. 'We do of course appear to reach the third kind of knowledge [..., but] the "transition" is only an appearance; in reality we are simply finding ourselves as we are immediately and eternally in God' (EP, 308). Once we thus reach the idea of God (after positive encounters with other modes, the derivation of common notions, and so on) then 'this idea, as an absolute principle, frees itself from the hypothesis from which we began in order to rise to it, and grounds a sequence of adequate ideas that is identical to the construction of reality' (EP, 138).

Our own inclusion in this generative sequence is the keystone of Spinozism and is fundamental to Deleuze's entire project. What is at issue is not the deduction or justification of the idea of God (since it is itself the sufficient reason of all necessity and deduction) but the removal of those constraints which hamper the thinking of this idea. We simply *are* facets of an infinite creativity and so it is enough for us to dissolve whatever hinders our awareness of this creativity in order for us 'to come into possession of what is innate in us'. The joy that accompanies this rediscovery is 'the joy of God himself insofar as he is explicated through our essence'.[52]

The crux of the sequence, then, is that we must actively construct the means of acquiring the idea that will explicate what we are. This construction must itself be undertaken *in actuality*, by experimenting with what a body can do and what a mind can think. 'We can know by reasoning that the power of action is the sole expression of our essence [...], but this knowledge remains abstract. We do not know what this power is, nor how we may acquire or discover it. And we will certainly never know this, if we do not concretely try to become active.'[53] There is nothing merely theoretical about the idea of God or the process of reaching it. To begin with, in other words, we only know (approximately) what affects or *happens to* our body; what we need to reach is the idea that *creates* our body and animates our mind.[54] This idea is our essence, the degree of God's power that we express. To reach it is to express it, i.e. to let it express itself through us. Though what enables our acquisition of insight is in reality just the power of this very insight, the actual process of its acquiring is a struggle against ignorance and impotence. Only the virtual *creans* that we express truly lives and thinks in us, but it is we ourselves as actual *creaturum* who must overcome whatever actually hinders this creating.[55] In the domain of cinema, for example, only the construction of a movement image can extract from moving bodies the 'pure movement' which moves them and makes up 'their common substance', but once constructed this image will retain nothing of these actual bodies as such. The extraction alone is all that matters, precisely because it is 'not an abstraction, but an emancipation' (C1, 23).

III

We can now pick up on the point we've already approached from several angles. Only the creature can overcome its own creatural limitations. This overcoming will involve experimentation and invention, the configuration of new actualities or bodies and new assemblings of bodies. But the purpose of such assemblings is not the consolidation but the dissipation of the actual, not the solidification of materials but their dematerialisation, not the preservation of embodiment but an intensive disembodiment. What matters is not so much the construction of additional forms as the removal of existing obstacles. The goal is less an actual construction than a virtual extraction. The real task is 'always to extract an event from things and beings' (WP, 33), a process which will eventually require the evacuation of those same things. As soon as light ceases to be mediated by the sensory-motor mechanism of an actual organism, for instance, it regains its power of absolute and immediate illumination.

> As soon as it stops being related to an interval as sensory-motor centre, movement finds its absolute quality again, and every image reacts with every other one, on all their sides and in all their parts. This is the regime of universal variation, which goes beyond the human limits of the sensory-motor schema towards a non-human world where movement equals matter, or else in the direction of that super-human world which speaks for a new spirit... (C2, 40).

If then our general question is, under 'what conditions does the objective world allow for a subjective production of novelty, that is, of creation?' (LB, 79), the answer is simplicity itself: under conditions which minimise the obstacles to creation. What Leibniz calls the best of all possible worlds is not 'the one that reproduces the eternal, but the one in which new creations are produced, the one endowed with a capacity for innovation or creativity' (LB, 79). In our previous chapter we examined the primary forms of anti-creation, and much of the agenda for creative counter-actualisation follows more or less automatically from this same diagnosis. Personality, identity, subjectivity, consciousness, signification: these are our primary obstacles. An adequate vehicle for creation must therefore become: impersonal or anonymous; unconscious, or asignificant; anorganic, or 'unlived'.

Perhaps the most serious and intractable obstacle to creation is posed by the reactive fiction of a thinking subject or self. In every inventive sequence 'the identity of the self is lost [...] to the advantage of an intense multiplicity and a power of metamorphosis' (LS, 297). Pierre Klossowski's exemplary work, for instance, 'moves toward a single goal: to assure the loss of personal identity and to dissolve the self. This is the shining trophy that Klossowski's characters bring back from a voyage to the edge of madness [...]; the dissolution of the self ceases to be a pathological determination in order to become the mightiest power, rich in promise and salutary promises.'[56] Like Blanchot, Klossowski writes in order to evoke only the most anonymous and impersonal voice, a voice incapable of saying the pronoun I, in which only an indefinite *one* speaks. We tap into the 'splendour of the pronoun "one"' when we are able to endure 'the advent of a coherence which is no more our own, that of mankind, than that of God or the world' (DR, xxi).

This advent requires the death of the self or I. The one will only live once the self is dead. Just as for Spinoza death allows us to become 'completely expressive' by extracting our eternal essence from its temporary actualisation in extensive parts (EP, 316), so too the artist is someone who 'has seen something in life that is too great, too unbearable also' and thus creates characters or sensations that 'are too alive to be liveable or lived' (WP, 171). For the subject who lives to bear it, 'every event is like death' (LS, 152).

Understood as an aspect of our redemptive counter-actualisation, death is 'an internal power which frees the individuating elements from the form of the I or the matter of the self in which they are imprisoned'. Death in this sense 'refers to the state of free differences when they are no longer subject to the form imposed upon them by an I or an ego, when they assume a shape which excludes *my* own coherence no less than any identity whatsoever' (DR, 259, 113). In this way Deleuze and Guattari seek to harness the death drive to a 'veritable institutional creativity', the vehicle of a generalised depersonalisation.[57] The death of the self clears the way for a new, still unlived and unlivable living. When one of Beckett's characters dies, for instance, 'it is because he has already begun to move in spirit. He is like a cork floating on a tempestuous ocean: he no longer moves, but is in an element that moves' (CC, 26). The moment when death starts to 'lose itself in itself' is also the moment in which dying 'indicates the figure which the most singular life takes on in order to substitute itself for me' (LS, 153). Deleuze will define a philosopher precisely as a person who can endure this substitution in its most extreme form. Through the exemplary death that is lived by any philosopher, 'the absolute inside and the absolute outside enter into contact, an inside deeper than all the sheets of past, an outside more distant than all the layers of external reality […]. The philosopher has returned from the dead and goes back there. This has been the living formulation of philosophy since Plato' (C2, 208–9).

Counter-actualisation doesn't require the death of the self alone. It also requires the sacrifice of that most precious sacred cow of contemporary philosophy – *the other*. The creative one creates as *one*, precisely, in the absence of others. In reality, it is always one and the same abstract animal or machine that creates, variously actualised.[58] For Deleuze the other as such is merely a component of actual individuation and mediated representation. The other is only an enabling condition of the self, the self in its actuality. The other is just 'the condition under which we *perceive* distinct objects and subjects […], and perceive them as forming diverse kinds of identifiable and recognisable individuals.'[59] This other is neither object nor subject *per se*, so much as a necessary condition of the normal perceptual field which sustains the actual self. The other distinguishes figure from ground. The other opens the gap between subject and object. The fundamental effect of the other is thus 'the distinction of my consciousness and its object' – the very root, as we have seen, of the long error of representation. For Deleuze, as in different ways for Girard and Blanchot, the other effects the mediation and consequent dis-association or alienation of desire, the triangulation of desire. 'It is always Others who relate my desire to an object […]. I desire nothing that cannot be seen, thought, or possessed by a possible Other' (LS, 305–10).

By the same token, a liberating return to the immediate and the impersonal will requires elimination of the other. Nothing is more foreign to Deleuze than an unconditional concern for the other qua other. An intuition adequate to real or intensive individuation requires penetration into 'those regions where the Other-structure no longer functions' (DR, 282). We only really know what we can feel or do, how fast we can move, in the absence of others. 'The absence of the Other is felt when we bang against things, when the stupefying swiftness of our actions is revealed to us' (LS, 306).

In this absence of the other, the whole of our actual or 'perceived world collapses in the interest of something else [...]. In the Other's absence, consciousness and its object are one. There is no longer any possibility of error [...]. Consciousness ceases to be a light cast upon objects in order to become a pure phosphorescence of things in themselves.' Reality appears through the disappearance of the other. Such is the redemptive lesson of Robinson Crusoe's story, reworked by Michel Tournier in his 1967 novel *Vendredi* as if in deliberate extension of Deleuze's early musings on desert islands (see above, Chapter 1, section VII). To begin with, of course, the newly marooned Robinson 'experienced the loss of Others as a fundamental disorder of the world'. Soon however he comes to learn that 'it is the Other who disturbs the world. The Other was the trouble.' Through the absence of the other, Robinson becomes a new vehicle for the creation of the island as such. In the end, 'Robinson is but the consciousness of the island [...], the island in itself.' Robinson finally becomes an inhabitant worthy of a truly deserted island. The death of the other thus paves the way for the 'detachment of a pure element which is at last liberated'. Thanks to this impersonal and otherless Robinson 'it is as if the entire earth were trying to escape by way of the island', in a single line of flight.[60]

IV

Deleuze's books are packed with other examples of subjects who manage to de-personalise or counter-actualise themselves and thereby become an adequate channel for creation as such. Two of the most striking are the subjects of masochism and of deterritorialisation.

As far as Deleuze is concerned, the main interest of Leopold von Sacher-Masoch's writings is that, for all their coldness and austerity, they offer a particularly instructive illustration of the 'necessary joy in creation'. They demonstrate that 'art is necessarily a liberation that explodes everything' (DI, 134). More specifically, they undertake a liberation from patriarchy. Patriarchy functions here as a configuration of the symbolic family system in which the son is forced into a defined role through identification with the father. The son is subjected via submission to the father. So whereas sadism negates or degrades the mother and exalts the punitive or castrating father, masochism begins, on the contrary, with the humiliation of this father. Masoch engineers situations in which 'the father is excluded and completely nullified'.[61] Inverting the famous Freudian fantasy, what is beaten and ridiculed in the masochist subject is not a child but rather the image of the father who oppresses that child. The immediate goal is to 'obliterate the father's role and his likeness in order to generate the new man' (MS, 99). Masochist ritual thereby allows its subject to 'liberate himself in preparation for a rebirth in which the father will have no part'; if the father is the ritual figure who forbids incest this is simply because he forbids this rebirth which excludes him.[62] The father is the principle of personality and conscience. The father is the super-ego. By excluding the father, Masoch invents a way of tapping into 'the great primary nature' which is in equal parts cold and sensual, impersonal and sentimental. Primary nature isn't the relentless violence imagined by Sade but rather the cold austerity of the nomadic steppe. Deleuze's Masoch writes in keeping with 'the messianic idealism of the steppe' (MS, 54–5). By the same token, if a woman is never more sensual and exciting than when she is cold or inhuman (a statue, a painting, an ideal...) this is because her coldness then excites a newly asexual sensuality and thus a new liberation from transcendent desire. What is new about the new man is his freedom from the constraints of genital sexuality, i.e. from desire oriented to the imperatives of reproduction and identity. By liberating himself from sexual love (and with it, from the constraints of family, property, work, the fatherland...), the new man attains a 'state of mystical contemplation' and acquires the strength required 'to create a pure ideal reality' (MS, 33).

The highly stylised sequences that recur in *Venus in Furs* and Sacher-Masoch's other books are good examples of what Deleuze calls, in *Logic of Sense*, a 'phantasm'. Like the other forms of counter-actualisation that Deleuze will develop in his later books, a phantasm is a vehicle for a new and properly asexual rebirth. The apparent sexualisation performed by a phantasm is geared in fact at a 'new desexualisation' and sublimation (LS, 220) – the sublimation, once again, that allows for the extraction of a virtual event. A phantasm represents neither an action nor a passion. It occurs as a 'pure event', and like any event a phantasm explodes the coherence of its subject so as to release the non-actual potential that swarms within it. 'What appears in the phantasm is the movement by which the ego opens itself to the surface and liberates the a-cosmic, impersonal and pre-individual singularities it had imprisoned. It literally releases them like spores and bursts as it gets unburdened.' Having thus merged the individuality of the actor with the force of the event, the phantasm presents 'the event according to its essence': it accesses its pure action or *verb*, 'an infinitive independent not only of all persons but of all time' (LS, 210, 213–14). The work of the phantasm is precisely to convert a merely actual, sexual energy into a channel for a purely virtual, purely spiritual thought. Proust's account of such conversion or extraction indicates the 'phantasm's path of glory', the metamorphosis which liberates an eternal infinitive for every body and every quality. By moving from his actual obsession (shall I marry Albertine?) to his virtual concern (the creating of *a* work of art) Proust's narrator retraces 'the path of the divine creation'. Setting out from a merely sexual couple, he attains a plane of immanence in which pure 'thought invests (or reinvests) that which is projected over its surface with its own desexualised energy', freed from any causal determination and liberated from whatever might happen in the depths of bodies or through the time of actuality. In this way,

> the phantasm recovers everything on this new plane of the pure event, and in this symbolic and sublimated part of that which cannot be actualised; similarly, it draws from this part the strength to orient its actualisation, to duplicate it, and to conduct its concrete counter-actu-alisation. For the event is *properly* inscribed in the flesh and in the body [...] only in virtue of the incorporeal part containing their secret, that is, the principle, truth, finality (LS, 220–2).

However ascetic it might seem, the logic of such constructive processes of impersonalisation and subtraction is thus poles apart from the sort of renunciation–extinction generally championed by Lacan or Žižek. The masochist is not the person who comes to terms with an allegedly constitutive gap or lack, but rather the person who success-fully hollows out a space of creative indetermination from within a psychological field that is otherwise always too full, too warm, too familiar.

Much the same effort motivates the process that Deleuze and Guattari famously dub 'deterritorialisation'. We know (from Bergson as much as from Darwin) that every living being owes its organic design and actual identity to the history of its interaction with its environment and with the other organisms that populate that environment. The creat-ural configuration of an organism is a function of the way it inhabits its territory, broadly understood – the creature qua creature, we might say, is indeed a function of its being *in* its world. Like several other French thinkers of his generation, Deleuze retains the essential lesson of Jakob von Uexküll's theory of the environment [*Umwelt*]: each organism only exists as an inhabitant of its particular environment, and every way of inhabiting or experiencing an environment is peculiar to each particular organism. For an organism then to escape its creatural configuration is at one and the same time the process whereby it manages to escape its territory. Deterritorialisation is a synonym for de-creaturation. A deterritorialised configuration of space (or what Deleuze will also call a 'smooth space' or de-actualised space: an 'any-space-whatever'), unlike a territori-alised or inhabited space, varies directly with the forces that produce or distribute it. Such a space conforms to

> a completely other distribution which must be called nomadic, a nomad nomos, without property, enclosure or measure […]. Nothing pertains or belongs to any person, but all persons are arrayed here and there in such a manner as to cover the largest possible space […]. To fill a space, to be distributed within it, is very different from distributing the space. It is an errant and even 'delirious' distribution, in which things are deployed across the entire extensity of a univocal and undistributed Being. It is not a matter of being which is distrib-uted according to the requirements of representation, but of all things being divided up within being in the univocity of simple presence (the One-All) (DR, 36–7).

In their conclusion to *A Thousand Plateaus*, Deleuze and Guattari distinguish between several different kinds or degrees of deterritorialisation (TP, 508–10).

Deterritorialisation is merely negative when it is corrected by and submerged under compensatory forces of reterritorialisation. Such is the usual fate of the actual migrant as opposed to the virtual nomad. Think for instance of those European colonists whose escape from the constraints of their traditional 'old world' directly prepared the way for a new regime of property and oppression in their new world, or of the way that a national state apparatus disrupts local relations of family or labour but only in order to submit its subjects to new forms of exploitation.

Deterritorialisation turns positive yet remains merely relative when it prevails over such reterritorialisations, but without managing to draw anything more than a discon-tinuous, compromised or segmented route of escape. A relative line of flight is not driven by the full power of its original impulse or élan. It remains 'divided into succes-sive "proceedings"' and thus vulnerable to forces of gravity and of recapture.

Deterritorialisation becomes positive and absolute, finally, when, rather than relate a creature to its environment, it is immediately expressive of the single energy (or movement, or line) that animates both creature and environment. Here as everywhere in Deleuze's work, 'absolute' has nothing to do with something transcendent or undifferentiated. 'A movement is relative, whatever its quantity and speed, when it relates a body considered as *One* [*Un*] to a striated space through which it moves, and which it measures with straight lines.' By contrast, 'a movement is absolute when, whatever its quantity and speed, it relates one or "a" body [*"un" corps*] considered as multiple to a smooth space that it occupies in the manner of a vortex.' Pure or absolute deterritorialisation is sustained by properly cosmic forces of creation. The earth itself is nothing other than 'the material through which human beings tap cosmic forces', and the process of deterritorialisation functions like 'the creator of the earth – of a new land, a universe', an earth directly 'connected with the Cosmos, brought into the Cosmos following lines of creation that cut across it as so many becomings. (Nietzsche's expression: Let the earth become lightness…).'[63]

Such is the dynamic incarnated by another Nietzschean figure: 'Dionysus has no territory because he is everywhere on earth' (CC, 104).

Since it is not transcendent, however, this absolute process must always proceed from and through particular territories. We come back here to the guiding principle of the present chapter: only an absolute, virtual or non-actual force creates, but it only creates *through* the relative, the actual, or the creatural. 'We can never go too far in the direction of deterritorialisation' (AO, 382), but as Deleuze and Guattari go on to explain, 'what complicates everything is that this absolute deterritorialisation necessarily proceeds by way of relative deterritorialisation, precisely because it is not transcendent.' Every deterritorialisation sets out from a particular territory, every line of flight takes flight from a particular place. But by the same token, absolute still means absolute. The creating *per se* is not itself relative or local and even relative deterritorialisation 'requires an absolute for its operation'. The force of deterritorialisation is itself absolute, in other words, though every occasion and application of this force is relative or local. Strictly speaking, 'the absolute […] does not appear at a particular place but becomes a nonlimited locality' (TP, 383). (Or in our theophanic terms: the difficulty, as always, is to remember that we reach God only via God and not via the creatural, yet the creatural provides the only site and occasion for our reaching). Hence the paradigmatic status of Deleuze and Guattari's virtual nomad, the exemplary hero of this local absolute:

> If the nomad can be called the Deterritorialised par excellence, it is precisely because there is no reterritorialisation *afterward* as with the migrant, or *upon something else* as with the sedentary (the sedentary's relation with the earth is mediatised by something else, a property regime, a State apparatus). With the nomad, on the contrary, it is deterritorialisation that constitutes the relation to the earth, to such a degree that the nomad reterritorialises on deterritorialisation itself […]. The land ceases to be land, tending to become simply ground [*sol*] or support. The earth does not become deterritorialised in its global and

relative movement, but at specific locations, at the spot where the forest recedes, or where the steppe and the desert advance […]; the nomad is in a *local absolute*, an absolute that is manifested locally, and engendered in a series of local operations of varying orientations: desert, steppe, ice, sea…[64]

Every deterritorialisation is accompanied by a reterritorialisation, but the most absolute deterritorialisation (which is the telos of every more relative deterritorialisation) reterritorialises only on the movement of deterritorialisation itself.

Melville's *Moby Dick* provides Deleuze and Guattari with one of their most powerful figures of deterritorialisation. Captain Ahab's delirious project doesn't just oblige him to sail his ship across an especially broad or especially dangerous expanse of territory. His nomadic voyage is less the exploration of an already constituted territory than the vector of an obsession that distributes oceanic space as the medium of its inexorably fatal actualisation.

Moby Dick further dramatises two additional features of any such process. It proceeds, first of all, not through association with a well-defined point of reference but through contamination by or complicity with a non-identical or 'anomalous' instance. Amidst the crowd of characters who make up the world of any given novel, Melville says, there is 'just one original Figure' who illuminates that world, 'like the beam of light that draws a hidden universe out of shadow' (WP, 65–6). The 'ungodly, god-like' captain of the *Pequod* does not represent a crew of people similar to himself. Still less does he become-whale through sympathy with whales in general, or with any sort of constituted whaleness. Ahab's obsession is with the altogether exceptional whale, the whale that incarnates its unnatural difference from the norm or pack. The becoming proceeds not with a typical whale or group of whales but with that anomaly who lives along the 'borderline' as such, along that singular line traced by 'the rough, cutting edge of deterritorialisation'.[65]

In the second place, the development of Melville's novel confirms the telos or tendency of every such line. The deterritorialising line leads towards an imperceptible illumination. By plumbing the inhuman depths of his becoming-whale, Ahab is caught up with an ever more immediate relation with the sea, until he is subsumed with a 'compound of sensations that no longer needs anyone: ocean' (WP, 169). And as he moves from the organic to the anorganic, from whale to ocean, his becoming crosses the threshold of perception as such. As his becoming-animal approaches its limit, this animal itself is consumed by its most distinctive trait, which is also the marker of its highest indistinction: its peculiar colour. As Ahab becomes animal, so must the animal 'become an unbearable pure whiteness, a shimmering pure white wall', 'pure vibration of white' (TP, 304; D, 73). Deterritorialisation can only become and proceed as absolute if it leads towards such a shimmering; otherwise it will remain compromised by the risk of its reterritorialisation (in the ocean, the voyage, the black hole of extinction).

Literature is no exception to the rule that 'we can never go too far in the direction of deterritorialisation'. In this as in every case, what the rule confirms is again the essential difference between activity and passivity – here, between the writing and the written. If Ahab's journey remains limited it is because it still holds out the possibility of 'reterritorialising oneself on the voyage' as such. In the end, Melville himself is compromised by his interest in geography, his attachment to the world of his actual travels and of the 'savages' he encountered (D, 38; TP, 188–9). Melville is overly drawn to the written voyage, whereas the only kind of voyage from which writing cannot recover is one undertaken by the writing itself. This the further step that is taken, in different ways, by Proust, Kafka, Blanchot, Sollers and the other contemporary novelists who Deleuze celebrates in *Difference and Repetition*. Literary writing enables the absolute and irreversible deterritorialisation of language.

Deleuze and Guattari illustrate what this involves in a compressed passage of their book on Kafka and minor literature. Like every animal, the human animal has evolved with its environment and in relation to the things it requires from its environment. To begin with, its mouth, tongue, and teeth 'find their primitive territoriality in food'. As they begin to devote themselves to the articulation of sounds, these organs deterritorialise. However, language ordinarily compensates for this first, relative or partial deterritorialisation by 'a reterritorialisation in meaning', i.e. by collusion in representation. A suitably creative or literary use of language will therefore have to ensure that, by evacuating and 'neutralising' meaning, 'sound itself will be deterritorialised irrevocably, absolutely'. Literary writing will duly send words hurtling along a 'line of escape – in order to liberate a living and expressive material that speaks for itself', independently of any actual meaning or representation.[66]

Deterritorialised (if not beatified), a nomad is that person who attains, in the domain of geo-philosophy, a vital virtual intensity comparable to that enjoyed, in the domain of psycho- and bio-philosophy, by the 'Body without Organs [*Corps sans Organes*]'. 'The BwO is the deterritorialised socius, the wilderness where the decoded flows run free, the end of the world, the apocalypse' (AO, 176). The BwO is the virtual, unformed body-potential that sustains any actual body. It is body as event, body that can become any body or anybody. It is *a* body subtracted from any bodily shape or norm, any organic or species coherence. As a virtual intensity, the BwO has nothing to do with space or place and everything to do with pure potential or becoming. Like absolute deterritorialisation, the BwO isn't so much a state or thing as a 'practice', and no actualised body or self can ever 'reach the BwO, you can't reach it, you are forever attaining it, it is a limit' (TP, 149–50). Nevertheless, what truly lives in you is nothing other than the BwO, and it is thus the BwO itself that strives to reach or attain itself, through you. Subtractive, the BwO only emerges through the dissolution of the organism; constructive, the BwO embodies the virtual event that determines *a* life. Like any virtual creating, 'the BwO is what remains when you take everything away'. The BwO remains when you strip away the whole domain of the created or creatural – the domain of signification, subjectification, and the self. Whereas a practice like psychoanalysis encourages its subjects to plumb the most threatening depths in search of their true self (i.e. their truest actual self), schizoanalysis says instead 'let's go further still, we haven't found our BwO yet, we haven't sufficiently dismantled our self' (TP, 151). The BwO, in other words, 'is not the child "before" the adult, or the mother "before" the child; it is the strict contemporaneousness of the adult, of the adult and the child, their map of comparative densities and intensities, and all of the variations on that map. The BwO is precisely this intense germen where there are not and cannot be either parents or children (organic representation)' (TP, 164). The BwO is an anorganic creating withdrawn from the mechanics of merely actual (socialised, sexualised) reproduction and merely chronological time. But equally, every BwO is *a* BwO; what you are is *your* BwO, this BwO, the BwO that lives through your actuality.

V

To deterritorialise is thus never simply to drop out of space altogether. To attain the body without organs is not to commit suicide. Like any form of counter-actualisation, deterritorialisation is not a matter of sheer renunciation or extinction. Creation cannot proceed in a void. What Deleuze and Guattari like to call a 'black hole' is precisely a form of virtual or molecular creating which turns back against itself or extinguishes itself. The only thing that can overpower a creating is this creating itself; a black hole is a creating whose energy has been harnessed to its own annihilation. Even 'lines of flight themselves always risk abandoning their creative potentialities' (TP, 506). We know that all creatures begin as ignorant and impotent: they must learn to master themselves and harness their power before rashly embarking upon a premature or merely self-destructive form of counter-actualisation. 'Every undertaking of destratification must observe concrete rules of extreme caution: a too-sudden destratification may be suicidal' (TP, 503). If deterritorialisation is too brutal, too abrupt or too precocious it may simply sap a creature's strength – Deleuze and Guattari cite 'the case of chaffinches that have been isolated too early, whose impoverished, simplified song expresses nothing more than the resonance of the black hole in which they are trapped' (TP, 334). A similar fate awaits those who misjudge their effort to break through the schizophrenic wall or limit and thereby doom themselves to confinement in an asylum – silent, immobile, caught in a sterile psychosis (AO, 136).

The further that Deleuze and Guattari strive to go in the direction of absolute deterritorialisation the more carefully they multiply such 'practical warnings'.[67] The subject of a becoming or a line of flight must overcome their fear of losing their molar or actual security and must resist the temptation to stop their flight and fix a new identity – but they must also resist the lure of annihilation pure and simple, i.e. 'the great Disgust, the longing to kill and die, the Passion for abolition' (TP, 227). With deterritorialisation, 'overdose is a danger' and Deleuze and Guattari respond with a new emphasis on the art of dosages. You don't deterritorialise 'with a sledgehammer, you use a very fine file' (TP, 160). Counter-actualisation is not to be confused with mere anti-actualisation. It is not enough simply and literally to reverse the process of your actualisation. You must become worthy of the events that will undo you. You must strive to align yourself with your own line of flight. Every 'line of flight creates, or turns into a line of destruction' (TP, 423). Which is it going to be? There's no way of knowing in advance, or in the abstract. 'No one can say where the line of flight will pass. Will it let itself get bogged down and fall back to the Oedipal family animal, a mere poodle? Or will it succumb to

99

another danger [...], annihilation, self-destruction, Ahab, Ahab?' (TP, 250). However violent his refusal of representation, an artist like Francis Bacon must be careful to avoid the risk of a black hole through the prudent handling of chaos, the production of a controlled 'catastrophe'. Such a catastrophe must be powerful enough to tear apart the merely actual order of the organism, of narration, communication and figuration, etc., but not so powerful as to obliterate the agent and continuation of this tearing itself. In Bacon's case, the production of this controlled catastrophe is achieved through a graph or 'diagram' (FB, 100). The diagram both undoes the actual and lends consistency to the virtual. It disrupts the world of representation and of clichés while fashioning a slice of stylised immanence, so to speak. A diagram is a productive manipulation of chaos, chaos made durable.

Suicidal extinction thus remains a genuine risk, but Deleuze and Guattari insist that 'there are criteria [...] sufficient to guide us through the dangers' (TP, 251) – the criteria of sustainable indiscernment or subtraction as such. Every line, every becoming or creating must pass the test of inclusion upon the 'plane of consistency, which is the ultimate Door providing a way out for them. This is the only criterion to prevent them from bogging down, or veering into the void. The only question is: Does a given becoming reach that point? Can a given multiplicity flatten and conserve all its dimensions in this way, like a pressed flower that remains just as alive dry?' (TP, 251).

As we shall see, it is for precisely this reason that counter-actualisation is properly a philosophical rather than a simply natural or vital process.

VI

If creatings do not take place within a territory or world, nevertheless they traverse and escape territories at certain points rather than others. A similar condition applies to the relation between creative time and historical time. In reality, genuine 'becomings always take place outside history'.[68] Without the becoming as such, 'nothing would come about in history' (WP, 112). Virtual determination takes place outside actual individuation. No more than Corbin or Henry, Deleuze firmly rejects the notion that the absolute might reveal itself progressively over actual time.[69] The absolute does not express itself mediately, through the course of history. The root of Deleuze's antipathy to Hegel is precisely here: though Hegel also seeks to develop a philosophy that will prove worthy of absolute creation, he invests far too much in the process of creatural mediation. Hegel's cosmic creativity is obliged to bide its time. Caught up in the slow drama of what actually happens, for that very reason it can acknowledge itself for what it is only at its end. 'Hegel betrays and distorts the immediate', for although he succeeds in stretching representation to its infinite limits he nonetheless fails to escape representation itself (DR, 10). The problem with Hegel is not the absolute per se, of course, so long as we remember that 'the Absolute as sense is becoming' and that 'absolute knowledge is not a reflection of humanity, but a reflection of the Absolute in humanity'.[70] The problem with Hegelian creation is not that it is too absolute or too immediate but on the contrary, that it takes far too long for it to become absolute enough. Hegel concedes too much to history.

History as Deleuze understands it is the time and space of actualisation alone. History is creatural time rather than creative time. 'What History grasps of the event is its effectuation in states of affairs or in lived experience, but the event in its becoming, in its specific consistency, in its self-positing as concept, escapes History.' History as such is a domain in which nothing becomes, in which what actually happens serves only to obscure what might really happen. History is an obstacle to creation. 'History today still designates only the set of conditions, however recent they may be, from which one turns away in order to become, that is, in order to create something new.'[71] What actually happens can never exhaust the virtual, and the creature that incarnates a creating itself adds nothing to its creative power. When an event or abstract machine 'constitutes points of creation or potentiality it does not stand outside history but is instead always "prior to" history'.[72] This priority is virtual rather than temporal. Such for instance is the relation between nomads and history, i.e. the history of their oppression or confinement. The relation between the nomadic and the sedentary cannot be understood, according to Deleuze and Guattari, in terms of any sort of historical development. 'The nomads do not precede the sedentaries; rather, nomadism is a movement, a becoming that affects the sedentaries, just as sedentarism is a stoppage that settles the nomads' (TP, 430). No more than the sedentary state-politics that oppresses them, nomads do not evolve or develop but spring immediately into being. The nomad is incompatible with any notion of 'development'. Strictly speaking, then, 'the nomads have no history; they have only a geography'.[73] As far as history or actuality are concerned, Deleuze and Guattari are quite willing to accept that 'the defeat of the nomads was such, so complete, that history is one with the triumph of States' (TP, 394). But as far as philosophy is concerned, this defeat is of no more consequence than are the actual politics of such states. No more than you might ever see an 'actual' schizo, no more than any process of becoming as such, you will not find these virtual nomads *in* history.[74]

On the other hand, however, what happens in history or actuality is always more or less favourable to the liberation of those becomings that animate it. There are moments in history that are more creative than others. Philosophy itself is a vehicle for absolute deterritorialisation, but (according to Deleuze and Guattari) it required first the 'relative deterritorialisation' of ancient Greek society in order to begin and then the more radical deterritorialisation of modern capitalism in order to develop; under the specific historical conditions of capitalism, lines of flight and movements of deterritorialisation 'take on a new character, and a new kind of revolutionary potential' (WP, 93; DI, 270). Along similar lines, we have already seen (in Chapter 2, section V) how what Foucault describes as the moment of our epistemological present is conducive to the emancipation of unbounded finity. The same coincidence, of course, favours the timing of Deleuze's own 'actual' contribution to philosophy. In virtual or creative time he simply provides a further vehicle for much the same insight that has already passed through the minds of people like Spinoza, Nietzsche and Bergson, and which could in principle be thought by anyone, anywhere and at any time. Deleuze's actual contribution to this insight was influenced, however, by the fact that the configuration of his own historical moment – the moment of Foucault, Klossowski, Lyotard, Godard, Beckett, Artaud, Michaux, Simondon, Guattari… – was particularly suited to the cultivation of this insight. It's no accident that *Difference and Repetition* (1968), in particular, 'should have been an apocalyptic book' (DR, xxi).

Over the course of his work Deleuze develops a number of accounts in which the (historical) orientation of the actual towards its counter-actualisation favours the extraction of a (supra-historical) series of events. One of the most straightforward is his alternative to a conventional history of cinema. Roughly speaking, the becoming of cinema as Deleuze conceives it divides into two distinct periods, corresponding to a before and an after. The *before* is dominated by the action-image, itself shaped by the logic of the organism and its sensory-motor mechanism (a hero who acts and reacts); the *after* then opens out onto a world liberated from organic or sensory-motor linkages, a world of overwhelming visions and de-actualised spaces. This shift is itself just an instance of counter-actualisation, a reversal of the movement from virtual to actual. But between this particular before and this particular after there is a specific historical hinge, namely the Second World War and its consequences: 'the unsteadiness of the "American Dream" in all its aspects, the new consciousness of minorities, the rise and inflation of images both in the external world and in people's minds, the influence on the cinema of the new modes of narrative with which literature had experimented, the crisis of Hollywood and its old genres', etc. (C1, 206). What Deleuze will call the virtual time-image, as opposed to the merely actual movement-image, is thus 'the phantom which has always haunted the cinema, but it took the modern cinema to give a body to this phantom' (C2, 41). As Christian Kerslake explains, if in its second or modern phase cinema comes to 'confront time in all its purity, and overcomes the traditional ideas about time as movement that were holding it back, this moment is *triggered* by a specific set of socio-historical conditions'. Modern cinema thus leads us into 'a new phase of history, governed by the tendency towards absolute deterritorialisation'[75] – which is precisely a tendency that owes and concedes nothing to history.

A similar temporality governs the trajectory of capitalism more generally. In *Capitalism and Schizophrenia* Deleuze and Guattari distinguish three general stages in its development. The point of departure is 'an undivided flow that has yet to be appropriated or compared, a "pure availability"', a pure elasticity of exchange without accumulation or stockpiling. Such is the 'primitive' stage, a time dominated by 'the continuous variation of free action, passing from speech to action, from a given action to another, from action to song, from song to speech, from speech to enterprise, all in a strange chromaticism…' (TP, 445, 491; cf. AO, 145–54). In a second moment, this availability is appropriated by the political vehicle of transcendence, the state. The state overcodes and channels the flow of primitive variation towards a resonant and definitive centre (a capital, a treasury, an emperor, a God…). Left to itself, however, this process remains incomplete. Caught within the constraints of their own transcendence, 'imperial myths are not able to conceive a law of organisation that is immanent in this universe' (AO, 219). The despotic drive to overcode the whole of public space simultaneously opens up pockets of interiority that eat away at transcendence from the inside.

The threat to imperial or despotic rule thus comes from the privatisation of citizenship and the decoding of wealth. 'Oedipus-the-despot will have to be replaced by Oedipuses-as-subjects, Oedipuses-as-subjugated-individuals' (AO, 217). This is the breakthrough that defines the third and still ongoing phase – the phase during which a previously external transcendence is internalised. Reterritorialisation now proceeds through the intimate form of the subject or self, matched by a more humane, more 'liberal' model of the state. The violently transcendent exploitation of land and work instituted by the despotic state is reorganised as a less violent, more efficient and more comprehensive process via Oedipus and the liberal state. Now there is neither slave nor slave-owner, but only a universal subjection, and through it the capitalist 'field of immanence – as delimited by the conjunction of the decoded flows, the negation of any transcendence [...] – institutes an unrivalled slavery, an unprecedented subjugation: there are no longer even any masters, but only slaves commanding other slaves' (AO, 254).

At each stage of this process, production takes another step towards its virtual limit (i.e. the limit of immediate creation or absolute deterritorialisation), and with each step it confronts another, more intensive form of resistance and containment. Insofar as the intensification and eventual universalisation of capitalism serves to decode or deterritorialise every configuration of values, so then it is 'correct to understand retrospectively all history in the light of capitalism' (AO, 140). The earth has never been more deterritorialised nor its inhabitants more 'molecularised' (TP, 345), and this is the result of a specific historical process. Deleuze and Guattari are the first to admit that they have little to add to Marx's description of this *actual* sequence. What they add is a new eschatology. The absolute limit to the de-coding of all values, the evacuation of every territory is a value or event beyond any conceivable presentation. The subject that may survive the dissolution of every presentable or actual subject will be an exclusively virtual or supra-historical subject – a nomadic or schizophrenic subject, one worthy of the end of history or the end of actuality. It's in this sense that, beyond capital's limit, schizophrenia is 'the end of history' (AO, 130). By striving to reach the 'furthest limit of deterritorialisation', Deleuze and Guattari's as-yet-unseen schizophrenic 'seeks out the very limit of capitalism: he is its inherent tendency brought to fulfilment', and thereby incarnates the very 'becoming of reality' itself (AO, 35). Their Kafka is likewise the quintessential artist of his time, insofar as he pushes the historical possibilities of actual deterritorialisation towards their virtual frontier. As the 'collective and social machines [of modernity] bring about a massive deterritorialisation of man, Kafka will take this process further, to the point of an absolute molecular deterritorialisation', to the exclusion of any merely critical or reflexive distance (K, 58).

In this, however, Kafka only undertakes for his time a version of the task undertaken by any artist for any time. Using the resources of his actual situation, he taps into the energy of that minimally compromised creating which, as we are about to see, is what powers any artistic project worthy of the name.

5

Creation Mediated: Art and Literature

'The path of salvation is the path of expression itself: to become expressive, to express God's essence, to be oneself an idea through which the essence of God explicates itself' (EP, 320).

What happens when we shift our perspective from that of an actual creature to that of a virtual creating as such? Everything accelerates, becomes more intense, more ethereal. The world of lived and recognisable experience dissolves to the advantage of forces beyond recognition, forces too powerful for both the lived and the world. We begin to participate directly in the production or making of things, rather than in their representation or interpretation. We start to approach the limits of infinite speed, the speed of a thought that immediately creates what it thinks.

Although (for reasons we'll take up in the next chapter) only philosophy can claim to have carried it through to its ultimate conclusion, art has an exceptionally important contribution to make to this reorientation. It isn't hard to see why art should enjoy a peculiar privilege in the Deleuzian universe. If being is creation then the more purely creative a practice or way of being becomes, the more intense it will be and the more being it will express; a practice geared to the exclusive criteria of creativity as such will be perfectly expressive of the intensity and vitality of being itself. The work of art, understood along these lines, can have nothing to do with the process of describing or redecorating a reality external to it. Art doesn't expose truths or realities that would pre-exist it: it *makes* truth and participates directly in the creation of reality. To the extent that truth can be affirmed independently of convention or correspondence, it must be thought as something that is 'produced' or made rather than exposed or represented (PS, 160). Rather than represent something external to itself, a work of art is a machine that generates its own reality. It doesn't produce it in order to make an impact upon something else: like any creating, art is self-sufficient. 'It is the work of art that produces within itself and upon itself its own effects [...]: the work of art is nourished by the truths it engenders' (PS, 154). Art conforms to a logic of creation rather than causation. Its effects are independent of any cause and indifferent to any application. Every great artist seeks to sustain a 'state of permanent creation', in which what matters is 'never what is known but rather a great destruction of what is already known, in favour of the creation of the unknown' (DI, 136).

But if artistic creation is self-sufficient in this sense this is not because it is distant from life but because, more than any actual facet of life, it participates directly in the creation that *is* life. If life is the creation of new forms, then nothing is more alive than art. 'Life alone creates zones where living beings whirl around, and only art can reach and penetrate them in its enterprise of co-creation' (WP, 173). Art lives with an intensity that no actual organism or experience can endure. Co-creators with life, artists are people through whom life lives. An artist is someone who hollows out the domain of the lived in favour of the pure or virtual living that courses through it. The artist (as creature) dies so that life (as creating) might live. Art will thereby emerge as 'the ultimate goal of life, which life cannot realise by itself [...]. Nature or life, still too heavy', will eventually find 'in art their spiritual equivalent' (PS, 155).

Art enables the full spiritualisation or dematerialisation of life.

Here again, Deleuze pushes one of Bergson's ideas to its limit. We have seen how Bergson's conception of the organism, of the organic coordination of body and mind, is stretched between two conflicting tendencies. On the one hand there is the tendency to be governed by the ordinary interests and needs of the organism. The more an organism's behaviour is geared towards this tendency, the more its experience of time is concentrated within the moment of a pure present, the more preoccupied it is with a particular set of stimuli or perceptions and the more devoted it is to the perfectly present-able imperatives of action. Taken to the extreme, an organism geared towards the present tends simply to react more or less instantaneously and automatically, on the model of a reflex response. The urgency of an actual reaction prevails here to the exclusion of all indetermination and all virtuality (and hence of all creativity, all thought, all reverie, all art...). On the other hand, then, the opposite tendency will tempt the organism to forego all concern for the present and for its actual interests or needs. A contemplative inaction can now prevail over action. Loosed from its concentration in the present, our experience of time stretches out in every direction. Eventually, we are exposed to the infinite expanse of time as a whole, as an indivisible continuum without beginning or end. Indifferent to the concerns of the present, we are free to wander through the labyrinth of memory for its own sake. This is the tendency that characterises dreamers and artists, people who are literally 'lost in their thoughts', detached from the concerns of actual life. And as Bergson speculates, if 'this detachment were complete [...], were the soul no longer to cleave to action by any of its perceptions, it would be the soul of an artist such as the world has never yet seen. It would excel alike in every art at the same time; or rather, it would fuse them all into one. It would perceive all things in their native purity.'[1] It would contemplate everything and do nothing. Incapable of action, it would become a being of pure sensation, of sensation in its most disinterested and non-reflexive state.

This is quite precisely the profile of a Deleuzian artist. As Deleuze understands it, the purpose of art is not to represent the world, still less to cultivate or enrich our appreciation of the world, but to create new and self-sufficient compositions of sensation, compositions that will draw those who experience them directly into the material vitality of the cosmos itself. 'The work of art is a being of sensation and nothing else' (WP, 164).

And what is sensation? Sensation is a force of creative intensity that pulses through actual bodies or materials. Rather like the Spinozist attribute of virtual extension, sensation is what *animates* the sensible. Sensation contracts vibrations that are dispersed through matter but that can be preserved through the soul, for 'only the soul preserves by contracting that which matter dissipates, or radiates' (WP, 211). At a maximum distance from the demands of interest or action, 'sensation is pure contemplation' and 'contemplation is creating, the mystery of passive creation, sensation' (WP, 212).

Conceived along these lines, sensation is not transitive. It isn't a matter of perceiving this or that object. Like any creative process, sensation is a form of counter-actualisation. The artist is not the more refined cousin of those ancient craftsmen who imposed beautiful form upon inert matter. Rather, via the composition of distinct creatings or lines of escape, the artist is the liberator of inventive potential within matter itself. Given an actual material or determinate state of affairs, the artist extracts a virtual bloc of sensation which then serves as a vessel for the conversion of that material. Through artistic composition, 'it is no longer sensation that is realised in the material but the material that passes [...], ascends, into sensation'. Art is that alchemy through which 'all the material becomes expressive' – expressive in the Spinozist sense of the word. Through a Rodin sculpture, for instance, 'the material passes into sensation' and enters into a virtual zone of indetermination, into the indefinition of *a* work (WP, 193, 173). Again, literary characters acquire an intensity more powerful than that of any actual individual or any lived experience 'because they do not perceive but have passed into the landscape and are themselves part of the compound of sensations. Ahab really does have perceptions of the sea, but only because he has entered into a relationship with Moby Dick that makes him a becoming-whale and forms a compound of sensations that no longer needs anyone: ocean' (WP, 169).

Through the transubstantiation or counter-actualisation of its material, art works towards the evacuation of a fully non-actual space, a space of creativity unhindered by the inertia of any creature, by the opacity of any obstacle. The artistic journey 'undoes all lands for the benefit of the one it is creating' (AO, 319). It opens up what Deleuze calls an *espace quelconque*, an any-space-whatever. Such a space is utterly indifferent to the coordinates of actuality. It has no stable time and place. It is not representable. Like any creating, it is in equal measure generic and remarkable, bland and unique, ordinary and extra-ordinary. It is this particular space, but its thisness is irreducible to any definable quality. In short, an indefinite any-space-whatever is the spatial equivalent of *a* virtual life. It is

a perfectly singular space, which has merely lost its homogeneity, that is, the principle of its metric relations or the connection of its own parts, so that the linkages can be made in an infinite number of ways. It is a space of virtual conjunction, grasped as pure locus of the possible. What in fact manifests the instability, the heterogeneity, the absence of link of such a space, is a richness in potentials or singularities which are, as it were, prior conditions of all actualisation, all determination [...]. The any-space-whatever retains one and the same nature: it no longer has co-ordinates, it is a pure potential, it shows only pure

Powers and Qualities, independently of the states of things or milieux which actualise them (have actualised them or will actualise them, or neither the one nor the other – it hardly matters) (C1, 109; 120).

<h2 style="text-align:center">I</h2>

Deleuze's univocal ontology, his equation of being and creation, sets several more specific conditions for artistic creation.

First of all, if art is to be creative rather than merely dynamic then the movements or blocs of sensation that it creates must endure. If 'novelty is the only criterion for any work of art', it is equally the case that 'the only law of creation is that it must stand up on its own'. This is the most difficult thing about creating a work of art: to make it autonomous of whatever triggers or causes it. Every genuine novelty must simultaneously present itself as 'eternal and necessary'. Before it is anything else, art is thus an answer to the question 'how can a moment of the world be made to exist by itself?', i.e. independently of the situation and the material in which it is actualised (RF, 200; WP, 164, 172). What preoccupies Deleuze and Guattari's Kafka, for example, 'is a pure and intense sonorous material that is always connected to its own abolition – a deterritorialised musical sound, a cry that escapes signification [...]. In sound, intensity alone matters' (K, 6). Art, we might say, creates an echo chamber in which pure sensation can vibrate in itself, in its undiluted intensity, free of both the *subject* that senses and the *object* that is sensed. Such a sensation is free of any actual object, because art is defined by its ability to make sensation or affect endure for its own sake, without regard for the transient existence of its material support. Art is the making of a smile without a cat (Carroll), the composing of a scream without occasion (Bacon), the composition of a childhood without experience (Proust). And it is thereby free of any subject as well: stemming from a 'gesture that no longer depends on whoever made it', works of art are conduits for the impersonal and inhuman creatings that proceed through them, channels for the nonhuman becomings of man. Rather than subject or object, art presents only affect and percept, only impersonal intensity and indifferent nature. Art frees virtual affects from lived emotions and virtual percepts from lived perceptions. 'Affects are precisely these nonhuman becomings of man', just as 'the percept is the landscape before man, in the absence of man'. Precisely because it is thus independent of all objective and subjective existence, 'art is the only thing in the world that is preserved' (WP, 172–3, 169, 163–4).

In the second place, in keeping with the univocal refusal of representation and metaphor, all art must be literal or immediate. Whatever art expresses must be expressed directly. 'No art can be imitative or figurative' (TP, 304), because art *is* reality as such. Art follows the movement of being-creation with a minimum of mediation. The intense 'matter-flow can only be followed,' and a genuine writer 'writes on the same level as the real of an unformed matter, at the same time as that matter traverses and extends all of nonformal language [...]. Writing now functions on the same level as the real, and the real materially writes' (TP, 512, 141; cf. CC, 11). Literary writing is 'a writing that is strangely polyvocal, flush with the real'.[2] Through literature, language becomes immediate to things, until language and things collapse together in a single plane of expression (CC, 16). The essays on literature collected in Deleuze's *Essays Critical and Clinical* adopt as their point of departure the presumption that language does not represent impressions or experiences *of* the world but is made up of the same 'stuff' as the creating of the world itself. Language expresses the world, it can become a vehicle for the world's own ex-centric movement. Appropriately used, language helps carry the world towards its 'outside'. Reality is not outside of language, it is rather literature that expresses the moving-outside of both language and reality.

An appropriately literary use of language will therefore tend to paralyse, estrange or desacralise its representational ambitions, so as to bring out those aspects of language – the way it sounds, stammers, leaps... – that allow it directly to convey the vitality of sensation and experience, always at levels of intensity that are indifferent to the limitations of the individual author. Both writer and critic should look, either by excessive inflation and excess (à la Joyce) or through sobriety and subtraction (à la Beckett), for ways of conveying intensities that remain properly pre- or post-individual and asignificant. What matters then is not what such a text might *mean* but what it can be made to produce or accomplish. Conventional interpretation is to be replaced with an appreciation for the mechanical and diagnostic potential of literary texts, as so many clinical experiments for investigating 'what a reader can do', for exploring how we might stretch or overcome the limits of our experience (and ultimately, the limits of ourselves: 'Artaud is the fulfilment of literature, precisely because he is a schizophrenic' [AO, 135]).

So third and most important, art must refuse any notion of personal or subjective interiority in favour of an anonymous distance or exteriority. If art is ultimately more creative (and thus closer to philosophy) than science, this is emphatically not because it is somehow more intimate or humane – less conventionally 'abstract' – than science. On the contrary: art's privilege stems precisely from its higher impersonality, its more radical power of abstraction, its ability to transcend, without abandoning the logic of sensation, the scientific plane of mere reference and actuality. Whereas science abandons any direct intuition of pure infinity (infinite chaos, infinite speed, infinite determination...) so as to isolate a plane of reference in which finite states of relative speed or relative complexity can be observed and analysed, art attempts, through its finite compositions, to serve as a conduit for an infinite compositional power. Science is concerned with the description of how virtual events are actualised; a work of art, by contrast, does 'not actualise the virtual event but incorporates or embodies it: it gives it a body, a life, a universe' (WP, 177). Art is a sort of intermediary between description of the merely actual (science) and intuition of the purely virtual (philosophy). Art allows the virtual to be experienced in the medium of sensation, i.e. as a form of life. The artist 'stops the world' (C1, 85; C2, 68) and strives to escape it, so as to grasp 'life in its pure state' (MS, 63).

There is nothing comforting about such experience, and there are good reasons why most people, most of the time, do all they can to avoid the traumatic depersonalisation and defamiliarisation demanded by art. In the interests of order and security, people normally take shelter from the creative chaos that is forever raging 'over their heads' under a comforting conceptual 'umbrella, on the underside of which they draw a firmament and write their conventions and opinions'. But artists and writers 'make a slit in the umbrella, they tear open the firmament itself, to let in a bit of free and windy chaos and to frame in a sudden light a vision that appears through the rent'. Without ever plunging us directly into the black hole of chaos itself, art lends consistency to the searing bolts of creativity that tear through us, through anyone and everyone.[3] Although artists are rare, there is thus nothing private or personal about what is created through them. In Deleuze and Guattari's terminology, artists *become* [*ils deviennent*], and to become is itself 'to become like everybody else; but this, precisely, is a becoming only for one who knows how to be nobody, to no longer be anybody' (TP, 197). Deleuze is audacious with his choice of examples: Proust is often read as a supremely intimate writer, and Kafka as obsessed with stifling forms of enclosure. But as Deleuze reads them they become allies of the great artistic project he associates with Anglo-American writing – the effort to escape, to break away from the familiar and the domestic. 'From Hardy to Lawrence, from Melville to Miller, the same cry rings out: go across, get out, break through.' At what price? 'At the price of a becoming-animal, a becoming-flower or rock, and beyond that, a strange becoming-imperceptible…'.[4]

On the one hand, then, the artist is indeed exceptional. The 'embodiment of cosmic memory in creative emotions undoubtedly only takes place in privileged souls' (B, 111). These souls, these artists and mystics, generally live in a profound state of actual solitude or isolation. Artists are the nomadic inhabitants of a virtual desert. Writers must endure the emptiness of what Blanchot called the *espace littéraire*. They must survive that personal evacuation or 'exhaustion' that Deleuze associates with Beckett.[5] As a rule, 'when you work, you are necessarily in absolute solitude' (D, 6). On the other hand, however, artistic work hurls you into direct contact with the anonymous expanse of creation as a whole. Precisely because it is not filtered through the idiosyncrasies of a constituted self, artistic expression opens onto an immediately universal plane. 'Kafka's solitude', for example, 'opens him up to everything going on in history today' (K, 17–18) for there is literally nothing and no-one to limit his expression of reality. It was in the moment of his greatest actual isolation that Nietzsche likewise came to identify with 'all the names of history' (AO, 21). The solitary artist always produces 'intensive quantities directly on the social body, in the social field itself. A single, unified process. The highest desire desires to be both alone and to be connected to all the machines of desire' (K, 71; cf. CC, 11). So what Deleuze and Guattari call a 'minor' literature is defined not only by its exceptional degree of deterritorialisation – these are literatures that develop at a distance from any actual or consolidated tradition, from state-mediated identity, from any sense of home or familiarity associated with a mother-tongue – but also by its insistently collective articulation. Everything in a minor literature is political, and its 'cramped space forces each individual intrigue to connect immediately to politics' (K, 17). By the same token, however, this remains a politics of minorities as such, that is of pure or virtual becomings, of movements that evade any communitarian identity or territorial definition.

Of the many artists and forms that Deleuze considers, there is space here to review three of his most suggestive examples, in three different media: the paintings of Francis Bacon, the cinema of the post-war avant-garde, and the writings of Marcel Proust.

II

There is nothing obscure about the creatural dimension in visual art: it depends on relations of representation and figuration, on the reliability of perspective and the stability of distinctions between perceiver and perceived, foreground and background, colour and line, etc. Figurative painting is designed to resemble the objects it represents, and to allow for the deduction of clear narrative or symbolic relationships among these objects. Based on an apparently natural coordination of hand and eye or of touch and sight, figuration conforms to the norms of fully actualised, fully 'striated' or metric space. And so long as the general system of representation remains in place, then painting can be dedicated to the illustration of concerns external to painting itself – for instance, of religious or political themes. All of these factors come together in the system of organic representation that dominated European art from the Renaissance through to the mid nineteenth-century. The result endures as a massive accumulation of visual clichés, so many 'figurative givens' that obstruct the work of painting before it even begins. The painter's point of departure is not the blank slate of an empty canvas but the stifling dominance of these figurative conventions. The painter's first 'problem is not how to enter into the canvas, since he is already there, but how to get out of it' (FB, 11, 87, 96).

To liberate creatings from within these constraints implies, in the first place, an end to the organic subordination of hand to eye. Deleuze distinguishes a number of possible routes to this goal. By emphasising colour over form, Byzantine art managed to develop a purely optic art, an art of the eye alone. Gothic art, by contrast, allowed the emergence of an irregular, mobile and disruptive line, a haptic art, an art of dynamic becomings, of linear connections and disconnections. Cézanne and Van Gogh were later to develop a sort of haptic colourism, an art of tonal variations and intensities.[6] Cézanne's work thus 'aims to extract directly the presences beneath and beyond representation': rather than look at things from a distance, 'it makes presence immediately visible' and 'gives us eyes all over' (FB, 52). To this extent Cézanne exemplifies the more general tendency of a visual art as such. 'By virtue of its most profound theme, the visual image points to an innocent physical nature, to an immediate life which has no need of language' (C2, 225). Once freed from the constraints of representation, painting can put 'the emancipated senses into direct relation with time and thought' (C2, 17). Rather than explore the perceptual relation between subject and object, visual art recognises that 'it is the same body which, being both subject and object, gives and receives the sensation' (FB, 35).

Although only modern art will develop the full potential of this logic of sensation, El Greco and Michelangelo anticipate some of its implications. El Greco's masterpiece *The Burial of the Count of Orgaz* (1588) is divided into two halves. The bottom half presents the burial itself, and conforms to many of the clichéd requirements of representation:

110

the figures are easily identified (as Saints Stephen and Augustine, as the artist's own son, as himself, etc.), their narrative relations are clear and distinct. But in the upper half of the painting, in which the count's soul is received by the heavenly Christ, 'there is a wild liberation, a total emancipation: the Figures are lifted up and elongated, refined without measure, outside all constraint. Despite appearances, there is no longer a story to tell; the Figures are relieved of their representative role', and freed from all figuration they 'enter directly into relation with an order of celestial sensations'. Precisely because they are sustained by this God of absolute sensation, so then 'the divine Figures are wrought by a free creative work, by a fantasy in which everything is permitted' (FB, 9–10).

Michelangelo's *Holy Family* (1504) is similarly traversed by a creative intensity which escapes the actual or organic limitations of its extension in space:

> It is as if the organisms were caught up in a whirling or serpentine movement that gives them a single 'body' or unites them in a single 'fact,' apart from any figurative or narrative connection [...]. The forms may be figurative, and there may still be narrative relations between the characters – but all these connections disappear in favour of a 'matter of fact' or a properly pictorial (or sculptural) ligature, which no longer tells a story and no longer represents anything but its own movement, and which makes these apparently arbitrary elements coagulated in a single continuous flow. Certainly there is still an organic representation, but even more profoundly, we witness the revelation of the body beneath the organism, which makes organisms and their elements crack or swell (FB, 130, 160).

Modern painting will embrace such counter-representation as its guiding ambition. 'The abandonment of simple figuration is the general fact of Modern painting, and still more, of painting altogether, of all time' (FB, xiv). Modern painting simply pushes the refusal of representation to its limit. It dismantles the order of cliché, and with it the creatural (organic, narrative, figurative...) order as a whole.

Deleuze distinguishes several dominant tendencies within the modernist project. The path of pure abstraction, exemplified by Mondrian's geometric compositions, abandons the domain of figuration or representation all at once. It cuts off any relation to nature or landscape. It doing so, however, it cuts off any relation with creative vitality as well. The result is an excess of order and control, a form of visual sterility; even Kandinsky's 'nomadic line' lacks genuine energy and 'tension'. Deleuze associates the opposite path, the path of abstract expressionism, with Pollock. Here 'the abyss or chaos is deployed to the maximum', in an attempt to sustain an unqualified proximity to catastrophic intensity. The result, says Deleuze, is *simply* chaotic – a 'mess'. Deprived of all clarity and precision, the canvas remains embroiled in an 'irremediably confused state' (FB, 109). One way or the other, both these options blur the distinction we established in the previous chapter, between subtraction and extinction. In order to trace a consistent line of flight, in order to sustain a viable creating, creatural disruption should avoid pure abstraction and proceed instead as a local absolute. It should develop as unlimited in its intensity yet focused in its time and space. It shouldn't consume the entire painting but allow for the extraction of a sensation that is 'clear and precise' (FB, 110). Such extraction will combine dissolution of the figurative together with creation of the *figural*, i.e. a counter-actualised figure, a virtual figure freed from all actual constraints.

This then is the third and final path, the path explored by Bacon himself when he takes up the task of painting pure sensation as such. Rather than paint the perception *of* horror, i.e. the relation between subject and object that justifies the reaction of horror, Bacon famously paints horror itself, horror as sensation. Bacon's Popes scream in the absence of any object or occasion that might motivate the scream. 'When Bacon paints the screaming Pope, there is nothing that might cause horror, and the curtain in front of the Pope is not only a way of isolating him, of shielding him from view; it is rather the way in which the Pope himself sees nothing, and screams before the invisible' (FB, 38). Isolated from the domain of perception, causation and action, free from the mediation of meaning or motivation, the sensation passes directly through the nervous system. The sensation simply resonates, here, in its thisness, in its pure or virtual intensity.

The mere elimination of a narrative dimension, however, is not enough to release the sensation. On the one hand, the order of narration and illustration must be actively broken up so as to allow the direct recording of a sensation or 'fact', via the introduction of involuntary marks and violent swipes of paint which block the revival of narrative clichés. These accidental strokes provide an initial 'graph' or 'diagram' which then guides the composition of the canvas and allows its figurative trajectory to endure.[7] As Bacon himself puts it, if a non-figurative or non-illustrative painting captures an image 'more poignantly' than an exact reproduction it's because it can come to acquire 'a life of its own', independently of the artist's conscious knowledge or will.[8]

It isn't difficult to reconstruct, from Deleuze's book on Bacon, the essential stages whereby a pure *living* comes to acquire a version of such independence. Everything begins with the catastrophic disruption of the actual or the clichéd, which allows for 'the emergence of another world' – a non-representative, non-narrative, non-figurative world (FB, 100). A canvas like Bacon's *Painting* of 1946 is dominated by the brooding menace of forces that promise to butcher what remains of organic form. Bodies become so many pieces of meat. Species are uncoupled from any stable essence and come to appear as purely contingent or accidental (FB, 135). The figure then emerges, improbably, abruptly, from the wreckage of the cliché. The forces that work through these dis-organised bodies now animate a figure that is irretrievably isolated from all 'sociable' interaction. The figure resists narrative or psychological interpretation. The figure coheres only as a vector for the intense sensations that tear through it and reshape it at will. Rather than emerge at a stable distance from its background, the figure is poised upon a ground or 'contour' only so as to establish the route of its imminent dissolution within that same ground. The figure then seeks 'to pass through a vanishing point in the contour in order to dissipate into the material structure', it 'tends to dissipate into the fields of colour' (FB, 17–18). The points of escape are variable – the figure can flow through an umbrella (as in the *Painting* of 1946 or 1971), or into a carcass, or down a drain (as in the 1976 *Figure at a Washbasin*), or simply into itself (as in Bacon's 1973 series of self-portraits).

Eventually, at the limit of such dissolution, as it fuses with 'cosmic dissipation', the figure is caught up with a pure 'becoming-imperceptible in which it disappears'. The figure enters into 'a space that will no longer be anything but the Sahara', a domain of absolute luminosity (FB, 29, 27). Especially in the great triptychs of the 1970s, the figures come to 'look like trapeze artists whose milieu is no longer anything but light and colour […]. An immense space-time unites all things, but only by introducing between them the distances of a Sahara, the centuries of an aeon'. And ultimately, once painting becomes thoroughly 'aerial' and attains the maximum intensity of light (its 'monochromatic eternity'), Bacon is at last free to leave the figure behind. In late paintings like *Jet of Water* (1979) and *Water Running from a Flowing Tap* (1982) Deleuze sees evidence of a final though still nascent period in Bacon's work, one 'characterised by an "abstraction" that no longer has any need of the Figure. The Figure is dissipated by realising the prophecy: you will no longer be anything but sand, grass, dust, or a drop of water.' In these and similar paintings the figure leaves only an indefinite or virtual trace of its former presence, and 'the scrambled or wiped-off zone, which used to make the Figure emerge, will now stand on its own, independent of every definite form, appearing as a pure Force without an object: the wind of the tempest, the jet of water or vapour, the eye of the hurricane…' (FB, 84–5, 31).

At this point Bacon's painting, like Ozu's cinema, attains the fully counter-actualised intensity of an any-space-whatever. In such a space the expression of intensity 'reaches the absolute, as instances of pure contemplation, and immediately brings about the identity of the mental and the physical, the real and the imaginary, the subject and the object, the world and the I' (C2, 16).

III

A variant of this same trajectory, oriented to this same telos, governs Deleuze's most widely read and most developed exploration of creative expression – his two-volume study of film. What cinema demonstrates above all, says Deleuze, is the machinery of time as such. As it evolves from its early confinement in Hollywood's entertainment industry through to the unconditionally experimental terrain of Europe's nouvelle vague, cinema progresses from an essentially indirect treatment of time – time filtered through *actual* movement, through the co-ordination of actions and reactions in a well-defined field of reference – to an ultimately direct or *immediate* treatment, one that blends with the pure creative virtuality of 'time in its pure state'.

Deleuze again depends heavily here on those Bergsonian distinctions between action and contemplation, interest and disinterest, that we reviewed in Chapter 2. An 'action-image' coordinates a situation or milieu to more or less appropriate forms of response or behaviour (C1, 134). Such an image is perceived through the mediation of organic interest and is shaped by criteria of pertinence and utility – it is geared towards recognisable stimuli and the anticipation of suitable reactions to those stimuli. Action-oriented or organic perception is thus one that presumes the independence of its object and that prepares the way for a useful subjective response to that object (C2, 126).

Perception is here incorporated within a sensory-motor schema that takes in information about the external world and channels it into functional and narratable sequences of actions and reactions. Given a threatening object, the subject will flee it or confront it, etc.; the (cowardly, indecisive, courageous, impetuous…) 'character' of such a subject can then be discerned in terms of a particular pattern of reactions. The 'sensory-motor image effectively retains from the thing only what interests us, or what extends into the reaction of a character' and this is why 'the sensory-motor schema is an agent of abstraction' in the merely privative sense (C2, 45). The sensory-motor mechanism is an instrument of drastic compression or limitation. Whereas every temporal moment is an aspect of the indivisible, unlimited and infinitely rich flow of time, the sensory-motor mechanism is interested only in the most compressed and presentable facet of time. The acting subject lives in a time reduced to an ephemeral present. The sensory-motor mechanism is attentive only to the immediate consequences of the present and to those fragments of the past that might be relevant to these consequences. The mechanism thus interrupts the indivisible flow of time by isolating, within the unpresentable flow, a dramatically impoverished slice of presentable *actualité*. As the commercial cinema has always understood, modes of perception that identify with the sensory-motor mechanism will be interested mainly in action images and thus in films that string together a series of adventures – action-adventure and character-development amount to essentially the same thing. Or as Bergson notes with his characteristic concision, 'before philosophising one must live, and life demands that we put on blinders'.[9]

On the other hand then, opposed to this concern for action and actuality, there is a mode of intuition that is oriented to contemplation and virtuality. Such intuition will be crystalline rather than organic. If sensory-motor or organic perception assumes the independence of its object, 'what we call a crystalline description stands for its object, replaces it, both creates and erases it' through the multiplication of 'purely optical and sound situations detached from their motor extension'. Whereas via organic perception characters respond to situations or behave in such a way as to disclose what is going on in a situation according to a particular set of interests or needs, crystallised characters 'cannot or will not react […]. Having lost its sensory-motor connections, concrete space ceases to be organised according to tensions and resolutions of tension, according to goals, obstacles, means or even detours.' In this way we penetrate zones of pure contemplation, in which the concerns of interest and action cease to impose any limit upon what is perceived. Perception becomes overwhelming, hallucinatory, unbearably intense. Through such crystalline intuition, characters become passive 'seers', indifferent to whatever might be present or actual, insensitive even to reflex reactions, 'so great is their need to "see" properly what there is in the situation'.[10]

The cost of such insight is perfectly explicit: the catastrophic paralysis of the actor, the dismantling of the organism. Starting with Italian neo-realism in the late 1940s and then continuing with the French new wave a decade later, the production of images mediated by moving actors is replaced by the production of pure 'time images', i.e. images that open directly onto the perception of creative time *as such*, 'cut off from the world' and purged of any actual creature (C2, 251). Through the films of Fellini, Godard, Resnais, and many others, the 'sensory-motor schema is shattered from the inside. That is, perceptions and actions cease to be linked together, and spaces are neither co-ordinated nor filled' but simply scattered in an errant distribution that generates the very dimensions that they occupy. Events no longer relate to the person who instigates them or responds to them but consist of 'immobilisings, petrifications and repetitions' (C1, 207; C2, 103). Actors become the victims of the events that befall them. Deliberation is replaced by chance, purpose is consumed by fate, journeys dissolve into aimless wanderings. Rather than integrated through action and narrative, the cinema of pure time images assembles dispersive situations characterised by the absence of plot and 'deliberately weak links'. The association of images becomes 'elliptical', 'irrational' and 'direct', without 'intermediaries' (C1, 207–10; 168). Stimuli no longer provoke reactions so much as summon up terrifying visions or dreams. Hence for instance the role of the child in the neo-realism of De Sica and Truffaut: thanks to their relative 'helplessness', children are 'all the more capable of seeing and hearing' and thus all the more open to the direct revelation of reality in its raw state, in that 'nakedness, crudeness and brutality which make it unbearable, giving it the pace of a dream or nightmare' (C2, 3).

The resulting images bend the dimensions of actuality back beyond the turn in experience, back to the virtual dimensions of its immediate determination. Through the creation of anorganic or crystalline images, 'the virtual detaches itself from its actualisations, starts to be valid for itself'. The creating extracts itself from its creatural incarnation. The time image is sufficient, it no longer leaves anything external to itself. The time image absorbs any out-of-field. 'The visual image has given up its externality; it has cut itself off from the world and conquered its reverse side; it has made itself free from what depended on it.' It has become absolutely 'autonomous', the master of its composition and framing (C2, 127, 251).

In the dimension of space, such virtual or crystalline perception intuits a purely non-actual, non-organic or uninhabitable any-space-whatever. Such spaces exist at a maximum distance from the domain of conventionally deliberate action – zones of disused or waste ground, 'the undifferentiated fabric of the city [...]. As Cassavetes says, it is a question of undoing space, as well as the story' (C1, 120–1; 208). Minimally constrained by any actual or constituted form of existence, an any-space-whatever is space in which literally anything is possible, the space of unhindered virtuality or potentiality as such (C1, 109). The question of 'how can any-space-whatever be extracted from a given state of things?' has of course received several different answers in the history of cinema. Expressionism, for instance, creates a Gothic 'world which drowns and breaks contours, which endows things with a non-organic life in which they lose their individuality, and which potentialises space, whilst making it something unlimited'. The lyrical-abstractionist approach emphasises a 'becoming-light', a movement towards a 'pure, immanent or spiritual light'. Colourism instead emphasises intensification and saturation, the absorption or obliteration of lines, figures, faces (C1, 111–19). Yasujiro Ozu is one of the great makers of *espaces quelconques*. Only very weak sensory-motor connections survive in Ozu's films. Through either 'disconnection or vacuity', Ozu transforms places into any-space-whatevers and through this conversion they 'reach the absolute, as instances of pure contemplation' – instances of pure creation in both the material and the spiritual plane (C2, 16–20).

In the dimension of time, crystalline perception opens directly onto indivisible continuity as such (or 'time in its pure state'). Once a character is consumed by sensory-motor helplessness there is nothing to filter the 'total and anarchic mobilizing of the past' in its continuous immediacy (C2, 55). Whereas sensory-motor perception strives to reduce temporal progression to an episodic series of successively present moments (a series that can be reconstructed in terms of causation, and anticipated in terms of interests or goals), in the films of someone like Robbe-Grillet 'there is never a succession of passing presents, but a simultaneity of a present of past, a present of present, and a present of future, which make time frightening and inexplicable'. Robbe-Grillet manages to abstract narration from the succession of actual time, and thereby replaces the movement-image with an immediate time image.[11] The time perceived in the time-image is virtual time in its infinite plenitude, i.e. a plenitude that is no longer mediated by any actuality. The time-image is thus precisely not an image in the usual (or actual) sense of the term. It is not a relation between perceiver and perceived, so much as 'a perception as it was before men (or after)', the perception of a time and space 'released from their human coordinates' (C1, 122). Crystalline perception proceeds, in other words, at the scale of cosmic creation itself. Grasped in their creative singularity, 'the little crystalline seed and the vast crystallisable universe' are aspects of one and the same self-differentiating whole. There is a 'homogeneity of seed and crystal, the whole of the latter being no more than a greater seed in the process of growth […]. What we are seeing in the crystal is always the bursting forth of life, of time' (C2, 81, 90–1). If, for example, Werner Herzog's *Heart of Glass* endures as one of the 'greatest crystal images in the history of the cinema' this is because it bends a counter-actualisation towards its properly spiritual and cosmic dimension:

> The search for the alchemical heart and secret, for the red crystal, is inseparable from the search for cosmic limits, as the highest tension of the spirit and the deepest level of reality. But the crystal's fire will have to connect with the whole range of manufacturing for the world, for its part to stop being a flat, amorphous environment which ends at the end of a gulf, and to reveal infinite crystalline potentialities in itself ('the earth rises up from the waters, I see a new earth…') (C2, 74–5).

As noted in the previous chapter, there is more than a passing resemblance between these crystal images and al-Suhrawardi's imaginal forms. In either case 'it is the whole of the real, life in its entirety, which has become spectacle' (C2, 84), a spectacle that transcends any possibility of reaction or intervention. In both cases the spectacle can be endured only by a seer or visionary strong enough to tolerate direct exposure to the 'iridescent chaos of a world before man' (C1, 81). In both cases the perception of such a virtual spectacle is a purely contemplative and essentially dematerialised or spiritual affair – 'the any-space-whatever is identical to the power of the spirit'. And in both cases, this spiritual intuition carries a properly redemptive force. It involves the intuition of a 'pure, immanent or spiritual light, beyond white, black and grey', and 'as soon as this light is reached it restores everything to us' (C1, 117). Such intuition restores 'faith in the world' precisely by tapping into the intensity that creates it. By giving up our creatural coherence we attain that non-organic life which pulses through the universe as a whole and maintains the immediate identity of 'brain and cosmos' (C2, 215; cf. C2, 151).

IV

However divergent their medium and material, Deleuze tends to read his privileged artists as contributors to one and the same creative project. It's not surprising that he should refer in his book on Bacon to Proust as a writer who, like the painter, sought to avoid a literature that was either merely figurative and narrative or else too deliberately abstract, in favour of a figural writing. Like Bacon, Proust seeks to evoke 'a kind of Figure torn away from figuration and stripped of every figurative function: a Figure in itself, for example, the Figure-in-itself of Combray' – a figure which allows for the extraction of an 'ineffable essence, an epiphany erected within the closed world' (FB, 67–8). Nor is it surprising that Deleuze should note, in his second book on cinema, that 'the direct time-image always gives us access to that Proustian dimension where people and things occupy a place in time which is incommensurable with the one that they have in space' (C2, 39). It's not surprising, in fact, that references to Proust should recur in most of Deleuze's books, since the general sequence he relates is typical of the general redemptive sequence that guides the whole of Deleuze's philosophy. Proust narrates the shift out and away from a position that is trapped within the actual world to a position invested with the power to create new worlds. Proust tracks the becoming-artist or becoming-visionary of his narrator: his narrator eventually stops building a prison for the worldly Albertine so as to dedicate himself to the temple of eternal art.

As Deleuze reads it, *In Search of Lost Time* is not a book about memory or recovering the past. It is organised, instead, as an 'apprenticeship', a learning process or initiation into a new artistic vocation (PS, 26, 92). Broadly speaking, the narrative trajectory of this initiation is comparable to that which led, in cinema, from the action image to the pure time image. The point of departure is an actual way of being in the world, a way of believing in the objective qualities of the world and in the subjective power to invest these qualities with meaning or depth. Over the course of his apprenticeship, the hero of the *Search* learns that these beliefs are delusions. His apprenticeship reorients him away from the world towards an insight that sees through the world. His path leads him through the worldly and the actual, through the snobberies of the society and the delusions of love, towards a purely contemplative intuition of essential reality in its raw state – an intuition of 'the original complication, the struggle and exchange of the primordial elements which constitute essence itself' (PS, 48). As much as Kafka and Artaud, Deleuze's Proust thus writes in pursuit of ever more absolute forms of counter-actualisation or deterritorialisation. If Proust's *Search* is 'a great enterprise of schizoanalysis' it's because 'all the planes are traversed until their molecular line of escape is reached, their schizophrenic breakthrough; thus in the kiss where Albertine's face jumps from one plane of consistency to another, in order to finally come undone in a nebula of molecules' (AO, 318). The narrator's journey pushes him further and further down the path of counter-actualisation, never ceasing to traverse territories and undo relationships until, eventually,

he reaches his *unknown country*, his own, the *unknown land*, which alone is created by his own work in progress, *In Search of Lost Time 'in progress'*, functioning as a desiring-machine [...]. He goes toward these new regions where the connections are always partial and nonpersonal, the conjunctions nomadic and polyvocal, the disjunctions included, where homosexuality and heterosexuality cannot be distinguished any longer: the world of transversal communications, where the finally conquered nonhuman sex mingles with the flowers, a new earth where desire functions according to its molecular elements and flows. Such a voyage does not necessarily imply great movements in extension; it becomes immobile, in a room and on a body without organs – an intensive voyage that undoes all lands for the benefit of the one it is creating (AO, 318–19).

The dual aspect of this trajectory is again familiar. On the one hand, the reaching of this new land, this creating without creature, will again involve the progressive paralysis of the actor, the collapse of all his worldly or romantic projects. The narrator's sensory-motor system will waste away until he becomes a purely passive spectator, incapable of reaction – a spectator who sees nothing because he intuits everything. And on the other hand, then, this same journey will allow the artist to attain an insight beyond action. As he learns to tap into 'time in its pure state', he becomes a disinterested seer, a witness who 'sees nothing, hears nothing, he is a body without organs [...], observing nothing but responding to the slightest sign'. Deleuze compares him to a sort of spider deprived of eyes and ears but infinitely sensitive to whatever resonates through his virtual web. Actual or constituted forms slip through the web and make no impression, for the web is designed to vibrate only on contact with virtual or intensive forms. The more fleeting or molecular the movement, the more intense its resonance through the web. The web responds to the movements of a pure multiplicity before it has taken on any definite shape. It is attuned to a purely 'intensive wave', and what Deleuze calls Proust's 'style' is the literary device he invents to capture and transmit this intensity.[12]

In his *Proust and Signs* (1964), Deleuze analyses the Proustian trajectory in terms of a progression through four regimes of signs or four levels of intelligibility, each distinguished by their relative proximity to the intuition of pure essence or 'absolute difference'. All four regimes express sense (in keeping with the characteristically Deleuzian meaning of *sens*) but they do so to degrees of intensity or purity: the purest expression of sense is simultaneously a differing that produces what it differs. Once again, the guiding priority of the Proustian apprenticeship will be the progressive liberation of virtual creatings from every trace of their creatural confinement.

The lowest degree of essence is expressed through worldly signs. Worldly signs are emitted through the way individuals behave as part of a group or clique – the way people evoke, more or less unconsciously, an air of distinction or superiority. Worldly signs decide the order of sociable interaction. They determine who dines with who, who receives who, who commands respect, who is capable of conferring prestige, etc. Worldly characters like the elegant but superficial Swann tend to 'think and feel in terms of subjects, forms, resemblances between subjects' (TP, 271). Like any vehicle of resemblance, worldly signs are essentially frivolous and empty, and the world is a place bereft of any genuine value. The world still signifies, however, insofar as worldly behaviour sends out obscure invitations to interpret the real mechanics of distinction or prestige. The more vacuous or snobbish the milieu, the more the world provokes the semi-detached observer to try to make sense of it.

As Swann is the first to discover, the signs of love occupy a slightly higher place on the expressive scale. The signs of love are not empty. The beloved person gives the impression of belonging to a secret or inaccessible world that is brimming over with meaning. This world remains closed to the lover, and it is precisely this inaccessible quality, of course, that provokes his desire. To love is then to seek to explicate or decipher the hidden world that the beloved person seems to evoke. The more passionate or jealous the lovers, the more of these signs they try to unravel – Swann's possessive love for Odette anticipates the pattern that will return, more intensely, when the narrator meets Albertine. Lovers seek to make these unknown worlds their own. Such, however, is the insurmountable contradiction of love. The lover seeks to possess or incarcerate a world that is lovable only *because* it cannot be possessed. The signs of love are thus irreducibly deceitful or deceptive. They attract with the same force and for the same reason that they exclude. They entice the lover only by hiding what they express. This is why jealousy is the veritable truth of love (PS, 9). Jealousy pushes the lover deeper and deeper into this world that excludes him. To persevere as a lover is to endure this torture. In the end, however, it will become intolerable. If it is sustained through to its limit love exhausts itself and eventually vanishes without trace. Of the narrator's beloved Albertine nothing will remain, not even a memory (nothing, that is, other than her transmutation into the work of art).

The third regime of signs, the signs of sensible or sensual reality, escape this fate. What these signs express is neither empty nor deceptive, neither frivolous nor ephemeral. Typically triggered by an experience of involuntary memory, they signify something real, something 'affirmative and joyous' – church steeples, hawthorn blossoms, a group of young girls on the beach, Venice, Balbec.... The most celebrated example is the scene in which the middle-aged narrator, after dipping a madeleine in his cup of tea, suddenly recovers, through the coincidence of this flavour with a memory of the same flavour, the whole of his childhood in Combray. Such an experience offers access to the very *essence* of Combray. What it reveals is not Combray as it actually was or as it was actually experienced. It doesn't recuperate a series of present moments that have since faded into the past but that might be more or less completely retrieved through conventional memory. Instead, Combray emerges here

in a form that is absolutely new. Combray does not rise up as it was once present [...]. This is no longer the Combray of perception nor of voluntary memory. Combray appears as it could not be experienced: not in reality, but in its truth; not in its external and contingent relations, but in its internalised difference, in its essence (PS, 60–1; cf. DR, 85).

Combray appears in its unique thisness, as an *event*. However, the access offered to essence or event through sensuous signs remains inadequate. It is limited precisely by its material or sensuous origin, by the actuality of its medium (taste, landscape, place…). It remains a matter of recovery. The sign involves the recovery of something external to itself – the recovery *of* Combray, precisely. On its own, the sensuous sign or experience of involuntary memory allows the narrator to bear witness to the process that individuates or produces the experience of Combray, the creating that then gave rise to Combray as it was lived (but that, as a creating, was not itself lived and never could be lived). But that is all: to bear witness is not yet to participate. The subject of involuntary memory remains passive. He is not yet a co-creator of reality. Essence here still expresses itself through something else, through a medium that is not yet perfectly transparent.

Artistic signs, finally, at the fourth and highest degree of this expressive scale, are wholly immediate to pure essence, beyond all actuality or specificity. 'Art is the finality of the world, and the apprentice's unconscious destination' (PS, 50). The signs emitted or refracted through a work of art are the highest or most intensive form of sign because, like Spinoza's highest form of knowledge, they *produce* the experience they signify. The essences revealed through art are immediately creative of what they express: they are nothing other than the event of a pure differing or individuating. 'An essence is a difference, the absolute and ultimate Difference. Difference is what constitutes being, what makes us conceive being' (PS, 41). More, 'essence individualises and determines the substances in which it is incarnated', and 'this is because essence is in itself difference' (PS, 48).

Whether he draws on Proust or Bacon, Spinoza or Nietzsche, Deleuze's definition of essence as a creating or differing remains broadly consistent. 'The essence of a thing is discovered in the force which possesses it and which is expressed in it' (NP, 77). In other words, an essence or differing isn't a sort of ideal object that we might see but a process that creates and sees in a single movement. An essence isn't something to be seen but a sort of absolute perspective which enables seeing itself – a 'superior' or 'irreducible viewpoint that signifies at once the birth of the world and the original character of a world'.[13] What we attain through Proust's work is Combray as pure seeing or vision, a virtual seeing liberated from anything actually seen – 'Combray as pure Viewpoint, superior to all that has been experienced from this viewpoint itself, appearing finally for itself and in its splendour' (PS, 119). Art allows us to see that essence isn't a merely actual individual, that it has no stable or constituted identity. Art reveals essence to be pure productive process, pure *creans*. Essence is the process of a unilateral individuating or individualising. Here as everywhere in Deleuze 'it is not the individuals who constitute the world, but the worlds enveloped, the essences that constitute the individuals' (PS, 43; cf. 110).

The expression of an artistic sign is thus nothing less than a fully self-sufficient creating. It is a creating that proceeds independently of any actual or creatural opacity.

Of course, as a creating, it is *also* incarnated in actuality – but this actuality is only a vessel for the creating, and it evacuates itself in the very movement of its expression. A work of art or pure creating is indeed incarnated in substances, but 'these substances are ductile, so kneaded and refined that they become entirely spiritual'. Deleuze's examples are not obscure. They include 'colour for the painter, like Vermeer's yellow, sound for the musician, words for the writer [...]. Art is a veritable transmutation of substance. By it, substance is spiritualised and physical surroundings dematerialised in order to refract essence, that is, the quality of an original world' (PS, 46–7). Take for instance the phrase of Vinteuil's music that so haunts Swann, or La Berma's performance of Phèdre:

> Of course Vinteuil's little phrase is uttered by the piano and the violin. Of course it can be decomposed materially: five notes very close together, two of which recur [...]. But the piano here is merely the spatial image of an entirely different keyboard; the notes are merely the 'sonorous appearance' of an entirely spiritual entity. 'As if the performers not so much played the little phrase as executed the rites necessary for it to appear' [...]. La Berma, too, uses her voice, her arms. But her gestures, instead of testifying to 'muscular connections', form a transparent body that refracts an essence, an Idea [...]. In her voice 'subsisted not one scrap of inert matter refractory to spirit'.[14]

Such is the source of art's superiority: unlike the signs of the world (bound up in the dynamics of the group), the signs of love (bound up in the face and body of the beloved) or the signs of sensual qualities (bound up in the materiality of what is sensed), the signs expressed through a work of art are utterly immaterial or spiritual and thus 'no longer have anything opaque about them'. Their transmuted substance is bound to their sense or essence in a 'perfect adequation'.[15] (And as we shall see in more detail in the next chapter, the only medium capable of such adequation is the non-medium of *thought* itself: what works through art is precisely 'pure thought as the faculty of essences' [PS, 86]).

To recap: Proust's *Search* is organised as a progressive learning sequence, a movement from ignorance to truth, from an indirect to a direct expression of essence. The sequence begins, as always, within the nullity of the world as such. Worldly signs are empty and have only a minimal, indirect relation to a sense that exceeds them – a sense they are able to evoke only insofar as they provoke the hero of the *Search* to search, and then to search elsewhere. The signs of love are deceitful or deceptive; they express something rather than nothing, but what they express is bound up in the contradiction of what they simultaneously reveal and conceal. Sensuous signs have a truthful meaning but the truth they express is external to them, their expression remains mediated and material. Only art expresses itself directly, adequately, in 'the splendid final unity of an immaterial sign and a spiritual meaning' (PS, 86). In each regime of signs, signs are emitted from within a material that more or less contains and constrains them. 'The signs emanate from objects that are like boxes or containers. The objects hold a captive soul, the soul of something else that tries to open the lid' – the soul of its essence. The lover consumed by jealousy, for instance, unfolds the secret world enclosed within the beloved, just as a sufficiently sensitive person 'liberates the souls implicated in things'

(PS, 90). Only art, however, allows for an absolute and genuinely transformative liberation–expression, precisely because what it liberates *is* nothing other than the liberating itself, the movement of pure spiritualisation or dematerialisation, which is to say: the movement of pure thought.

V

In anticipation of our next chapter it may be worth emphasising the peculiar and unabashedly philosophical privilege of artistic signs in this Proustian configuration, since it is a privilege that sheds an unusually clear light on the orientation of Deleuze's project more generally.[16] We have seen how art expresses an essence that determines or produces what it creates, and how art expresses this creating in an adequate or immaterial form. But this is not all. Artistic adequation is also equipped to surmount the obstacles that otherwise limit the expression of essence. Art is thus able to redeem or spiritualise that which is originally given as other than art. Once art has revealed the true nature of essence it allows us to see, retrospectively, that *everything* was more or less expressive of essence. In the process art can express the ultimate wholeness of being as open creation, i.e. the transversal unity of time grasped as the time of creation as such.

What, to begin with, are the obstacles that limit the expression of essence? Just as you would expect, the first and most serious obstacle is 'objectivism' – a belief in the primacy of the actual or 'self-evident' object. Objectivism is our natural tendency to attribute directly to the object the signs it emits, and thus to think that a particular social group is indeed a place of intrinsic distinction or prestige, or to think that it's a person's innate qualities that make him or her lovable. Objectivism depends on a merely 'voluntary memory', one that is oriented (along broadly Bergsonian lines) towards pleasure or utility (PS, 29). We know this to be the creatural delusion par excellence, and Proust's narrator begins his apprenticeship in a characteristically deluded state. He 'participates more or less in all the objective beliefs' (PS, 31). He believes in the intrinsic value of friendship and sociability; in the privileged wisdom of artists and mentors (Swann, Bergotte, Elstir…); in the inherently desirable qualities of a woman; in the urgency of addressing his love to the actual person loved; in the importance of paying attention to objects in general, of describing them appropriately, paying homage to their particularity, and so on. Every one of these beliefs is groundless, and each leads to an inevitable disillusionment. One after another, each of the narrator's much anticipated encounters results in a crushing disappointment. Slowly, the narrator learns that he must 'renounce this belief in an external reality' and give up the temptation to observe, admire or describe the actualities that surround us. He must learn that literature has nothing to do with observation or description. Literature never represents objects, and still less does it ennoble or beautify objects.

This realisation is delayed, however, by the second major obstacle confronting artistic expression. This obstacle emerges precisely as a form of compensation for the disappointment generated by objectivism. It amounts to a sort of subjectivism. No sooner has he stopped believing in the innate qualities of the object than the narrator instead tries to steady his belief by enfolding it in a series of subjective associations. Disappointed by La Berma's performance as an actor, he takes comfort by comparing her to a statuette. Unable to penetrate Odette's secret world, Swann will instead associate her with Vinteuil's music and with Renaissance paintings. But such chains of association are no more expressive of essence than is a belief in its factual existence.

Neither subject nor object offer access to the essence or sufficient reason of a place, person or experience. Such an essence can be accessed only through itself, by participating in its immediate self-expression. 'It is the essence that constitutes the sign insofar as it is irreducible to the object emitting it; it is the essence that constitutes the sense [*sens*] insofar as it is irreducible to the subject apprehending it' (PS, 37–8). Access to this constituting, we know, is here the privilege of the artist alone. The same La Berma who disappoints the narrator when he tries to see her as an object, when he tries to appreciate her apparently innate or actual qualities, is a genuine artist precisely insofar as she is able to counter-actualise these qualities and act as the vehicle for an intensity that is not her own. What La Berma presents is reducible neither to an objective state of affairs nor to a subjective chain of associations. Instead, when she takes on the role of Phèdre she creates a viewpoint on a new 'spiritual milieu populated by essence. La Berma, bearer of signs, renders them so immaterial that they grant access to these essences and are filled by them' (PS, 37).

The essences of *Proust and Signs*, in other words, are another vehicle for those virtual creatings that Deleuze describes in terms of events in *Difference and Repetition* and in terms of sense in *Logic of Sense*. Essences are not fixed creatural forms, they are the dynamic creatings which generate every possible form but which themselves have neither identity nor stability. Essences proliferate in their discrete and fragmented multiplicity, as aspects of an immediate and eternally sufficient production. If then Deleuze's Proust is no mere Platonist this is not because he shies away from the notion of an idea or ideal as the sufficient reason for what there is. On the contrary, it's because Plato's version of such an idea isn't sufficient or determinant *enough*. Plato doesn't lend his ideas a fully immediate creative force. His ideas do not directly determine or individuate actuality. Rather, Plato's actuality merely 'imitates the Idea as best it can, according to its powers'. The Platonic idea, moreover, is itself trapped within its own definite actuality or stability. It is an essence that has become static, inert (PS, 109). Plato can only think of an essence cut off from its real power. A Platonic essence (according to this reading) is merely one that allows actuality to resemble it via imitation, approximation or generalisation, rather than one that directly produces the actual in its unique, non-typical or non-general thisness.

Whereas the Platonic essence remains general or typical, a Proustian or Deleuzian essence is always radically singular. It is always, again, a matter of *an* event, *an* essence, *a* life, *this* life. If essence can 'individualise and determine the substances in which it is incarnated' (PS, 48) this is because it is nothing other than a force of pure individuation. Essence is not mediated by general categories: it expresses itself as this or that creating, immediately. Expressions of an 'absolute internal difference', essences are monadic or non-relational. Just like Leibnizian monads, each essence subsists in its radical isolation, in its self-sufficiency, without any actual doors or windows, precisely because an essence is itself a pure viewpoint that intuits the whole of reality.[17] An essence requires no window out upon the world, no window that allows us to see the world (as an object), since an essence is nothing less than the creating or unfolding of the world. Through art we come to understand that 'the world enveloped by essence is always a beginning of the World in general, a beginning of the universe, an absolute, radical beginning' (PS, 44).

Now precisely because art reveals the immediately differing or individualising force of essence, precisely because *all* individuation stems from essence, so then once the narrator understands the signs of art he realises that what all the other regimes of signs signified was itself nothing other than essence, only to lesser degrees. In every domain, any given 'material sense [*sens*] is nothing without an ideal essence that it incarnates' (PS, 13). Once we reach the signs of art then we realise that sensuous, amorous and even worldly signs '*already* referred to an ideal essence that was incarnated in their material sense. But without art we should not have understood this' (PS, 14tm). Art is necessary to this understanding because 'essence is always an artistic essence', i.e. essence can be grasped for what it truly is (or does) only through signs of art. But then, once we have grasped this, we can see that essence 'is incarnated not only in spiritualised substance, in the immaterial signs of the world of art, but also in other realms, which will henceforth be integrated into the work of art. It passes then into media that are more opaque, into signs that are more material' (PS, 50–1). The more material the signs, the more essence tends towards the zero degree of worldly expression, the more its own purely creative intensity or spirituality is diluted. The signs we access through deliberate or voluntary memory, for instance, are bound to the limitations of their actual form, their *presence* – they appear only as a series of static impressions or snapshots, tied to the place and circumstances in which they were once presented. Even the signs expressed through Proust's famous involuntary memories, although more expressive of essence, remain inferior to those of art because 'their substance is more opaque and refractory, their explication remains too material', too 'local' (PS, 54, 61).

The *work* that is art, however, will allow even worldly signs to recover the true force of their own expression. Art transforms its material. Art is a dematerialising. Art enables the counter-actualisation of all the lower signs, insofar as they are transubstantiated through incorporation into the diffractive whole that is the working of art.

> All the stages must issue into art, we must reach the revelation of art; then we review the stages, we integrate them into the work of art itself, we recognise essence in its successive realisations, we give to each degree of realisation the place and the meaning it occupies within the work […]. The absolute Self of art encompasses all the different kinds of Self (PS, 66, 88).

Illuminated by art, we are able, for instance, to go back through the serial sequence of our loves, and through the equally serial stages of each love affair, and understand them as they really were – as organised by a guiding idea or essence, which even our jealousy

124

and despair was able to evoke. 'We extract from our particular despairs a general Ideal; this is because the Idea was primary, was already there', unconsciously guiding our experience. Love too is thus an incarnation of essence, albeit one that is necessarily limited to a serial and consequently general form, a form that depends 'on extrinsic conditions and subjective contingencies'.[18] The further away that we move from such generality and contingency, the further we move away from love and the world, the more singular and the more necessary the incarnation of essence (PS, 89). Through art and only through art can we thus make *sense* of life. Once we have grasped essence in and through itself we can then look back and 'recognise the marks of its attenuated, loosed splendour' in other realms, and in the process 'recover all the truths of time, and all the kinds of signs, in order to make them integral parts of the work of art itself'. And only then do we acknowledge the full power of essence. Only then can we appreciate that it works through even that which is distant from itself. Creation creates even the lowliest of creatures and these too must be appreciated as such – even though only a creation that is most removed from these creatures is capable of such appreciation. In his early article on Hyppolite (1954), Deleuze allowed himself a more Hegelian formulation of much the same conclusion: 'in both the empirical realm and in the absolute, it is the same being and the same thought; but the difference between thought and being has been surpassed in the absolute by the positing of Being which is identical to difference'.[19]

Two last points need to be made about this openly teleological configuration. First of all, if art comes to be seen as 'the ultimate goal of life' (PS, 155), the searching movement *towards* this insight remains irreducible. Just as Spinoza doesn't start out from the idea of God but instead tries to reach it as quickly as possible (so as then to use it to explain everything else, including the process through which it was reached), so too is the idea of art an idea that must be *learned*. Although it will explain everything, it is only grasped as such at the end of an apprenticeship. Once the creating has taken place then we can easily see how one and the same movement led up to its achievement. But to claim instead that Proust knew what he was making from the beginning, that the *Search* was written in conformity with a goal or method that pre-existed it, as if the guiding idea was already there, animating the whole project from the start – this is a mistake. The process of counter-actualisation is itself a creative and thus unpredictable one. We do not begin from art but from the world. We do not begin from the whole for the whole is never given, or giveable. Even as readers of Proust's own work, we can set out only from the 'disparity, the incommensurability, the disintegration of the parts of the *Search*' (PS, 116). And if there is a method that shapes this *Search* then it only emerges retrospectively. The method wasn't given in advance so much as revealed at the end, and it is revealed not as in some sense appropriate or typical but as unique to this particular creating. The method will be revealed, once the work is made, as having been the 'only method capable of operating in such a way as to allow this particular work to be produced' (RF, 44–5).

Nevertheless, once reached, art is indeed a sufficient vehicle for an intuition of reality as a whole. This is the second point. The apprenticeship that leads to art must indeed progress, more or less blindly, through the thicket of worldly and sensuous signs; we would never become artists if sensuous signs didn't first 'give us a foretaste of time regained, and prepare us for the fulfilment of aesthetic Ideas. But they do nothing more than prepare us: a mere beginning' (PS, 54). Art enjoys a qualitative advantage over every other domain, precisely because it alone is adequate to a *comprehensive* vision of creative time as whole:

> The signs of art give us a time regained, an original absolute time that includes all the others [...]. It is in the absolute time of the work of art that all the other dimensions are united and find the truth that corresponds to them [...]. The time regained by art encompasses and comprehends all the others, for it is only within time regained that each line of time finds its truth, its place, and its result from the viewpoint of truth (PS, 24–5, 85–6).

Needless to say, the whole that is time regained is not an actual (totalisable, presentable) whole. If there is unity then it cannot reside in what is seen but in the seeing itself.[20] If there is unity, it isn't the attribute of anything within time. It is indivisible time itself that unifies things by dividing and distributing them as facets of creation. It is time that transverses things, insofar as time is nothing other than the indivisible creating of all things. The same movement that generates the virtual whole ensures that there can be no *actual* whole – time is not an actual unity or whole 'for the simple reason that it is itself the instance that prevents the whole', i.e. the disruptive or differing instance that prevents actuality from ever appearing as whole (PS, 161).

The whole that is creation is a movement that exceeds any actual unification, any possible presentation or *actualité*. It's precisely because time is creation or difference that the whole of time must be virtual, unpresentable or ungiveable. And it's precisely because time thus coheres in a fully virtual dimension that it can be expressed only through utterly pure or creative thought, thought liberated even from the media of art. Only pure thought will prove adequate to time, precisely because this adequation is itself *timeless*.

Philosophy is the name that Deleuze gives to this adequation, and the aim of the next and final chapter is to explain how it works.

6

Creation Unmediated: Philosophy

'Creation will appear to the mystic as God undertaking
to create creators, that He may have, besides Himself,
beings worthy of His love.'[1]

There is surely no recent or contemporary philosopher who writes about a wider range of topics and materials than Deleuze. His frame of reference extends from the ancient to the modern and from the microscopic to the cosmic. He engages, in detail, with figures from virtually every branch of the arts and sciences. In fact he engages with just about anything under the sun: anthropology, universal history, genetics, psychoanalysis, alcoholism, calculus, mental illness, cartography, evolution, cognition, linguistics.... What then is the place of philosophy itself in the midst of all this? Why does Deleuze insist on describing what he writes as philosophy? What does he mean when says that his books on cinema, for instance, are books of pure philosophy and nothing but philosophy, or that *A Thousand Plateaus* consists simply of 'philosophy in the traditional sense of the word'? (RF, 163; C2, 280).

From the perspective developed over the course of this book, these are quite easy questions to answer. If being is creation and if being becomes more creative the less its creatings are obstructed by creatures, then the privilege of philosophy is that it is the discipline most adequate to our expression of being as such. Philosophy is our most becoming expression of being. Philosophy simply *is* the expression of being, insofar as it articulates absolutely pure creatings, i.e. creatings liberated from any residual mediation through the creatural or the actual. And furthermore, once equipped with this understanding of creation, philosophy is the discipline that can then go back and see that what sustains even unphilosophical (or more creature-bound configurations) is again nothing other than creation, albeit in a less pure or less intensive form.

Whereas the various arts differ in their 'respective substances, their codes and their territorialities', they all serve to trace an abstract line that invariably leads from the perceptible to the imperceptible, from the constituted to the constituting. Philosophy is the thinking of this line itself. 'Everything that becomes is a pure line which ceases to represent' what it might actually be, and 'when we come to trace the line, we can say "it is philosophy"' – not because philosophy interprets the line or provides suitable ways of representing the line but because it *is* the very line as such. 'Philosophy is necessarily produced where each activity gives rise to its line of deterritorialisation' (D, 74).

The privilege of philosophy is thus perfectly consistent with the privilege of art that we considered in the previous chapter. Both disciplines express creatings as such, and the more immaterial the expression, the purer and more creative it becomes. With Proust, it is because artistic signs are utterly 'spiritualised and dematerialised' that they are adequate to the articulation of pure essence, i.e. essence understood as an instance of absolute and immediate self-individuation. Conceived along these lines, there is already a sort of hierarchy within the arts themselves, depending on the materiality or opacity of the art. It's not only that an art becomes less artistic the more it relies on the creatural norms of représentation, figuration, interpretation, and so on; from time to time Deleuze also suggests some arts are less artistic than others, because the medium of their expression is itself more solid or opaque and thus more resistant to counter-actualisation. Architecture, sculpture and dance do not figure prominently in the Deleuzian pantheon of the arts, and it's not surprising that Deleuze should pay more attention to the luminous art of film than to the more corporeal art of theatre, the art of *représentation* par excellence. For the same reason, even in the middle of his book on Bacon, Deleuze is prepared to acknowledge a certain 'superiority of music'. Up to a point, 'music begins where painting ends [...]. Music strips bodies of their inertia, of the materiality of their presence: it *disembodies* bodies.' Whereas painting exposes the 'material reality of bodies' as such, music passes through bodies and lends only a 'disembodied and dematerialised body to the most spiritual of entities'.[2]

But beyond music? Is there a process more spiritual than any entity at all? Since 'a spiritual movement cannot be separated from the process of its own disappearance or dissipation' (CC, 170), is there anything more dissipative than music? Yes: such a process is simply pure thought itself. This conclusion is already perfectly clear, in fact, in Deleuze's writings about art. Take the case of cinema. Deleuze explains that 'the essence of cinema has nothing but thought as its higher purpose', and if Resnais' work is particularly significant here it's because he does for cinema what Deleuze himself does for philosophy – he 'creates a cinema which has only one single character, Thought' (C2, 168, 122; cf. C1, 215). Or again, we know that Proust's artistic initiation concludes with a realisation that 'only pure thought discovers essence, only pure thought is forced to conceive essence as the sufficient reason of the sign and its sense' (PS, 100tm). Although in his book on Proust Deleuze is appropriately discreet on this point, it's quite clear that, once reached, there is nothing specifically artistic let alone aesthetic about this insight. On the contrary, Deleuze simply attributes to art the quintessentially metaphysical capacity – the capacity to articulate an adequate conception of pure essence. Such art is independent of memory, it bears no particular relation to language or technique in the usual sense of the term, it is even independent of 'imagination and unconscious figures. The signs of art are explained by pure thought as a faculty of essences', nothing more or less (PS, 55). Deleuze's work on literature more generally has nothing to do with textual criticism or commentary, deconstructive or otherwise, since what matters is only what can be created, experimented or lived through the text, on the assumption that 'a text is nothing but a cog in a larger extra-textual practice' (DI, 260). Understood in this way, art or literature is simply one of several available vehicles for immediate intellectual intuition (i.e. intuition of the sort that Kant and the neo-Kantians sought to foreclose). Beyond the materiality of this or that art, what is essential is the immediate identity of thinking and creating. Like any artist, Proust leads us to the conclusion that

> the act of thinking [...] it is the only true creation. Creation is the genesis of the act of thinking within thought itself [...]. It is no longer a matter of saying: to create is to remember – but rather, to remember is to create, it's to reach that point where the associative chain breaks, leaps over the constituted individual, is transferred to the birth of an individuating world [...]. To remember is to create, not to create memory, but to create the spiritual equivalent of the still too material memory, to create the viewpoint valid for all associations, the style valid for all images [...]. It is no longer a matter of saying: to create is to think – but rather, to think is to create and primarily to create the act of thinking within thought.[3]

Both art and philosophy, in other words, are facets of pure thought, and pure thought is the most adequate medium of being, i.e. of creation. Of course (for reasons discussed in Chapter 2, section III), that such thought is 'pure' and abstract doesn't mean that it lacks any correlation with virtual extension; it means that this correlation is liberated from any mediation through the actual, the individuated, or the constituted. To purely creative thought will correspond purely creative forms of extension – the unpredictable flight of an abstract line or the free indetermination of an any-space-whatever.

If, then, philosophy has any privilege over art it is simply that it is able to go still further in the spiritualisation of its medium. Or rather, philosophy is precisely that form of thinking which requires no medium at all. Whereas art works through sound, or light, or paint, or words, philosophy as Deleuze conceives it works through nothing other than itself. Whereas art creates vehicles for sensation and life, philosophy is concerned *only* with spirit and concept, thought and implication. Whereas art lends an event a new body, philosophy extracts only the event as such. This is what is at stake when Deleuze says that philosophy is dedicated to the 'creation of concepts'.[4] Whereas art's 'sensory becoming is otherness caught in a matter of expression', philosophy's still purer 'conceptual becoming is heterogeneity grasped in an absolute form' (WP, 177). Philosophy, in short, is the most immediate discipline of thought – indeed, 'the immediate is precisely the identity of the thing and its difference as philosophy rediscovers or "recaptures" it' (DI, 25). Pure thought creates the material it thinks through, without reference to *anything* outside itself. Though the difference is only one of intensity or degree, it is thought, rather than life, that has the final word of Deleuze's philosophy of creation.[5]

Just as it takes Proust time (the whole time of the apprenticeship) to arrive at the insight which will then provide, retrospectively, the organising principle of his work, so too Deleuze and Guattari only spell out the precise disciplinary privilege of philosophy in their last collaborative project, when they finally address the question *What is Philosophy?* (1991).[6] As they note in the first paragraph of the book, this is properly a question you can ask only once you have already become a philosopher, at the point when you begin to wonder 'what is it I have been doing all my life?' (WP, 1). They address the question in fairly conventional fashion, by distinguishing philosophy from science on the one hand and art on the other. But their version of this distinction makes it depend more or less entirely on the degree of relative approximation to a purely creative point of view.

The first thing they have to re-establish is the difference between creation and chaos. As we have seen, chaos is the point where innovation becomes so instantaneous that it simply dissolves – chaos names the point where the crucial difference between subtraction and extinction becomes unsustainable. Chaos is not indeterminant but hyper-determinant. Whereas every viable creating establishes a certain consistency or trajectory, chaos is inconsistent.

> Chaos is characterised less by the absence of determinations than by the infinite speed with which they take shape and vanish. This is not a movement from one determination to the other but, on the contrary, the impossibility of a connection between them, since one does not appear without the other having already disappeared […]. Chaos undoes every consistency in the infinite (WP, 42).

This is one reason why a creative ontology requires the intervention of appropriately creative *thought* rather than a merely receptive faculty or passive intuition – it isn't a matter of reflecting chaos but of inventing forms of consistency that 'stand up' to and in chaos. Deleuze and Guattari name science, art and philosophy as the three forms of thought capable of such invention. They are the 'three Chaoids, realities produced on the planes that cut through chaos in different ways'.[7]

The difference that distinguishes these ways isn't complicated, or unfamiliar. Science is preoccupied with the domain of actuality alone. Science considers the ways in which infinite or virtual intensity comes to be extended or explicated in material situations or actual states of affairs. 'Science passes from chaotic virtuality to the states of affairs and bodies that actualise it', for example through the individuation of a chemical element, an organism, a population. If the concern of philosophy is always the event of a creating, the concern of science is the creature that results. Whereas 'philosophy wants to save the infinite by giving it consistency', science abandons the infinite and the virtual in favour of reference and the measurable. As if on top of the virtual plane of constant variation, science lays out an empirical plane through which actual movements and propositions can be distinguished and assessed (WP, 197). Confronted with virtual chaos, the scientist seeks to isolate 'variables that have become independent by slowing down', i.e. variables whose actualisation separates them from the immediate intensity that engendered them (WP, 156). Thus actualised, these variables can be observed or modelled, measured or analysed. Science thereby 'relinquishes the infinite, infinite speed, in order to gain a reference able to actualise the virtual'. As soon as creation is perceived through a plane of reference, its speed slows down dramatically, as if caught in a freeze-frame. Science operates in slow motion. Even those values which limit the coordinates used to measure movement on the plane of reference – values assigned 'to the speed of light, absolute zero, the quantum of action, the Big Bang', and so on – impose radical limits upon the *scientifically* incoherent notion of infinite speed or infinite action (WP, 118–19). Moreover, whereas fully creative or unconditioned philosophical concepts maintain 'the inseparability of variations' internal to their consistency, science analyses its plane of reference in terms of functions that presume 'the independence of variables, in relationships that can be conditioned' and ordered in terms of relatively stable equations or formulae. Insofar then as science limits itself to the physical, it necessarily stops short of an exploration of the meta-physical, which can alone think the sufficient reason of the physical (WP, 126). But despite its orientation to the actual, science as Deleuze and Guattari describe it remains a form of thought, rather than a merely thoughtless means of representation. Science itself demonstrates that 'a state of affairs cannot be separated from the potential through which it takes effect' (WP, 153). Science may only observe actuality at a distance from the creating that gives rise to it, but even so it is 'inspired less by the concern for unification in an ordered actual system than by a desire [...] to seek out potentials in order to seize and carry off a part of that which haunts it, the secret of the chaos behind it, the pressure of the virtual'.[8] Science, in short, analyses actuality so as to *prepare* it for its eventual counter-actualisation.

We already know how art undertakes the first phase of such counter-actualisation. If science moves from the creatively virtual to the derivatively actual, art is a step in the opposite direction. Whereas science withdraws from the infinite to so as to measure the finite, art enjoys the 'peculiar' power of being able 'to pass through the finite in order to rediscover, to *restore* the infinite'.[9] Art's aim is to tap into a virtually infinite creative power from within the medium of actual materiality, to arrange patterns of sensation in such a way as to reorient them towards their creative source. Art configures blocs of sensation that can be detached from the actual organism or situation in which they are actualised – blocs that can then serve as an adequate vessel for an anorganic or intensive sensation, for a pure life lived at a coherence beyond the organism. Art aligns the actual towards the virtual. Or alternatively, if science considers how events are actualised in a state of affairs, art does 'not actualise the virtual event but incorporates or embodies it: it gives it a body, a life, a universe' (WP, 177). Art thus works on the active interface of being, *between* a creating and its creature: its medium is actual or material, the stuff of embodiment, but art itself is nothing other than the process whereby this material is 'transmuted' or 'spiritualised'. Art is the process whereby actual incorporation becomes virtual incarnation.

The further and final phase of counter-actualisation begins when creations finally break free of embodiment and actuality altogether. Science is concerned with the actualisation of an event and art with its incarnation; the proper concern of philosophy is with an event's *extraction*. 'Through its functions, science continually actualises the event in a state of affairs, thing, or body that can be referred to', whereas through the invention of its concepts 'philosophy continually extracts a consistent event from the state of affairs – a smile without the cat, as it were' (WP, 126). Philosophy's concern is with the virtual event as such and for its own sake. 'Philosophy's sole aim is to become worthy of the event', which is to say to 'counter-effectuate the event' (WP, 160, 211). Philosophy thinks creation through creations *alone*, by extracting them from the actuality of their consequences. The extraction or counter-effectuation of events and the invention or 'setting up' of concepts are one and the same thing: both are creations pure and simple. So while science has 'no need of the concept and concerns itself only with states of affairs', by contrast,

> the task of philosophy when it creates concepts, entities, is always to extract an event from things and beings, to set up the new event from things and beings, always to give them a new event [...]. The philosophical concept does not refer to the lived [...] but consists, through its own creation, in setting up an event that surveys or flies over [*survole*] the whole of the lived no less than every state of affairs (WP, 33–4tm).

Unlike science or art, philosophy can claim to think at the highest degree of proximity to absolute chaos or infinite difference. Every philosophical 'concept is a chaoid state par excellence; it refers back to a chaos rendered consistent, become Thought'. For the same reason, only the philosopher can bring back from chaos variations that remain infinite (WP, 208, 202). Only philosophy can think *exclusively* virtual variations that still pulse with the infinite speed of thought itself.

Indeed, the only real 'problem of philosophy is to acquire a consistency without losing the infinite into which thought plunges'. In order to deal with this problem, Deleuze always insists on the necessary elaboration of a relatively stable *plane* of immanence. Always at the risk of its submersion in chaos, thought can only think immanence by endowing it with the consistency of a surface or plane. So while science renounces the infinite in exchange for reference and art seeks to release infinite movements from within the finite, philosophy alone, through the invention of concepts upon a plane of immanence, will manage to 'retain infinite movements that turn back on themselves in incessant exchange, but which also continually free other movements' (WP, 202; 42). In the process, philosophy will allow each 'individual to grasp itself as event'. Philosophy is the universal discipline that allows an individual to grasp itself as a facet of that infinitely creative movement which passes 'through all the other individuals implied by the other events, and extracts from it a unique Event which is once again itself, or rather the universal freedom' – the only freedom consistent with the full univocity of being (LS, 178–9).

We are now in a better position to confirm a point first suggested back in Chapter 1, section V – the privilege that Deleuze accords to philosophy is an extension of much the same power that Bergson eventually attributes to mysticism. Somewhat like Deleuze,

Bergson invests philosophy with more expressive power than art. Art certainly 'dilates our perception'. Art 'enriches our present, but it scarcely enables us to go beyond it', into the virtual continuity of time as a dynamic whole. Through philosophy, however, we come to realise that every present moment is a facet of indivisible creation. Every present moment then 'affirms itself dynamically, in the continuity and variability of its tendency [...]. Everything comes to life around us, everything is revivified in us. A great impulse carries beings and things along. We feel ourselves uplifted, carried away, borne along by it.'[10] More, philosophy allows everyone to feel this way. Whereas the artistic release from actuality is enjoyed only by a few privileged individuals, philosophy pursues a similar objective 'in another sense and in another way, for everyone'.[11] Philosophy cultivates the insight that is already implicit in every ordinary intuition of movement and change, the realisation that we are facets of a creative energy that is itself wholly virtual or immaterial. Philosophy thus 'introduces us into spiritual life, at the same time [as] it shows us the relation of the life of spirit to the life of the body'.[12] And because he goes still further into the pure life of the spirit, because he is nothing other than the intensification or dematerialisation of life, so then the mystic completes the move begun by the philosopher. As Deleuze explains at the end of his own book on Bergson, philosophy can extract 'the lines that divided up the composites given in experience', and thereby manage to extend thought to a virtual point beyond the actual limit of experience. But this extension remains indeterminate until it gains a 'new kind of determination in mystical intuition – as though the properly philosophical probability extended itself into mystical certainty'. Thanks to this 'final transmutation into certainty', thanks to the power of this pure affirmation it is then

> the mystic who plays with the whole of creation, who invents an expression of it whose adequacy increases with its dynamism. Servant of an open and finite God (such are the characteristics of the *Élan Vital*), the mystical soul actively plays the whole of the universe, and reproduces the opening of a Whole in which there is nothing to see or to contemplate (B, 112).

Or as Bergson himself puts it: 'the task of the great mystic is to effect a radical transformation by setting an example. The object could be attained only if there existed in the end what should theoretically have existed in the beginning, a divine humanity.'[13] As we will see in a moment, precisely this originary outcome (complete with its tangled temporality) is what is at stake in Deleuze's version of the eternal return.

Now in order to present it as the discipline adequate to pure or unmediated creation, Deleuze must lend his post-mystical philosophy several distinctive attributes. It must be grounded in the purity of its own self-affirmation. Purely conceptual creation, it must be fully spiritualised or dematerialised, i.e. independent of any medium external to itself. It must sustain an ultimately immediate (or timeless) conception of time. And in the end, it must sustain a singular, unilateral or non-relational understanding of individuation. In what remains of this chapter I'll take up each of these four points in turn.

II

Deleuze is not a anti-foundational philosopher. Unlike pragmatist, post-metaphysical or even post-philosophical thinkers, Deleuze is just as concerned as Plato, Descartes or Hegel with questions about the ultimate nature of reality. Deleuze always accepts that philosophy is essentially a reflection on fundamental and perfectly traditional questions: what is being? how does thought think?

Attempts to answer such questions (and thereby to provide an ultimate metaphysical foundation) can draw on a number of different strategies. Given a certain set of phenomena or experiences, a philosopher might try to model the ideal laws or patterns to which they appear to conform, or to deduce the transcendental conditions that make it possible for us to experience them, or to establish secure rules of reliable observation and logical inference that would allow us to make generalisations about them: one way or another, these philosophers might then be able to *justify* their answers to questions about the ultimate nature of being and thought. Descartes, for instance, combines an apparently reliable method (based on mathematical reasoning) with an apparently reliable experience (of thinking) in order then to justify deductions about the existence of God and the immortality of the soul (which thus provide the retrospective ground for both the method and the experience). In somewhat the same way, Kant's critique of precisely such deductions, his critique of any attempt directly to demonstrate metaphysical principles or ideas, is itself a fundamental part of his project to justify them by other means – 'to deny knowledge in order to make room for faith', to displace speculation in favour of moral action. As Kant concludes, 'I cannot even assume God, freedom and immortality for the sake of the necessary practical use of my reason unless I simultaneously deprive speculative reason of its pretension to extravagant insights.'[14]

Deleuze adopts a very different approach. For Deleuze the ultimate means of legitimation do not involve judgement and justification but *affirmation*, and affirmation in a quite emphatically extravagant sense. The ultimate basis for metaphysical affirmation – for affirming our triple equation of being, creation and thought – can only be the exercise of affirmation itself. To try to think affirmation other than directly through affirmation is already to distort it. The affirmation of absolute creation must be unconditionally affirmative by definition. Only an infinitely affirmative or infinitely creative thought (the thought that classical metaphysics conventionally associates with the idea of God) is adequate to the expression of an infinitely creative conception of being or life. 'It is life that justifies; it has no need of being justified' or 'rationalised' (CC, 81).

This is another point common to all of Deleuze's philosophical allies, one that unites his naturalist forbears precisely against the critical tradition of Descartes and Kant. 'From Lucretius to Nietzsche, the same end is pursued and attained. Naturalism makes of thought and sensibility an affirmation' (LS, 279). Whereas the Cartesian–Kantian tradition is concerned with the norms of representation, rationalist naturalism affirms the immediate (and unrepresentable) positivity of nature as production or process. As usual, Spinoza sets the decisive example. 'Spinoza's philosophy is a philosophy of pure affirmation. Affirmation is the speculative principle on which hangs the whole of the *Ethics*'

(EP, 60). In particular, via Spinoza 'univocity becomes the object of a pure affirmation', such that 'there is no question of deducing Expression: rather it is expression that embeds deduction in the Absolute, and that renders proof the direct manifestation of absolutely infinite substance'.[15] Through the infinite perfection that is affirmed via the idea of God, Spinoza asserts a power of 'thinking which conquers an absolute speed', 'the absolute speed of figures of light' (CC, 186–7). According to Deleuze's post-Leibnizian conception of things, each line of creation or differentiation unfolds in its radical singularity, as absolutely divergent, and precisely this 'divergence is the object of affirmation. It is indistinguishable from the great work which contains all the complicated series, which affirms and complicates all the series at once' (DR, 123). Nietzsche's transmutation or transvaluation of values ensures, likewise, that 'only affirmation subsists as an independent power [...]. There is no other power but affirmation, no other quality, no other element'. The primary and ultimate element of all things is the affirmative power of active forces, and only this power can *return*, via the self-destruction of all reactive or negative forces.[16] In other words, 'in its essence, affirmation is itself difference' (DR, 52).

There can be no deducing such affirmation from anything resembling a demonstration of its conditions of possibility, since its exercise determines these conditions all by itself. Affirmation affirms its own power to affirm, on the model of a self-causing power that exists in and through itself. Affirmation neither requires nor tolerates any external justification: to step back from affirmation so as to judge or justify it is simply to abandon one philosophical orientation for another. Every affirmative philosophy must 'have done with judgement'.[17] After Nietzsche, Deleuze realises that 'of course one may ask in what sense and why noble is "worth more" than base' or indeed 'why affirmation should be better than negation?', but these very questions are themselves symptoms of a base or reactive orientation. Active forces express themselves through an affirmative power that is utterly indifferent to the business of justification, according to a logic most concisely suggested by the metaphor of a singular throw of the dice – that divine or super-human move whereby 'Nietzsche turns chance into an affirmation' (NP, 86, 26; DR, 198). It is precisely the unconditional affirmation of the whole of chance that eliminates any 'arbitrariness' in the outcome, and with it any need for a mechanism of legitimation as such.

This image of the radically affirmative dice-throw figures prominently in *Difference and Repetition, Logic of Sense* and Deleuze's work on Nietzsche. Up to a point, it compresses the whole logic of difference and repetition in a single motif. The dice-throw is one of those 'magic formulae' through which Deleuze embraces the one and the multiple in a single line of thought. It's a multiple affirmation in which 'all the parts, all the fragments, are cast in one throw; all of chance, all at once'. Whereas a good or absolutely affirmative throw consumes the whole of chance in a single movement, the 'bad player counts on several throws of the dice' (NP, 29, 26–7). On the basis of a general spread of results, bad players try to calculate and predict probable outcomes. They remain tied to a set of *actual* expectations, to the domain that subsists between a cause and effect or an experience and its interpretation. Chance remains arbitrary, in other words, to the extent that it is not affirmed or not adequately affirmed, such that its consequences are distributed within a space of already existent possibilities (rather than embraced as distributing the space of reality itself). But 'once chance is affirmed, all arbitrariness is abolished every time' (DR, 198). The good player thus escapes from a probability distributed across several throws by embracing an utterly fatal necessity (cf. NP, 27). Players should identify with the fate that works through them. They should not throw so much as allow themselves to be thrown – absolute affirmation can only be the affirmation of something that happens through you, as a 'necessarily winning throw' (DR, 283).

If we rephrase this sequence in our familiar theophanic terms we can isolate the essential components of a purely affirmative orientation easily enough – 'creation or throw', they amount to much the same thing (DR, 199). First of all, in its being, the act of creation is always one and same: a creating *is* always a facet of creation, pure and simple. There is one 'single ontologically unique throw, the same across all occasions'. Since creation is absolute and self-grounding, so then there is strictly speaking only one act of indivisible creation, a single event for all events, the singular movement of an aleatory point that races through every actual combination of points. 'An aleatory point is displaced through all the points on the dice, as though one time for all times' (DR, 283).

In the second place, though, this singular act is itself the production of infinite divergence or difference. Since creations are *creative*, precisely, each creating is always absolutely different or new. Each outcome of the dice-throw is itself singular or non-generalisable, and the different outcomes 'distribute themselves in the open space of the unique and non-shared throw: nomadic rather than sedentary distribution' (DR, 283). Once the disparate outcomes of the dice-throw are affirmed they begin to resonate together and form what Deleuze calls a distinct 'problem' (problems, or ideas, are what virtual events or creations determine in the dimension of pure thought[18]). A work of literature, for example, is composed here as a problem that issues from the imperative to affirm the whole of chance, and the work is 'all the more perfect and total in a single throw as the problem is all the more progressively determined as a problem'. Hence the exemplary value of writers like Roussel, Blanchot, and the 'many modern novelists [who] install themselves in this aleatory point, this imperative and questioning "blind spot" from which the work develops like a problem' and who thereby 'make the work a process of learning or experimentation, but also something total every time, where the whole of chance is affirmed in each case, renewable every time, perhaps without any subsistent arbitrariness' (DR, 199).

As for the nature of the player, finally, this is again perfectly explicit. Only a divine or super-human artist is capable of this game. By definition, 'man does not know how to play'.[19] The problems that come to resonate through the divergent throws enjoy an absolute power of immediate determination, a power infinitely beyond the capacity of any actual organism or subject. This power is not ours and nor are we capable of sustaining any relation *with* it. It works through us with an intensity that is both more intimate than any proximity and more excessive than any distance. Our only real decision is either to affirm or not to affirm – to allow ourselves to be infused by this power of determination, or to resist it.

> Problems are inseparable from a power of decision, a fiat which, when we are infused by it, makes us semi-divine beings […]. The power of decision at the heart of problems, this creation or throw which makes us descendant from the gods, is nevertheless not our own […]. The imperatives and questions with which we are infused do not emanate from the I: it is not even there to hear them. The imperatives are those of being, while every question is ontological and distributes 'that which is' among problems. Ontology is the dice throw.[20]

Deleuze takes us back in this way to the central theophanic conviction – that only God is capable of affirming God, only God is capable of thinking the idea of God, only God can think with an infinite power of thought. We express God by allowing God to work (think, create, act…) through us, or as Eckhart puts it, 'I never see God except in that in which God sees Himself'.[21] De-theologise the terms and the logic stays much the same: only being can affirm itself. Only affirmation itself can affirm a power of infinite affirmation.

As far as actual thinkers are concerned, then, absolute or unconditional affirmation is again always a matter of being-affirmed or being-infused. To think is to allow thought to work through us. This is one of the most insistent themes in Deleuze's various reflections on the nature of thought or spirit. 'Subjectivity is never ours, it is time's, that is, soul [*l'âme*], spirit, the virtual' (C2, 82–3). If 'the act of thinking is the only true creation', if creation is nothing other than 'the genesis of the act of thinking within thought itself' (PS, 97), this is because to think isn't part of actual or creatural behaviour. We do not own our thoughts. 'We' are not ordinarily capable of thought, and 'man', the molar or constituted subject par excellence, does not think. Thinking is not the exercise or action of an actual individual or species. As far as the individual is concerned, to think is always experienced as a force of imposition or violence. Thinking is never willed or deliberate. 'There is only involuntary thought' (DR, 139; cf. PS, 15, 95). Thinking begins when we are forced to think or infused by thought. It is always its unconscious or involuntary exercise that marks 'the transcendent limit or the vocation of each faculty' of the mind. Why? Because, grounded in an absolute power of thinking, the 'activity of thought applies to a receptive being, to a passive subject which represents that activity to itself rather than enacts it […]. Thought thinks only on the basis of an unconscious […], the universal ungrounding which characterises thought as a faculty in its transcendental exercise.'[22]

Consequently, the highest exercise of thought can only be undertaken by a version of what Deleuze, after Spinoza, names the 'spiritual automaton'. According to a Spinozist conception of things 'we have a power of knowing, understanding or thinking only to the extent that we participate in the absolute power of thinking' (EP, 142). The automaton is simply a mode defined by maximal participation in this power. It offers no resistance to the expression of the attribute that is expressed through it. The automaton is a mode of thought through which thought thinks without hindrance. Precisely because it is 'dispossessed of its own thought', the automaton is a mode in which 'thought thinks itself' on the sole basis of its own laws.[23] The automaton is thus to thought what *amor fati* is to the event. Like any creative figure (artist, thinker, philosopher…) in Deleuze, the automaton has been stripped of its own or actual interests and capacities of action. The automaton is 'petrified' and isolated. Incapable of action, it is 'cut off from the outside world'. But precisely on this condition, the automaton is a vessel of that power that breathes life into this same world, a power more distant than any outside. Once the automaton has cut itself off from any *actual* outside, 'there is a more profound outside which will animate it', an outside which now acts immediately on its evacuated inside, via the virtual 'identity of brain and world' (C2, 179; 206–7).

The automaton animates in this way an austerely redemptive logic. Through the figure of the automaton we 'reach a spiritual space where what we choose is no longer distinguishable from the choice itself'. Such a space is what we have already encountered as a wholly counter-actualised or wholly virtual any-space-whatever [*espace quelconque*]. In the end, 'the any-space-whatever is identical to the power of the spirit, to the perpetually renewed spiritual decision: it is this decision which constitutes the affect, or the "auto-affection", and which takes upon itself the linking of parts' (C1, 117). What is this decision, this choice indistinguishable from what it chooses? It is of course nothing other than the decision to affirm affirmation itself. Precisely because the choosing choses itself (through us), so then 'only he who is chosen chooses well or effectively', in line with the immediate movement of 'the Spirit, he who blows where he will' (C2, 178). For the same reason, 'choice as spiritual determination has no other object other than itself: I choose to choose'. Or rather, choosing chooses itself through me, and what 'I' choose is a choosing that is 'not defined by what it chooses but by the power that it possesses to be able to start afresh at every instant, of starting afresh itself, and in this way confirming itself by itself, by putting the whole stake back into play each time'. Just as a wholly affirmative throw of the dice cannot lose, so then 'the true choice, that which consists in choosing choice, is supposed to restore everything to us. It will enable us to rediscover everything, in the spirit of sacrifice, at the moment of the sacrifice' (C1, 114–16). It will recover, through our creatural sacrifice, the whole of creation.

The main mistake to avoid here is the confusion of such purely affirmative choice with anything like the conventional notion of 'free choice' – a notion which applies only to the unfreedom that characterises the whole creatural domain of actual preferences, probabilities and causes. Conventional notions of free will or free choice have no place in a Deleuzian universe. A creating simply does everything that it is capable of doing, without deliberation or reflection. Whatever the circumstances, 'the philosopher creates, he doesn't reflect' (N, 122). As a rule, 'creators only do what they absolutely need to do' (RF, 292) and so 'necessity everywhere appears as the only modality of being' (EP, 212). In Spinoza's exemplary vision of the world the decisive questions are always a matter of capacity and power alone, to the exclusion of all moral judgements: 'in a sense every being, each moment, does all it can'.[24] For Deleuze's Leibniz, likewise, a free act is never determined by the preference of one motive or option over another. Motives are simply invented by their subject, after the fact; perhaps the subject amounts to nothing more than the requisite support for such invention. The question is then precisely, since 'everything is sealed off from the beginning and remains in a condition of closure', how might we 'conjoin liberty with a schizophrenic automaton's inner, complete and preestablished determination?' Since any given monad is 'nothing other than a passage of God', then an act is free if it eliminates all resistance to this passing. A free act 'expresses the entire soul at a given moment of its duration'. What a free monad does, in other words, is fully to express what inheres in it – 'inherence is the condition of liberty and not of impediment'. A free act is one that embraces and identifies with the absolute necessity of its (divinely ordained) determination (LB, 69–73).

If freedom means anything for Deleuze it isn't a matter of human liberty but of liberation *from* the human – of 'liberty become the capacity of man to vanquish man'.[25] Precisely because he offers no resistance to the fate that befalls him, 'only the free man can comprehend all violence in a single act of violence, and every mortal event in a single Event which no longer makes room for the accident' (LS, 152). The immediate political implication of such a position, we might note in passing, is clear enough: since a free mode or monad is simply one that has eliminated its resistance to the sovereign will that works through it, so then it follows that the more absolute the sovereign's power, the more 'free' are those subject to it. As Spinoza himself puts it, the 'more absolute a government [...] the more suitable [it is] for the preservation of freedom' (and 'no matter how unfair a subject considers the decrees of the commonwealth to be, he is bound to carry them out').[26]

III

We are now in a position to consider the full consequences of Deleuze's definition of philosophy as the creation of concepts. 'The question of philosophy is the singular point where concept and creation are related to each other.' Philosophy is the discipline through which creative events can be expressed in pure thought. 'With its concepts, philosophy brings forth events', and a concept is itself produced as 'pure event or reality of the virtual'.[27] Concepts allow the unpresentable to be thought. As usual in Deleuze, whatever may seem difficult about this definition is not the result of its complexity but rather of its literal and uncompromising simplicity. The main thing to remember is that a concept is here simply a creating in its purest or most affirmative form. This has at least five closely related implications.

In the first place, as a *creating*, a concept is obviously not something already made but a making. It is not an object but a process. When they use the word 'concept' in *What is Philosophy?*, Deleuze and Guattari certainly do not mean a pre-fabricated form of representation that would be 'indefinitely the same for objects which are distinct' (DR, 13). A concept doesn't operate here like a notional definition, on the model of a generic conceptual dog designed to encompass every actual variety and living instance of dog. That philosophy creates concepts means it does not contemplate, reflect upon or communicate concepts that it encounters external to itself. 'If ready-made concepts already existed they would have to abide by limits.' A characteristic feature of conceptual creatings, by contrast, is that they have 'no other limit than the plane they happen to populate' – and this plane is itself precisely 'limitless', the space of a 'measureless creation' (WP, 77–8). What Deleuze and Guattari call a minority is a good example of a concept in this sense, since 'a minority never exists ready-made, it is only formed on lines of flight' – and though lines of flight are formed from and through particular times and territories, such lines themselves have no territory or temporality other than the temporo-territoriality of flight itself (D, 43, 50).

The more stable, static or blandly universal a concept the more skeletal, unremarkable or uncreative it becomes. Plato, for Deleuze and Guattari, is the philosopher who forgets this lesson. Like any philosopher, Plato creates concepts but he then goes on 'to set them up as representing the uncreated that precedes them'. He configures his concepts in such a way that they seem to attest to the pre-existence of an ideal or objective transcendence (WP, 29). And although they replace Plato's ideal eternity with a dynamic temporal development, Hegel and Heidegger are guilty of the same kind of mistake insofar as their historicism leads them to 'posit history as a form of interiority in which the concept necessarily develops or unveils its destiny' (WP, 95). The absolute creation that is a concept is as intolerant of such historical mediation as it is indifferent to eternal fixity. A concept is a pure becoming or event, and as we saw in Chapter 4, section VI, history presents only the actualisation of events: 'the event in its becoming, in its specific consistency, in its self-positing as concept, escapes History' (WP, 110).

Furthermore, the fact that the creation of concepts occurs through philosophy *alone* means that the actual occasion of such creation is literally immaterial. Anyone who has read even a little of Deleuze's work knows that he creates his own concepts through the most diverse situations of thought, through material drawn from literature, mathematics, cinema, geology, etc. Nevertheless, the conceptual creating per se is always independent of the actual configuration of such situations. The work of philosophy is precisely to extract a concept from the circumstances of its actualisation. In *What is Philosophy?*, where only philosophy creates new concepts (whereas art creates new sensations and science new functions), Deleuze and Guattari pause to consider what happens when the operations of these disciplines seem to converge. What happens 'when a philosopher attempts to create the concept of a sensation or a function (for example, a concept peculiar to Riemannian space or to irrational number)'? What happens when an artist creates a new sensation from a concept (as with abstract or conceptual art)? Their answer is simple: 'in all these cases the rule is that the interfering discipline must proceed with its own methods' (WP, 217). Philosophy remains philosophy, whatever the occasion or material. This is why Deleuze's cinema books, for instance, are books of philosophy and of philosophy alone. Deleuze's books are not about actual cinema but create the concepts that philosophy can extract from the virtual processes that compose cinema. 'Cinema's concepts are not given in the cinema. And yet they are cinema's concepts, not theories about cinema. So there is always a time, midday-midnight, when we must no longer ask ourselves, "What is cinema?", but "What is philosophy?" Cinema itself is a new practice of images and signs, whose theory philosophy must produce as conceptual practice.'[28]

In the second place, as *a* creating, a concept is always singular, indivisible and discrete. 'Every creation is singular, and the concept as properly philosophical creation is always a singularity' (WP, 7tm). Conceptual creations are always accompanied by the signature of the thinking through which they were made – Plato's idea, Aristotle's substance, Descartes' cogito, Leibniz's monad, Bergson's duration, Derrida's *différance*, etc. Every conceptual creating thus injects a certain stability into the otherwise undifferentiated flux of pure chaos in which thoughts disappear as soon as they appear. 'Nothing is more distressing than a thought that escapes itself, than ideas that fly off, that disappear hardly formed' (WP, 201). The invention of singular concepts makes it possible for thought to proceed and develop. A concept renders *a* slice of chaos available for thought. A conceptual creation achieves this by imposing a certain consistency upon its various elements. A concept connects and renders inseparable a certain number of heterogeneous components by traversing them 'at infinite speed': as a pure creating, a concept is 'immediately co-present to all its components or variations, at no distance from them'. What is thus 'distinctive about the concept is that it renders components inseparable *within itself*' (WP, 19–21). Heidegger's concept of being, for instance, renders inseparable movements of veiling and unveiling. The foundational certainty that Descartes' attributes to his concept of the cogito is likewise extracted from the integration of its three components: doubting, thinking and being. It focuses this certainty through the central point of the subject or 'I', and it does this in a way that is independent of any other concept of the subject (e.g. scholastic notions of man as a rational animal). When Kant then introduces a fourth component into the cogito, the dimension of time as the element in which the otherwise undetermined existence of the I is determined as a merely phenomenal self (i.e. the self as an *other*), he thereby transforms the concept and with it the configuration of truth and error as a whole (WP, 27, 31; cf. KT, viii–ix).

Our third point is already implied in the notion of absolute affirmation or infinite speed. As a pure creating, a concept *becomes* in the absence of any medium external to itself. Conceptual inventions are creatings that generate only the most evanescent, most immaterial of creatures – creatings with the minimal degree of creatural opacity. A concept is defined by the requirements of its consistency alone. Even in his earliest essays, Deleuze always seeks to affirm (against Kant and against the logic of representation) a notion of the concept that is 'identical to its object'.[29] Indistinguishable from the object it creates, a concept has no actuality or reference. A concept is not a proposition that might refer to something beyond what it does or says. A concept is 'purely self-referential; it posits itself and its object at the same time as it is created [...]. The concept is neither denotation of states of affairs nor signification of the lived; it is the event as pure sense that immediately runs through the components' (WP, 22, 144). As theorists of absolute creation have always recognised, every unconditional creating must also be self-affirming or self-positing.

> The concept is not given, it is created; it is to be created. It is not formed but posits itself
> in itself – it is self-positing. Creation and self-positing mutually imply each other because

what is truly created, from the living being to the work of art, thereby enjoys a self-positing of itself, or an autopoetic characteristic by which it is recognised. The concept posits itself to the same extent that it is created. What depends on a free creative activity is also that which, independently and necessarily, posits itself in itself: the most subjective will be the most objective (WP, 11).

What does it mean, after all, to say that the concept is 'thought operating at infinite speed' (WP, 21), that 'from Epicurus to Spinoza and from Spinoza to Michaux the problem of thought is infinite speed' (WP, 36)? Infinite speed is the speed of a movement that no longer passes through any dimension external to itself. Infinite speed is not mediated by time or space. Infinite speed thus describes a movement that no longer has anything to do with actual movement, a purely virtual 'movement' that has always reached its destination, whose moving is itself its own destination. It is the movement of an aleatory point that is already everywhere and nowhere. Such a point will pass through every possible point in space during one and the same point 'in' time (in time or out of time – as we shall see in a moment, from the perspective of absolute creation this is not a meaningful distinction).

Any notion of a positive infinity must be affirmative or self-positing (if not axiomatic) as a matter of course. Since it is not mediated by anything external to itself, since it creates the very time and space that it works through, infinite speed is simply the speed of affirmation as such. This is what thought claims by right: pure thought, thought that proceeds independently of any medium, 'demands "only" movement that can be carried to infinity. What thought claims by right, what it selects, is infinite movement' (WP, 37). In the end, this means that philosophy will pursue its invention of concepts in the absence of any already constituted world or people that might in some way hinder or deflect such invention. Rather than work through the actual world, philosophy posits a new, still virtual world as the counter-actualised correlate of creation itself. 'Art and philosophy converge at this point: the constitution of an earth and a people that are lacking as the correlate of creation' (WP, 108). Or again, from the perspective of the earth itself: its counter-actualisation or 'deterritorialisation is absolute when the earth passes into the pure plane of immanence of a Being-thought […]. Thinking consists in stretching out a plane of immanence that absorbs the earth (or rather, "adsorbs" it).' (WP, 88). The only medium of philosophy is the immediate movement of thought itself, i.e. of thought extracted even from the organic mediation of the brain. Philosophy can work through the non-medium of the brain once the brain has been conceived exclusively as thought, or what Deleuze and Guattari evoke in the conclusion to their book as a 'Thought-Brain'. This brain then lays out the plane of immanence upon which a philosophy thinks. Such a singular brain, or 'cosmos-brain', has all of the characteristics of pure creation as such:

it is an absolute consistent form that surveys itself independently of any supplementary dimension, which does not appeal therefore to any dimension, which has only a single side whatever the number of its dimensions, which remains copresent to all its determinations without proximity or distance, traverses them at infinite speed, without limit-speed, and which makes of them so many inseparable variations on which it confers an equipotentiality without confusion. We have seen that this was the status of the concept as pure event or reality of the virtual (WP, 210).

A concept is not only self-positing and self-referential, however. The creation of concepts also has a redemptive or transformative aspect – infinite speed is itself a characteristic of the redemptive conceptions of thought defended by Pascal and Spinoza.[30] This is our fourth point. We know that actualisation is an unavoidable part of differentiation, that creatings tend to be concealed by the creatures they produce. To create a concept and to extract an event are one and the same process of counter-actualisation or counter-effectuation. If science tracks the movement that passes from chaotic virtuality to actual bodies and states of affairs, philosophy inverts the process. But such inversion does not simply return the system to its original state. It intensifies or enhances the creating as such. Counter-actualisation allows the creating itself to *become*. If its actualisation or effectuation confines a creating within a creature, its counter-effectuation restores it to its fully creative potential or virtuality. 'To the extent that the pure event is each time imprisoned forever in its actualisation, counter-actualisation liberates it, always for other times' (LS, 161). The initial actualisation (e.g. the individuation of an organism, or a territory) was still too chaotic or thought-less. The counter-actualisation (the deterritorialisation or destratification, the dis-organisation of the organism) liberates the creating and makes it *consist* in the purity of its own dimension, i.e. in the dimension of concepts or thought. The process of liberation or destratification generates, all by itself, a sort of 'surplus value' or 'gain in consistency' (TP, 335–6). So when we move from science to philosophy, when

we go back up in the opposite direction, from states of affairs to the virtual, the line is not the same because it is not the same virtual [...]. The virtual is no longer the chaotic virtual but rather virtuality that has become consistent, that has become an entity formed on a plane of immanence that sections the chaos. This is what we call the Event [...]. The event is actualised or effectuated whenever it is inserted, willy-nilly, into a state of affairs; but it is *counter-effectuated* whenever it is abstracted from states of affairs so as to isolate the concept (WP, 156, 159).

Only through such isolation can creation return to its unlimited intensity or infinite speed. A redemptive philosophy will therefore seek to demonstrate, after Leibniz, that 'everything has a concept!', or in other words, that only the singular 'individual exists and it is by virtue of the power of the concept: monad or soul'. What is a monad, if not a concept conceived as a creating? A monad acquires this power not by lending form to matter or by specifying some more general category or genre, but by condensing and extending events, nothing but events and 'the droplets of events'. Monads are the elementary units of creation as process. They are 'genuine or absolute forms', 'primary forces, essentially individual and active primary unities, that actualise a virtuality or a potential, and that are in harmony with each other without any one being determined by the other' (LB, 41, 64, 103).

In the fifth and final place conceptual creation thus implies, together with the existence of virtual 'conceptual personae' who oversee the coordination of a concept's components,[31] the existence of a plane in which several concepts can, more or less harmoniously, co-exist or consist. However disjunctive or divergent the process of their becoming, the creation of any given series of concepts must at least presuppose the shared dimension of their creation as such. If the problem of thought has always been infinite speed, then in order for it to be sustained, the infinite speed of creation 'requires a milieu that moves infinitely in itself' (WP, 36). What Deleuze and Guattari call a plane of immanence provides such a milieu. This is a plane in which a certain number of creations can hold together or consist, without compromising their divergent self-positing or autonomy. Deleuze and Guattari's 'constructivism requires every creation to be a construction on a plane that gives it an autonomous existence' (WP, 7) and that prevents it from sliding back either into undifferentiated chaos or the mere communication of actualities. In other words, not only are conceptual creations singular and discrete, they also resonate together in a sort of localised absolute. 'The philosophy that creates them always introduces a powerful Whole that, while remaining open, is not fragmented: an unlimited One-All, an "Omnitudo" that includes all the concepts on one and the same plane.' If concepts are like individual waves, the plane of consistency or immanence that they agitate is like a tidal movement that lends them a more general orientation. Or again, 'concepts are events, but the plane is the horizon of events, the reservoir or reserve of purely conceptual events: not the relative horizon that functions as a limit, which changes with an observer and encloses observable states of affairs, but the absolute horizon, independent of any observer, which makes the event as concept independent of a visible state of affairs in which it is brought about' (WP, 35–6).

The plane is thus a purified plane of creation alone, which lends a certain consistency to the creations that proceed through it. The plane 'presents only events', to the exclusion of any actuality or lived experience (WP, 47). The important point is that such a plane cannot itself be directly thought. Philosophy thinks concepts and nothing but concepts. The plane is not itself thought, then, but is rather the 'image' that thought, as it thinks concepts, 'gives itself of what it means to think, to make use of thought, to find one's bearings in thought' (WP, 37). The plane orients thought. Philosophy thinks creations and nothing but creations but by doing so it *implies* the plane upon which a given set of creations can take place. This is not all. Beyond the implication of any given plane of immanence, beyond each particular plane that corresponds to each particular set of creations, there hovers the horizon of a still more inclusive plane – the horizon that would be 'THE plane of immanence', the sole dimension of *all* creation in and of itself. The existence of such a plane would be doubly implicated or implied (the French verb *impliquer* can carry both meanings). It would exist at a double remove from any thinkable creating. It would be not only the unthinkable horizon for any singular act of thinking, but the unthinkable horizon of every unthinkable horizon. To try directly to present such a plane would be to annul the difference between creation and chaos. The whole of creation can be presented to thought only as mere chaos, i.e. as the dissolution of any plane and hence as the dissolution of any configuration of thought; there must be a multiplicity of planes, 'since no one plane could encompass all of chaos without collapsing back onto it' (WP, 50).

However, the equation of being and creation just as certainly *implies* the existence of this unique plane, THE plane in which creation creates nothing other than itself, a plane of immanence that is immanent only to itself. And the certainty of this implication is enough to provide Deleuze and Guattari with the basis for a whole history of philosophy – the *becoming* of philosophy conceived as a progressive approximation to this plane. Over the course of such approximation, immanence ceases to be immanent to the One (with Plato) or to a divine transcendence (with Nicholas of Cusa) or to the personal subject of consciousness (with Descartes, Kant, Husserl…) so as to become immanent to nothing other than itself. Such a plane would be 'traversed by movements of the infinite' alone. It would consist solely of infinite speeds, the articulation of an absolute freedom. The evocation of such a plane, we know, was Spinoza's particular achievement, and this is why Spinoza figures here as the 'fulfilment' of philosophy. Spinoza is the 'infinite becoming-philosopher', the philosopher who once managed to think 'that which cannot be thought and yet must be thought, as Christ was incarnated once, in order to show, that one time, the possibility of the impossible' (WP, 46–8tm, 60).

With this conclusion we arrive at the last and no doubt most significant reason why the highest or most absolute form of creation must also proceed in the exclusive dimension of pure thought. By definition, only thought can express a pure implication; only thought can posit that which can be presented exclusively as unthought. Only thought is adequate to a properly spiritual redemption, once we realise that 'redemption, art beyond knowledge, is also creation beyond information' (C2, 270). Or again, since every thinking is *a* creating, it is not possible to think creation as whole (without thereby changing it, or creating it anew). The process of thinking, however, *implies* the dimension of creation as an unhindered whole, i.e. the reality of THE plane of immanence in which creation encounters neither limit nor obstacle. This implication is the 'non-thought within thought. It is the base of all planes, immanent to every thinkable plane that does not succeed in thinking it [...]. Perhaps this is the supreme act of philosophy: not so much to think THE plane of immanence as to show that it is there, unthought in every plane, and to think it in this way as the outside and inside of thought.'[32]

A similarly implicit or implicative status applies, in fact, to all of Deleuze's central concepts – the virtual, of course, but also sense, the event, pure difference…. Since only the actual is presented and experienced, so then from within the confines of experience the reality of the virtual is only ever implicit. Virtual difference cannot be presented, let alone represented. As virtual difference tends to be suspended in the actual systems that explicate it, and as 'difference creates these systems by explicating itself' so the reality of difference as such is a matter for pure thought alone – precisely because it can only be accessed in terms of its implication. 'It is not surprising that, strictly speaking, difference should be "inexplicable". Difference is explicated, but in systems in which it tends to be cancelled; this means only that difference is essentially implicated or implied [*impliquée*], that its being is implication.'[33]

<h1 style="text-align:center">IV</h1>

The same logic of implication that conditions Deleuze's notion of infinite speed is also the guiding principle behind his notoriously complex conception of time. There isn't space to engage with this complexity here – but nor is there any need to do so, since in terms of the argument developed in this book, the question of time emerges as a fairly straightforward sort of paradox. Time is the essential medium of creation, insofar as a creating (as opposed to chaos) must consist, proceed and *become*. On the other hand, if it is to be absolute, creation must proceed immediately and all at once, at a literally infinite speed. Bergson (creation as it evolves) points Deleuze in the first direction, Spinoza (creation *sub specie aeternitatis*) in the second. Deleuze needs a theory of time that allows him to square this circle, and he claims to have found it in a version of Nietzsche's eternal return.

We are already thoroughly familiar with the crucial preliminary distinction – the difference between actual and virtual time. The ordinary metric or chronological conception of time, time measured in terms of hours and days or projects and goals, applies only to the domain of actuality. (The French term *actualité* connotes both what is actual and what is present or current). Actual time is the medium through which creatures coordinate their perceptions, actions, and reactions. The time of the creature qua creature, the time of its birth and growth, its living and acting, its aging and death – this is time in which nothing becomes. Actual time is time that only a creature has. It is time for this or that. It is time to grow up, time to move on, time to eat, sleep or act. Drawing on Stoic vocabulary, Deleuze calls it the time of Chronos. Chronos is the time of historical development as much as it is of personal experience. Chronos can be lived, remembered, chronicled, measured (TP, 262). Chronos, in short, is the time of representation. Chronos is time conceived as a series of presents, each of which can be more or less accurately re-presented.

The time of creation, by contrast, coheres in a wholly virtual dimension. Creative time is the time of events alone, and events are not mediated by the actualities they produce. Events emerge and develop according to their own rhythm on the plane of immanence, i.e. a plane which cannot be measured or represented but only thought. Such is the time of Aion, the time of events which do not themselves 'have' time, and that in particular have no present. Aion is 'never an actuality [...]. Always already passed and eternally yet to come, Aion is the eternal truth of time: pure empty form of time, which has freed itself of its present corporeal content' (LS, 63; 165). Aion is thus 'the pure moment of abstraction' of an event as such, the time of the un-actual or un-timely. Aion is 'time out of joint'.[34] In other words, events do not happen in a time that pre-exists them; rather, what is primary is that events occur, and their occurring gives rise to time. Events come first, and their occurring produces time as a dimension of their occurring. 'Events are ideational singularities which communicate in one and the same Event. They have therefore an eternal truth, and their time is never the present which realises them and makes them exist. Rather, it is the unlimited Aion, the Infinitive in which they subsist and insist [...], an infinitive independent not only of all persons but of all time' (LS, 53, 214). By the same token, if 'univocal Being is the pure form of the Aion', this is because 'univocity wrests Being from beings in order to bring it to all of them at once, and to make it fall upon them for all times' (LS, 180).

By privileging Aion over Chronos or the virtual over the actual, Deleuze thus reverses (after Kant and the post-Kantians) the traditional relation of time and event.[35] Events no longer punctuate a regular, orderly time, and their time is not measured and linked according to the regularity of movement. Instead, the immediate occurring of singular events generates an aberrant time as the dimension of their incompossible coordination. Such aberration 'sets time free from any linkage; it carries out a direct presentation of time by reversing the relationship of subordination that time maintains with normal movement [...]. What aberrant movement reveals is time as everything' (C2, 37). Time ceases to be the medium of sensory-motor reactions, oriented towards the pressing demands of the present, so as to become the very element of creation itself. As Spinoza explains, creative eternity is something altogether different from ordinary duration or time, even duration imagined as 'without beginning or end'.[36] Creation does not occur within an already constituted time. Creative time emerges only insofar as creation makes time, 'an absolute, original time' (PS, 17).

As far as the creature is concerned, however, it takes time to understand time. Rather as Spinoza cannot set out from the idea of God (or Proust from the idea of art), an actual individual must arrive at this idea of virtual time, precisely through a process that explodes the limits of creatural temporality.

In *Difference and Repetition*, Deleuze charts the shift from creatural to creative time via three successive syntheses. The first establishes the apparent primacy of the present and the actual. The creature's time, as we have seen, is the time of actions and interests, and this first synthesis organises time as a 'living present, and the past and the future as dimensions of this present' (DR, 75–6). A second and deeper synthesis then combines present and past through the *passing* of the present. The succession of present moments now appears as 'the manifestation of something more profound – namely, the manner in which each continues the whole life', such that each present moment is grasped as 'no more than the actualisation of [...] the relations of virtual coexistence between the levels of a pure past' (DR, 83). As Bergson has already taught us, this is the time that unfolds or explicates itself with the events it contains – this is creation as it proceeds over time.

The third and final synthesis involves, by contrast, the immediacy of an absolute creation that affirms and *implicates* the whole of time in a single moment. This is a time that presents itself as pure and empty form, 'time freed from the events which made up its content [...]. Time itself unfolds instead of things unfolding within it' (DR, 88). As far as the creature or self is concerned, affirmation of such non-creatural time 'must be determined in the image of a unique and tremendous event, an act which is adequate to time a whole' – for example, 'to throw time out of joint, to make the sun explode

[...], to kill God or the father' (DR, 89). Active individuals (Hamlet, Oedipus...) must become equal to the events they bear, to the act that will destroy them. In this third moment, the event and the act come to 'possess a secret coherence which excludes that of the self; they turn back against the self which has become their equal and smash it to pieces, as though the bearer of the new world were carried away and dispersed by the shock of the multiplicity to which it gives birth' (DR, 89–90). Geared to the violent immediacy of creation in itself, of creation in its immediate yet unpredictable future, this third synthesis 'subordinates the other two to itself and strips them of their autonomy' (DR, 94). The third synthesis unites all three syntheses and orients them to itself alone. The future is the 'ultimate synthesis' since 'the future is the deployment and explication of the multiple, of the different and of the fortuitous, for themselves and "for all times"' (DR, 115). More, the third synthesis not only determines the two others 'but also eliminates them, determining them to operate only once and for all, keeping the "all times" for the third time alone' (DR, 297). The future is thus the finality of time as a whole – it is the synthesis, precisely, of time as *everything* and of time as *pure and empty form*.

Absolutely creative time, in other words, can only be thought as both empty and full. It is full, naturally, because it creates all there is. But it must also be empty, if each new act of creation is to be fully creative, i.e. unhindered by any previous creation. Since only creatures get in the way of creation, creative time will be creatureless; since only the present interrupts or divides time, creative time will be presentless. Such has always been the paradox of eternal and unlimited creation, and Deleuze resolves it in a perfectly classical manner – through a definition of time that allows it to divide itself between 'explicated' and 'implicated' states.[37] On the one hand, time in its pure state is full or is everything insofar as it is the time of every possible event, the time of all makings or creatings or thinkings (to the exclusion of all preservings or representings) – for example, the creating of Combray as a way of seeing, not as something seen. Insofar as these creatings occur and develop they 'take time' by unfolding or distributing it as the dimension of their occurring. Needless to say, events do not take place all at once. Time as explication is what ensures that everything isn't given in one and the same moment, it is the instance that blocks any presentation of an actual whole. On the other hand, however, time is a pure and empty form insofar as the occurring of events is itself determined or distributed by a force that is beyond occurring (or that is simply the 'occurring' of the One-All itself). Not only does the occurring of change and becoming occur within a form that 'does not itself change' (DR, 89; C2, 17), but every event is a facet of one and the same Event. Time is the production of self-differing differences, but in the end 'there is only a single time, a single duration, in which everything would participate [...], a single time, one, universal, impersonal. In short, a monism of Time' (B, 78). Every singular creating is a facet of absolute creation, in which all that occurs inheres in a state of infinite implication. If this dimension of time is a sort of eternity it remains a creative or 'expressive' eternity, precisely (PS, 45) – eternity conceived not as the static absence of change but as an unthinkably compressed instance of all thinkable change, as a single aleatory point moving at infinite speed, as a single throw of the dice.

Deleuze's philosophy of time is precisely the time of 'an eternity that can only be revealed in a becoming' (CC, 5). It is the time of a revelation that promises to reconcile Spinoza with Bergson.

The literal convolution of Deleuze's conception of time is a simple consequence, in fact, of his inaugural equation of being and absolute creation or difference. Deleuze's ontology obliges us to think of creation both as the ongoing production or occurring of new events and as a single event in which all such production is immediately affirmed. Such, remember, was already the lesson of Proust's notion of essence as 'the birth of Time itself'. Essence is a power of pure individuation or 'absolute difference', and essence emerges with the 'absolute speed of figures of light' (CC, 151). Essence or difference does not assemble an actual totality but differentiates a virtual whole. Time will then be defined as the power that both distributes and transverses these differings in an immediate but non-integrative unity, a single self-dividing 'auto-affection'.[38] Essence scatters fragmented parts over time, but time remains 'the power to be the whole of these parts without totalising them [...]. Ultimate interpreter, ultimate act of interpretation, time has the strange power to affirm simultaneously fragments that do not constitute a whole in space, any more than they form a whole by succession within time. Time is precisely the transversal of all possible spaces, including the space of time.'[39] Whereas what is created is bound to a particular span of time, time itself is the medium of the timelessly creative as such.

What inhibits our thinking of time in this way is of course any notion of it as *actual* synthesis or dialectical totality. Against Hegel, Deleuze insists that being does not need to pass through cumulative, creatural, or historical time in order to become what it is. Creation is immediately creative; there is no transcendent or negating subject of creation that might need time in order to become conscious of itself or otherwise catch up with itself. Precisely because creative difference is self-differing or internally differing, so then 'what differs from itself is *immediately* the unity of substance and subject' (DI, 38tm). If Hegel is his most obvious philosophical antagonist, it is because Deleuze's project precludes, from start to finish, the time and space of mediation itself.

Against Hegel, Nietzsche provides Deleuze with his chief philosophical resource for thinking creative time. What Nietzsche's doctrine of eternal return allows Deleuze to say, in a nutshell, is that only differings or creatings have being.[40] Creations return, creatures do not — or rather, what returns of a creature is its creating alone. '*Return is the being of that which becomes*. Return is the being of becoming itself, the being which is affirmed in becoming.'[41] Eternal return is the most radical and uncompromising version of Deleuze's most general conviction – that only creations *are*.

The eternal return is said only [...] of the pure intensities of that Will which are like mobile individuating factors unwilling to allow themselves to be contained within the factitious limits of this or that individual, this or that Self. Eternal return expresses the common being of all these metamorphoses, the measure and common being of all that is extreme [...]. In all these respects, eternal return is the univocity of being, the effective realisation

149

of that univocity. In the eternal return, univocal being is not only thought and even affirmed, but effectively realised.[42]

Negatively, eternal return simply confirms that all of becoming-actual or 'becoming-reactive has no being' (NP, 71–2). All that is actual or creatural comes into existence but never *is*: it exists and then passes away, never to return. Created individuals occur only once, once and for all, and are 'thereafter eliminated for all times' (DR, 300). Only creatings return, since creatural forms are not forms of being but forms in which being is suspended or cancelled. 'It is quality and extensity that do not return, in so far as within them difference, the condition of eternal return, is cancelled' (DR, 243). The same fate awaits all that applies to actuality – equality, identity, similarity, resemblance, representation, reaction, negation, etc.

Positively, eternal return figures as 'the highest affirmation' in this whole philosophy of affirmation. 'Difference is recovered, liberated, only at the limit of its power – in other words, by repetition in the eternal return.' Return is the affirmation of the whole of chance in a single gesture.[43] Eternal return affirms only the new or different as such, the new in its *producing*, liberated from its causes, conditions or agents. Return thus confirms the eternal 'independence of the work' or of a producing as such, conceived as a facet of one eternally recurring production (DR, 90–1). Eternal return affirms every event in a single event: 'returning is everything but everything is affirmed in a single moment [...]. The complete formula of affirmation is: the whole, yes, universal being, yes, but universal being ought to belong to a single becoming, the whole ought to belong to a single moment' (NP, 72). The eternal return is 'the same of the different, the one of the multiple' (DR, 126). Eternal return, in short, is just another name for creative time itself, insofar as such time is nothing other than the power to combine its two divergent aspects: time explicated through the differentiation of creatings, and time implicated through their immediate affirmation.

The process of eternal return is thus less a conventionally temporal dynamic than a principle of ontological discrimination. The function of return is 'never to identify but to authenticate', i.e. to serve as a principle of 'creative selection'. The primary purpose of return is to distinguish once and for all between active and reactive aspects of being. Return separates superior or absolute forms of affirmation from more measured or moderate ones – more precisely, 'the words "separate" or "extract" are not even adequate [...], since the eternal return creates the superior forms' (DI, 124–5). As Deleuze explains in *Difference and Repetition*, eternal return is what differs or makes difference by creating the superior form of everything that is, and this 'superior form is not the infinite, but rather the eternal formlessness of the eternal return itself, throughout its metamorphoses and transformations'. The superior form, in short, is again nothing other than the pure creating of creatings as such, unbound from any creatural constraint or creatorly stasis. The shortcoming of every philosophy that accepts such stasis or constraint (a philosophy of representation, of identity, or resemblance...) is its need 'to remain relative to what it grounds, to borrow the characteristics of what it grounds, and to be proved by these' (DR, 88). With Descartes, for instance, the ground upon which things differ or are made to differ is provided by an 'external and transcendent divine causality' that creates substances which conform as closely as is possible to our capacity to represent them (EP, 31). The eternal return, by contrast, effects a sort of 'universal ungrounding', or rather it enables the unrestricted 'freedom of the non-mediated ground, the discovery of a ground behind every other ground' – the ground of a differing liberated from the differed (DR, 67).

This creative temporality has one last implication – an implication which is notoriously difficult if embraced as an initial point of departure, but which should now follow on from the preceding discussion more or less as a matter of course. If every new event is also a facet of the one Event, if every creating is a facet of Creation, this means that every new difference is also the moment of a pure or immediate repetition. 'The form of repetition in the eternal return is the brutal form of the immediate, that of the universal and the singular reunited, which dethrones every general law, dissolves the mediations and annihilates the particulars subjected to the law' (DR, 7). Pure repetition, repetition that does not wait for the mediation of a time or routine through which it would repeat, is *immediately* (rather than eventually) indistinguishable from pure difference. Every new creating is also a repeating or renewal of one and the same act of creation. Every new throw of the dice is another instance of the same ontological throw. The act of creation is always the same, in the same absolute sense that what it creates is always different. Eternal return, in this sense, completes the affirmation of ontological univocity: we can fully affirm a single voice for the whole of the multiple only on condition that each voicing gives voice to that excessive movement which creates it as eternally different from itself (DR, 304).

This the central idea of *Difference and Repetition* is already anticipated in an important passage of *Proust and Signs*, which is clear enough to be worth quoting at length. We know that essence individualises the substances in which it is incarnated, because

essence is in itself difference. But it does not have the power to diversify, and to diversify itself, without also having the power to repeat itself, identical to itself. What can one do with essence, which is ultimate difference, except to repeat it, because it is irreplaceable and because nothing can be substituted for it? This is why great music can only be played again, a poem learned by heart and recited. Difference and repetition are only apparently in opposition [...]. This is because difference, as the quality of a world, is affirmed only though a kind of autorepetition that traverses the various media and reunites different objects; repetition constitutes the degrees of an original difference, but diversity also constitutes the levels of a repetition no less fundamental. About the work of a great artist, we say: it's the same thing, on a different level. But we also say, it's different, but to the same degree. Actually, difference and repetition are the two inseparable and correlative powers of essence. An artist does not 'age' because he repeats himself, for repetition is the power of difference, no less than difference the power of repetition. An artist 'ages' when, 'by exhaustion of his brain', he decides it is simpler to find directly in life, as though ready-made, what he can express only in his work, what he should have distinguished and repeated by means of his work (PS, 48–9).

What applies to the work of an individual artist or creator holds still more absolutely for the greatest 'creator' of all, i.e. the work of immanent creation as such: at every level of its production, 'what is produced, the absolutely new itself, is in turn nothing but repetition' (DR, 90).

V

There is now just one last question to address, a question that has been present but mostly implicit in this study thus far.

The logic of difference and repetition, and with it the logic of eternal return and of creative temporality in general, reinforces one of the conclusions that emerged from our discussion of the virtual and actual in Chapter 2, section V – Deleuze's theory of difference is clearly a theory of 'unilateral distinction'. Deleuzian 'difference makes itself' (DR, 28). We have seen how any given event is determined and distributed as a facet of one all-creating Event, how all events 'form one and the same Event, an event of the Aion where they have an eternal truth' (LS, 64).

The question is then: how are we to think the relation between individual events and this unique Event? Is it thinkable, in fact, as any sort of *relation* at all? How are we to think the being-together of 'fragments whose sole relationship is sheer difference – fragments that are related to one another only in that each of them is different'? (AO, 42). By 'relation' I mean a process that operates between two or more minimally discernible terms, in such a way as to condition or inflect (but not fully to generate) the individuality of each term. A relation is only a relation in this sense if its terms retain some limited autonomy with respect to each other. A relation is only a relation if it is *between* terms that can be meaningfully discerned, even if the means of this discernment proceed at the very limit of indiscernment. In other words, the question is: can Deleuze's theory of difference provide a coherent theory of relation between terms, for example, relations of conflict, solidarity, ambivalence, and so on (and thus a coherent theory of the circumstances and decisions that serve to orient relations between subjects, between priorities, between perspectives, between political classes…)? Or, on the contrary, is his theory of difference not only non-relative but non-relational as well?

Most commentary on Deleuze has tended to assume that what he's proposing is a relational account of being as difference. There might seem to be a fair amount of evidence for such a reading. Doesn't he privilege multiplicity over unity? Doesn't he denounce every recourse to a transcendent principle of individuation? Doesn't he emphasise the way becomings take place 'in the middle', in a 'between'? Doesn't he privilege *et* [and] over *est* [is] – the serial syntheses of the 'AND AND AND' over any definitive determination of what is? Doesn't he provide an account of the generation of ideas and problems in terms of the 'differential relations' modelled on the infinitesimal relations of calculus (dx/dy)?

The answer is of course yes, he does all these things – but he does them, nevertheless, in such a way as to ensure the exclusive primacy of non-relational difference, a notion of strictly intra-elemental rather than inter-elemental difference. From start to finish, Deleuze's concern is always with a logic of difference whereby, before it differs with other anything external to itself, a differing 'differs with itself first, immediately', on account of the internal and self-differing power that makes it what it is.[44] We know that what animates such force is a power of unconditional, self-affirming creation. What Deleuze calls 'an absolute, ultimate difference' is never an actual or 'empirical difference between two things or two objects' but rather is 'something like the presence of a final quality at the heart of a subject: an internal difference' (PS, 41). A differing differs itself by itself, and its determination of what is differed is immediate and absolute. An affirmation affirms itself by itself, on the basis of its own integrity; a creating does what it is, in the absence of any constituent relation either to other creatings or to the creature it creates. Think back to the example in Chapter 1, section IV, of Riderhood and the spark that individuates *a* life – we attain the beatitude of such a life only when the individual who incarnates it and who is alone capable of actively relating to other individuals is literally put out of action (so as to reveal the spark as the indefinite correlate of an immediate and impersonal intuition).

Given any relation of contradiction or negation between two terms, Deleuze's whole effort is to say that 'the opposition of two terms is only the realisation of the virtuality which contained them both' (DI, 43tm). No less than Simondon, Deleuze always affirms the primacy of disparity and 'disparation' over any form of relation, including relations of opposition, integration, tension, and so on (DI, 87). A becoming, which is to say a becoming-other, is not something that operates *between* two terms in the usual sense of this word, for instance via their antagonism, synthesis, or solidarity. Given a becoming that might seem to 'relate' two terms, what is properly at issue is 'a third which always comes from elsewhere and disturbs the binarity of the two, not so much inserting itself in their opposition as in their complementarity', i.e. in the process that 'carries them off' in a shared becoming-indiscernible (D, 131). Strictly speaking, multiplicities or becomings have no distinct terms at all, since whatever becomes is immediately 'taken up in another becoming' (TP, 238; cf. 249). In the end, what is eliminated in the Deleuzian conception of difference is 'simply all value that can be assigned to the terms of a relation [*un rapport*], for the gain of its inner reason, which precisely constitutes difference'. Difference will no longer exist primarily *between* the polygon and the circle, for instance, but rather 'in the pure variability of the sides of the polygon' (LB, 65). The parts of a desiring machine, likewise, exist in an anarchic dispersal that is held together only through 'the very absence of a link [*lien*]' (AO, 324). Such too is the lesson of Deleuze and Guattari's alternative to psychoanalysis: 'you will not have reached the ultimate and irreducible terms of the unconscious so long as you find or restore a *link* [*lien*] between two elements'.[45] The things collected together through a schizophrenic assemblage only cohere 'as a result of their having no relation' (RF, 18).

Absolute difference, in short, creates rather than relates what it differs. A differing that is not mediated by what it differs, a virtual event that is independent of any actual state of affairs, a creating that determines its creature – these are all processes that can only be interpreted in unilateral or non-relational terms. Once Deleuze rejects every notion of mediated difference he rejects any viable theory of inter-individual relation as well. The multiplication of virtual 'connections' that characterise any creative becoming or desire have nothing to do with relations between discernible terms: they proceed, on the contrary, through their indiscernment. The primary forces in Deleuze's universe are always processes subtracted from discernment as such. Any social configuration, for instance, is shaped first and foremost by forces of dissipation, dissemination, deterritorialisation, and so on – processes of distinction and actual differentiation are secondary. And since such deterritorialising 'lines of flight are the primary determinations', what requires explanation is not our ability to resist mechanisms of discernment and identity (since we *are* this ability) but rather the ordinarily stifling impact of such mechanisms (RF, 118; cf. 261).

At best, if Deleuze has a theory of relation it is one that makes relation indistinguishable from non-relation, i.e. one that makes it difficult to *relate* relation to non-relation – what I would prefer to call a non-relational theory of non-relation. Even those forms of 'reciprocal determination' he associates with the differential relations of dx/dy, as we saw in Chapter 2, section V, 'allow no independence whatsoever to subsist' among their elements (DR, 183). A differential relation is not a relation between two discernible terms, however indefinite they might be, so much as the primary power that generates and differentiates these very terms. In this as in every comparable case, individuation does not presuppose any actualisation or differenciation but 'gives rise to it'. Since 'every individuating factor is already difference and difference of difference', individuation does not proceed through the distinction of 'qualities and extensities, forms and matters, species and parts', but generates all these things as secondary phenomena of its own 'full, positive power' (DR, 247, 257–8). Or if you prefer, individuation is a relation conceived as a *pure* or absolute between, a between understood as fully independent of or external to its terms – and thus, a between that can just as well be described as 'between' nothing at all.

Deleuze encourages us to draw this conclusion in a number of ways. To begin with, he retains from Hume and the empiricists 'the truly fundamental proposition that relations are external to ideas [...]. We will call "nonempiricist" every theory according to which, in one way or another, relations are derived from the nature of things' (ES, 98, 109). Why are relations thus external to their terms? Terms figure here as distinct impressions, perceptions or ideas, which are given as primary. Relations (of causality, equality, similarity, distance, etc.) are then merely imposed upon terms by the subject who considers them. To quote Hume himself: 'since equality is a relation, it is not, strictly speaking, a property in the figures themselves, but arises merely from the comparison, which the mind makes betwixt them'.[46] Such a relation is discerned by mind once it has been subjected through the principles of association (and it is precisely this subjection, of course, which must then be undone by a philosophy oriented to a reality whose intensity explodes any merely subjective coherence). The mere effect of those principles of association which 'naturalise and give constancy to the mind' (ES, 100), relations figure here as entirely external and irrelevant to the processes through which ideas themselves are individuated. As a general rule, 'a multiplicity is never in terms, however many there are, nor in their set or totality. A multiplicity is only in the AND, which does not have the same nature as the elements, the sets or even their relations […]. The AND has a fundamental sobriety, a poverty, an ascesis' (D, 57). The AND is not itself properly a relation at all but rather the sufficient and animating principle of all relations.[47]

What Deleuze retains from the rational theophanists Spinoza and Leibniz is a stronger version of a similar configuration. In Spinoza, the essential distinction that must be preserved is the one between the immediately creative (or divine) process that determines *a* modal essence as a degree of absolute power, on the one hand, and the general laws of modal existence and interaction on the other (i.e. the laws in compliance with which a mode composes its earthly existence and its relations with other modal existences). 'We must, above all, avoid confusing essences and relations, or a law of production of essences and a law of composition of relations […] Relations are composed and decomposed according to their own laws' (EP, 211–12). Relations have no effect on the determination of essence, which remains forever primary and self-sufficient. Intermodal relations should simply be aligned with the coordinated development of nature or reality as an unfolding whole, on the model of a commonwealth that acts as 'a multitude which is guided, as it were, by one mind'.[48] We have seen how Leibniz's monads are likewise 'absolute forms' or 'primary forces, essentially individual and active primary unities […] that are in harmony with each other without any one being determined by the other' (LB, 103). Since they lack doors or windows, there can be no relations between monads. Whether it is inspired by Leibniz or Proust, Deleuze's conclusion is the same. 'Our only windows, our only doors are entirely spiritual; there is no intersubjectivity except an artistic one', precisely because an artist is not a subject at all (PS, 42).

Now as Deleuze notes in the larger of his two books on Spinoza, the question of a modal or monadic coordination is directly linked to the main difference between Leibnizian pluralism and Spinozist monism. 'If Leibniz recognises in things an inherent force of their own, he does so by making individual essences into so many substances. In Spinoza, on the other hand, this is done by defining particular essences as modal, and more generally, by making things themselves modes of a single substance.' Leibniz then has to coordinate this plurality by subjecting monads to the agreement of an externally imposed harmony or finality – in other words, Leibniz is forced to presume the transcendence of a divine purpose above and beyond the workings of the world, above the laws of mechanical motion, and so on. If then Deleuze insists that in the end he remains more of a Spinozist than a Leibnizian, it is above all because Spinoza has no need for any such externality, finality or transcendence. Since all that exists is a facet of one and the same dynamic substance, so then all that happens in the world is already coordinated by an 'absolutely immanent pure causality'.[49]

What then are we make of the twist that seems to set Deleuze apart from his rationalist predecessors – the fact that unlike Leibniz he affirms an 'incompossible' perspectivism (a discordant monadology, a theodicy without harmony or finality), the fact that against Spinoza he makes substance turn around the modes?[50] To my mind, these moves towards a still more radically divergent or differential conception of things serve only to intensify the non-relational orientation of Deleuze's theory of individuation. Whereas Leibniz compensates for the lack of monadic relations by coordinating them through God's selection of the best of all possible worlds, Deleuze stretches monadic divergence to the point where it can thought solely as the object of a still more radical or unconditional affirmation. Whereas Spinoza attributes the individuation of essence to substance, Deleuze multiplies and scatters it across the infinite dissemination of modes themselves, each of which becomes a sufficient creating in itself.[51] The effect (if there is an effect) is clearly to render the power of difference more absolute and more non-relational, rather than less. Rather than distinct facets of one and the same substance, the being-together of absolutely divergent modes can again only be thought via the pure affirmation of that unthinkable plane upon which their aberrant creating or deviant differing 'consists'.

As far as the idea of absolute creation itself is concerned, however, what does this change? No less than Martial Gueroult, Deleuze knows perfectly well that what 'unifies' the field of being or creation in Spinoza isn't the idea of substance per se but the notion of *God*, i.e. the notion of an 'infinity and perfection of essence'.[52] Nowhere in his work does Deleuze put in question such infinity or perfection; on the contrary, his philosophy presupposes them at every turn. Eventually, Deleuze will even recognise that this shift in attribution from substance to modes is already accomplished over the course of Spinoza's *Ethics* itself (RF, 177). To privilege modes over substance isn't itself to block the implied or implicative reality of a single and all-inclusive plane of immanence, any more than it denies, among other things, the 'uninterrupted continuum of the Body without Organs'. In the medium of desiring production, THE plane of consistency re-establishes the 'ontological unity of substance', precisely, by gathering together the 'totality of all BwOs'; this totalisation establishes nothing less than 'a continuum of all of the attributes or genuses of intensity under a single substance' (TP, 154). Deleuze never wavers in his affirmation of this immanent continuity. In any case, whether it be attributed to either substance or modes, what's clear is that the notion of infinite and self-grounding perfection is not itself up for qualification. And once carried to the absolute, there can be no 'substantial' difference between a purely self-differing unity and a purely self-scattering multiplicity, since in either case there is no place for any relational conception of 'self'.

More generally, one of the most characteristic features of Deleuze's work is his tendency to present what initially appears as a binary relation in such a way as to show that this relation is in fact determined by only one of its two 'terms'. The difference between active and reactive force, for instance, turns out to be internal to the self-differentiation of active force, which alone *is*. For the same reason, the apparent distinction (in *Kafka* and *Capitalism and Schizophrenia*) between a schizophrenic immanence and a paranoid transcendence is unilaterally subsumed by schizophrenia as 'universal primary production' (AO, 5) – in the end, the 'paranoid law gives way to a schizo-law' (K, 73). As the subject of universal desiring production, the schizo is 'not simply bisexual, or between the two, or intersexual', but 'transexual'. He does not reconcile opposed or contradictory elements by providing an occasion for their encounter or elaboration. Instead, he affirms pure disjunction 'through a continuous overflight spanning an indivisible distance'. He does not relate man to woman or adult to child; he immediately activates within himself 'this distance that transforms him into a woman', into a child, and so on

(AO, 76–7). Likewise, the difference between molar and molecular (or major and minor) forces turns out to be a difference of degree – molar forces are weakened versions of molecular forces, versions which have been captured within a transcendent framework of identity. There can consequently be 'no question of establishing a dualist opposition between the two types of multiplicities, molecular machines and molar machines [...]. There are not two multiplicities or two machines; one and the same machinic assemblage produces and distributes the whole' (TP, 34). If everywhere the molecular initially seems to exist 'with' the molar, nevertheless only the molecular is primary or productive. No deterritorialisation proceeds without a subsequent reterritorialisation, but what is invariably 'primary is an absolute deterritorialisation, an absolute line of flight, however complex or multiple – that of the plane of consistency or body without organs' (TP, 56; cf. 484–5). In this and every comparable case, 'dualism is therefore only a moment, which must lead to the re-formation of a monism'.[53] Reality is one of a kind, and it excludes relation along with negation and representation.

Of the many further illustrations of this point that recur in Deleuze's work, two last examples of its non-relational orientation might to help decide the argument: I extract them, more or less at random, from Deleuze's interpretation of Bacon's painting and from his account of structuralist methodology.

The artistic logic of sensation might seem to be a perfectly relational process, insofar as it envelops 'a plurality of constitutive domains' and continually 'passes from one "order" to another, from one "level" to another'. Nevertheless, the key to Deleuze's analysis turns on 'what makes up the sensing or sensed unity' of any particular passing (FB, 36–7). The separation of each level of sensation (as colour, taste, touch, etc.) is itself 'possible only if the sensation of a particular domain is in direct contact with a vital power that exceeds every domain and traverses them all. This power is rhythm, which is more profound than vision, hearing, etc. Rhythm appears as music when it invests the auditory level, and as painting when it invests the visual level'. Relations between or across senses, in other words, are themselves enabled by a singular power which determines the distribution of sense. The ultimate ground is this 'rhythmic unity of the senses', which can only be discovered by 'going beyond the organism'.[54]

A still more most suggestive example of such singular and unilateral determination is provided by Deleuze's answer to the question 'How do we recognise structuralism?' in an essay first published in 1967 (and then reworked in parts of *Difference and Repetition* and *Logic of Sense*). Based on readings of familiar texts by Lacan, Lévi-Strauss and Barthes, among others, this essay is perhaps the most accessible illustration of that differential logic which finds its purest and most difficult form in Deleuze's adaptation of post-Leibnizian calculus. In a first moment, what Deleuze presents as characteristic of a structuralist account might again appear to be relational through and through. Distinct places and functions emerge only in their difference with other places or functions, along the well-worn lines of Saussure's linguistics and its application in Lévi-Strauss's anthropology. The phonetic values of 'p' and 'b' emerge only in relation to each other; the same holds for places in an order of kinship (DI, 176). Phonetic or social structures are here distributed through the reciprocal determination of pure differentials, on the abstract model of dx/dy (where dy is undetermined in relation to y and dx is undetermined in relation to x, but where the relation dy/dx is 'totally' and 'reciprocally' determined). Lévi-Strauss's landmark reading of the Oedipus myth, for instance, is structured by the relations between two differential pairs (the overvaluation of kinship as opposed to its undervaluation; negation of the aboriginal or autochthonous origins of humanity as opposed to their affirmation). These unconscious differentials then determine the singular points that lend the myth its narrative trajectory (Oedipus is named club-foot, marries his mother, kills his father, dispatches the Sphinx, etc.), and the very 'terms of each series are in themselves inseparable from the slippages or displacements that they undergo in relation to the terms of the other' (DI, 183). Relations, here, would no longer seem to be external to their terms.

Up to this point, Deleuze's account remains perfectly conventional. What is distinctive about his reading of these structuralist texts depends on a second and unequivocally non-relational phase of the argument. Everything now depends on the isolation of a singular principle of individuation or differentiation, a virtual, aleatory and indefinite 'object = x'. This absolute object is what 'distributes series, displaces them relatively, makes them communicate with each other'. It is a sort of object-event. Deleuze's examples of such an object include Miller's non-identical zero, Lévi-Strauss's mana, Foucault's empty place of representation, Sollers' blind-spot. His most familiar example is the letter in Lacan's famous seminar on Poe's 'The Purloined Letter' – the letter which is forever missing from its place and that determines the positions taken up, in sequence, by the Queen, the minister, and Dupin. In each case, Deleuze insists that

> in fact, it is in relation to [this] object that the variety of terms and the variation of differential relations are determined in each case [...]. The *relative* places of the terms in the structure depend first on the *absolute* place of each, at each moment, in relation to the object = x that is always circulating, always displaced in relation to itself [...]. Distributing the differences through the entire structure, making the differential relations vary with its displacements, the object = x constitutes the differenciating element of difference itself (DI, 185–6).

It is this singular and self-differing displacement that 'drives the whole structure'. Differentiated structures are thus characterised by their symbolic form, their singularities, their differential relations – but 'above all, by the nature of the object = x that presides over their functioning'. Lacan's emphatically non-relational concept of the phallus, for instance, is precisely that which 'founds sexuality *in its entirety* as system or structure, and in relation to which the places occupied by men and women are distributed'. All by itself, the phallus 'determines the relative place of the elements and the variable value of relations'.[55]

And what is this object = x, this instance of pure self-displacement, if not another vehicle for the one and only force that is itself displaced and renewed through each of Deleuze's texts – the unilaterally and immediately determining force of absolute creation as such?

Conclusion

'From now on, therefore, we regard no one from a human
point of view; even though we once knew Christ from a
human point of view, we know him no longer in that way.
So if anyone is in Christ, there is a new creation: everything
old has passed away; see, everything has become new!'[1]

As Deleuze is the first to recognise, it is futile to argue about whether a philosophy or a
concept is literally right or wrong. Before you disagree with a work that is worthy of dis-
agreement, you have to admire it and rediscover the problems that it poses. 'You have to
work your way back to those problems which an author of genius has posed, all the way
back to that which he does not say in what he says, in order to extract something that
still belongs to him, though you also turn it against him. You have to be inspired, visited
by the geniuses you denounce' (DI, 139). A philosophy unworthy of admiration is
unworthy of critique. Before we embrace or reject a concept, what matters is to figure
out how it works, to appreciate what it allows you to do and to take stock of what it
prevents you from doing. A philosophy, after all, is nothing other than 'an elaborately
developed question; by itself and in itself it is not the resolution to a problem but the
elaboration, *to the very end*, of the necessary implications of a formulated question' (ES,
106; cf. WP, 27). What matters is the depth and provocative power of the question, in
comparison with other philosophical questions.

   This book has tried to show that Deleuze's work is itself guided by a single question,
the question of absolute creation, elaborated through the distinction of actual creatures
and virtual creatings. Deleuze's tireless engagement with this question allows him to
accomplish a good many things. Negatively, it allows him to mount an uncompromising
assault on notions of representation, of interiority, of interpretation, of mediation, of
figuration, and so on. It allows him to avoid any inane reverence for the other as much
as for the self. Positively, it allows him to revive a classical (or non-Kantian, non-critical)
tradition of metaphysics. It allows him to embrace an unabashedly 'inhuman' philosophical naturalism. It allows him to think artistic and conceptual innovation in dramatically
cosmological terms. It allows him to embrace a univocal and wholly affirmative conception of thought without collapsing the difference between subtraction and extinction. It
allows him to acknowledge that whatever genuinely acts, thinks or creates is less the work
of an individual than of forces that work *through* the individual – that every cogito masks

a deeper cogitor. It allows him, in short, to make the single most compelling contribution to an immanent understanding of creative thought since Spinoza. Along with his contemporaries Henry Corbin, Christian Jambet, and Michel Henry, Deleuze may eventually be remembered mainly for the part he played in the late-modern revival of a post-theophanic conception of thought.

What is distinctive about this contribution should be immediately obvious through even superficial comparison with several of his contemporaries – for instance Heidegger, Agamben and Foucault.

Martin Heidegger is the philosopher who revived the classical question of being, being insofar as it is not reducible to the merely ontic qualities of beings. No less than Deleuze, Heidegger affirms a dynamic conception of being that has more to do with the verb than the noun – being as creative process or event.[2] But he does so, at least to begin with, by framing it precisely in terms of being-in-the-*world*, on the one hand, and being within creatural or mortal *time* on the other.

Giorgio Agamben's work is in a sense poised between that of Heidegger and Deleuze. Like Deleuze, Agamben's chief concern lies with a creative virtuality or potentiality. Only if it is never fully enacted or actualised but remains open to an as yet indeterminate potentiality (itself based on a still deeper im-potentiality or withdrawal from action) can what Agamben calls a 'form of life' resist its ultimately murderous actualisation as merely 'bare' or disposable life.[3] It is because it retains this potential character, its capacity to both be and not-be, its capacity to exceed any actual identification, that indefinite or 'whatever-being' remains resistant to the increasingly coercive modern tendency to define and enclose life.[4] Unlike Deleuze, however, Agamben insists that '*there is truly potentiality only where the potentiality to not-be does not lag behind actuality but passes fully into it as such*. This does not mean that it disappears in actuality; on the contrary, it *preserves itself* as such in actuality.' This would be a 'potentiality that conserves itself and saves itself in actuality'.[5] Whereas Deleuze looks for ways to evacuate the creatural so as to renew the creating that sustains it, Agamben looks to bear witness to what *remains* of the creating within the creatural as such. For Agamben (after Benjamin), it is the creature qua creature that will be redeemed and it is the actual in its actuality that will regain its potential.[6]

A comparison with Deleuze's close friend Michel Foucault is still more instructive. The several points of convergence between their two philosophical perspectives have often been noted. The points of divergence, however, are no less fundamental. It is hard to imagine a more non-Deleuzian definition of thought than the one offered by Foucault in a late interview: 'thought is freedom in relation to what one does, the motion by which one detaches oneself from it, establishes it as an object, and reflects on it as a problem'.[7] Whereas Deleuze seeks to write a philosophy of creation without limits, Foucault writes a philosophy of the limit as such – a practice of thought that operates at the limits of classification, at the edge of the void that lies beyond every order of recognition or normalisation. Whereas Deleuze maintains an ultimately non-relational theory of difference, Foucault always affirmed 'the strictly relational character of power relationships'.[8] Whereas Deleuze would like to get rid of the relational subject altogether, Foucault wants to *purge* the subject, to eliminate everything that specifies or objectifies the subject (as deviant, perverse, criminal, as much as rational, sensible, law-abiding...). Whereas Deleuzian creatings or events presume a virtual but immediately adequate determining instance, Foucault's historically specific investigations are 'free of any constituent activity, disengaged from any reference to an origin' or foundation.[9]

Even Foucault's early essays like 'Preface to Transgression' (1963) and 'Thought from the Outside' (1966), the essays in which he is no doubt closest to Deleuzian concerns, what is mainly at issue is not the liberation of a singular creative energy so much as the absence of determination that confronts a fully de-specified subject. In all the limit experiences that Foucault garners from Bataille, Roussel, Artaud and others, the void which defines their limit remains precisely that: void. It is the 'absolute void' or 'essential emptiness' left by the dissolution of the classical subject that resonates in Foucault's early essays.[10] Quite unlike Deleuze's plane of immanence (which lacks nothing), Foucault's 'outside cannot offer itself as a positive presence – as something inwardly illuminated by the certainty of its own existence – but only as an absence that pulls as far away from itself as possible'.[11] So when Foucault carefully distinguishes his outside from any merely mystical intuition, he also provides us with a useful way of distinguishing his position from Deleuze's cosmic vitalism. 'The characteristic movement of mysticism', says Foucault, 'is to attempt to join – even if it means crossing the night – the positivity of an existence by opening a difficult line of communication with it', i.e., by becoming one with the creative presence that sustains the world. But, Foucault continues, 'the experience of the outside has nothing to do with that [...]. It opens a neutral space in which no existence can take root.'[12] At this radical edge of the specific, subtracted from every positive specification, what individuates an individual, writer, or work is simply 'its own particular way of being anonymous', its particular way of evading specification.[13] Contrary to what we might initially expect, it may be that Foucault's work has less in common with Deleuze's subtractive vitalism than with Badiou's still more subtractive pursuit of the generic as such.

Now Deleuze understands perfectly well why 'most of the objections raised against the great philosophers are empty'. Indignant readers say to them: 'things are not like that [...]. But, in fact, it is not a matter of knowing whether things are like that or not; it is a matter of knowing whether the question which presents things in such a light is good or not, rigorous or not' (ES, 106). Rather than test its accuracy according to the criteria of representation, 'the genius of a philosophy must first be measured by the new distribution which it imposes on beings and concepts' (LS, 6). In reality then, Deleuze concludes, 'only one kind of objection is worthwhile: the objection which shows that the question raised by a philosopher is not a good question', that it 'does not force the nature of things enough' (ES, 107; cf. WP, 82).

Deleuze certainly forces the nature of things into conformity with his own question. Just as certainly, however, his question inhibits any consequential engagement with the constraints of our actual world. For readers who remain concerned with these constraints and their consequences, Deleuze's question is not the best available question.

Rather than try to refute Deleuze, this book has tried to show how his system works and to draw attention to what should now be the obvious (and perfectly explicit) limitations of this philosophy of unlimited affirmation.

First of all, since it acknowledges only a unilateral relation between virtual and actual, there is no place in Deleuze's philosophy for any notion of change, time or history that is mediated by actuality. In the end, Deleuze offers few resources for thinking the consequences of what happens within the actually existing world as such. Unlike Darwin or Marx, for instance, the adamantly virtual orientation of Deleuze's 'constructivism' does not allow him to account for cumulative transformation or novelty in terms of actual materials and tendencies. No doubt few contemporary philosophers have had as an acute a sense of the internal dynamic of capitalism – but equally, few have proposed so elusive a response as the virtual 'war machine' that roams through the pages of *Capitalism and Schizophrenia*. Like the nomads who invented it, this abstract machine operates at an 'absolute speed, by being "synonymous with speed"', as the incarnation of 'a pure and immeasurable multiplicity [...], an irruption of the ephemeral and of the power of metamorphosis' (TP, 386, 352). Like any creating, a war machine consists and 'exists only in its own metamorphoses' (TP, 360). By posing the question of politics in the starkly dualistic terms of war machine *or* state – by posing it, in the end, in the apocalyptic terms of a new people and a new earth or else no people and no earth – the political aspect of Deleuze's philosophy amounts to little more than utopian distraction.

Although no small number of enthusiasts continue to devote much energy and ingenuity to the task, the truth is that Deleuze's work is essentially indifferent to the politics of this world.[14] A philosophy based on deterritorialisation, dissipation and flight can offer only the most immaterial and evanescent grip on the mechanisms of exploitation and domination that continue to condition so much of what happens in our world. Deleuze's philosophical war remains 'absolute' and 'abstract', precisely, rather than directed or 'waged' [*menée*].[15] Once 'a social field is defined less by its conflicts and contradictions than by the lines of flight running through it',[16] any distinctive space for political action can only be subsumed within the more general dynamics of creation or life. And since these dynamics are themselves anti-dialectical if not anti-relational, there can be little room in Deleuze's philosophy for relations of conflict or solidarity, i.e. relations that are genuinely *between* rather than external to individuals, classes, or principles.

Deleuze writes a philosophy of (virtual) difference without (actual) others. He intuits a purely internal or self-differing difference, a difference that excludes any constitutive mediation between the differed. Such a philosophy precludes a distinctively relational conception of politics as a matter of course. The politics of the future are likely to depend less on virtual mobility than on more resilient forms of cohesion, on more principled forms of commitment, on more integrated forms of coordination, on more resistant forms of defence. Rather than align ourselves with the nomadic war machine, our first task should be to develop appropriate ways of responding to the newly aggressive techniques of invasion, penetration and occupation which serve to police the embattled margins of empire. In a perverse twist of fate, it may be that today, in places like Palestine, Haiti and Iraq, the agents of imperialism have more to learn from Deleuzian rhizomatics than do their opponents.[17]

As we have repeatedly seen, the second corollary of Deleuze's disqualification of actuality concerns the paralysis of the subject or actor. Since what powers Deleuze's cosmology is the immediate differentiation of creation through the infinite proliferation of virtual creatings, the creatures that actualise these creatings are confined to a derivative if not limiting role. A creature's own interests, actions or decisions are of minimal or preliminary significance at best: the renewal of creation always requires the paralysis and dissolution of the creature per se. The notion of a constrained or situated freedom, the notion that a subject's own decisions might have genuine consequences – the whole notion, in short, of *strategy* – is thoroughly foreign to Deleuze's conception of thought. Deleuze obliges us, in other words, to make an *absolute* distinction between what a subject does or decides and what is done or decided through the subject. By rendering this distinction absolute he abandons the category of the subject altogether. He abandons the decisive subject in favour of our more immediate subjection to the imperatives of creative life or thought.

Deprived of any strategic apparatus, Deleuze's philosophy thus combines the self-grounding sufficiency of pure force or infinite perfection with our symmetrical limitation to pure contemplation or in-action. On the one hand, Deleuze always maintains that 'there are never any criteria other than the tenor of existence, the intensification of life'. Absolute life or creation tolerates no norm external to itself. The creative movement that orients us *out* of the world does not depend on a transcendent value *beyond* the world. After Spinoza, after Nietzsche, Deleuze rejects all forms of moral evaluation or strategic judgement. Every instance of decision, every confrontation with the question 'what should we do?', is to be resolved exclusively in terms of what we *can* do. An individual's power or capacity is also its 'natural right', and the answer to the question of what an individual or body should do is again simplicity itself – it should go and will always go 'as far as it can' (WP, 74; EP, 258). But on the other hand, we know that an individual can only do this because its power is not that of the individual itself. By doing what it can, an individual only provides a vessel for the power that works through it, and which alone acts – or rather, which alone *is*. What impels us to 'persevere in our being' has nothing to do with us as such.

So when, in the conclusion of their last joint project, Deleuze and Guattari observe that 'vitalism has always had two possible interpretations', it is not surprising that they should opt for the resolutely in-active interpretation. Vitalism, they explain, can be conceived either in terms of 'an Idea that acts but is not, and that acts therefore only from the point of view of an external cerebral knowledge; or of a force that is but does not act, and which is therefore a pure internal Feeling [*Sentir*]'. Deleuze and Guattari embrace this second interpretation, they choose Leibnizian being over Kantian act, precisely because it disables action in favour of contemplation. It suspends any relation between a living and the lived, between a knowing and the known, between a creating and the created. They embrace it because what feeling 'preserves is always in a state of detachment in relation to action and even to movement, and appears as a pure contemplation without knowledge'.[18]

As Deleuze understands it, living contemplation proceeds at an immeasurable distance from what is merely lived, known or decided. Life lives and creation creates on a virtual plane that leads forever out of our actual world.

Few philosophers have been as inspiring as Deleuze. But those of us who still seek to change our world and to empower its inhabitants will need to look for our inspiration elsewhere.

Notes

Introduction

1 Deleuze, 'On Philosophy' (1988), N, 136.

2 Deleuze, 'Cours Vincennes: Leibniz', 15 April 1980, available online at http://www.web-deleuze.com/php/texte.php?cle=48&groupe=Leibniz&langue=1.

3 In this as in so many aspects of his philosophy, Deleuze follows Spinoza's lead. From a Spinozist perspective, 'the identity of power and essence means: power is always an act or, at least, acting [*en acte*]' (EP, 93tm). Every Deleuzian verb should be understood on the model provided by Spinoza's *naturare*, 'to nature', a process that immediately divides into an actively naturing (*naturans*) and a passively natured (*naturata*). It is perhaps no accident that the term 'expression' which Deleuze adopts as the basis for his reading of Spinoza is only used by Spinoza himself in the verbal form of *exprimere* (e.g. Spinoza, *Ethics* ID6). As Pierre Macherey notes, 'the order of expression does not correspond to a system of things, frozen in the inert reality that their names designate, but is nature in so far as it is effected in action' (Macherey, 'Deleuze in Spinoza', *In a Materialist Way*, 123).

4 Spinoza, *Ethics* V36P.

5 Nietzsche, *Ecce Homo* I, §8; *Ecce Homo* II §9.

6 K, 13; cf. TP, 31–3, 248, 273.

7 TP, 279; cf. D, 45; C2, 190.

8 See below, Chapter 4, section I.

9 See in particular Prigogine and Stengers, *La Nouvelle alliance*, 387–9.

10 See in particular Christian Jambet, 'The Stranger and Theophany', 27–41. Jambet describes theophany as 'a way of perceiving what exists in such a way as to confer upon it, without delay, the strange power of reflecting divine operations […]. Theophany is the determinate existing thing itself when the absolute does not absent itself from it but offers itself in the mode of a paradoxical presence' (27).

11 On the very rare occasions when Deleuze himself mentions Eriugena, it is in order to emphasise his failure (by comparison with Spinoza) to affirm a fully immanent theory of creation or expression, i.e. his characteristically Neoplatonic reliance upon a transcendent creator. Cf. EP, 177–8, 180.

12 Eriugena, *Periphyseon* III 681A.

13 Eriugena, *Periphyseon* III 678C, V 982C.

14 Eriugena, *Periphyseon* II 528B.

15 Ibn al-'Arabi, *Les Gemmes de la sagesse*, in Corbin, *L'Imagination créatrice*, 147.

16 Hegel, *Science of Logic*, 538–9. The 'oriental theory of absolute identity […] of the finite and

the infinite in God […,] all this is an echo from Eastern lands' (Hegel, *Lectures on the History of Philosophy*, vol. 3, 252).

17 LB, 72. As Deleuze and Guattari will conclude in their final joint project, 'the grandiose Leibnizian or Bergsonian perspective whereby every philosophy depends upon one intuition that its concepts constantly develop through slight differences of intensity is justified if intuition is conceived as the envelopment of infinite movements of thought that constantly pass through a plane of immanence' (WP, 40tm).

18 EP, 321; ES, 106tm; cf. WP, 4–5, 27.

1 The Conditions of Creation

1 Spinoza, *Ethics* IP36D, quoted EP, 13–14; TP, 43.

2 WP, 59–60, 48; cf. N, 140. Rather than merely influenced by Spinoza, there is a real sense in which Deleuze strives to participate in the co-creation of Spinoza's own work. Macherey puts it very well: Deleuze's project involves 'dynamically producing, rather than reproducing, the intellectual movement through which [Spinoza's] philosophy has become what it is. Instead of "following" Spinoza […] it is as if Deleuze preceded him' (Macherey, 'Deleuze in Spinoza', *In a Materialist Way*, 120).

3 Hegel, *Lectures on the History of Philosophy*, vol. 3, 281. Hegel goes too far, however, when he draws from this refusal the conclusion that 'there is therefore no such thing as finite reality' (281).

4 Spinoza, *Ethics* IP15, IP17S1.

5 TP, 153, 335; cf. LB, 7; ES, 119.

6 AO, 19tm, 87. Or again, the 'coextension of man and nature [is] a circular movement by which the unconscious, always remaining subject, produces and reproduces itself […]. The sole subject of reproduction is the unconscious itself' (AO, 107–8).

7 DI, 154. 'The human mind has an adequate knowledge of God's eternal and infinite essence' (Spinoza, *Ethics* IIP47).

8 Spinoza, *Ethics* IIP40S2.

9 N, 143. 'The essential thing for me [is] this "vitalism", or a conception of life as non-organic energy' (Deleuze, Lettre-Préface, in Buydens, *Sahara*, 5; cf. FC, 93; B, 106–7; DI, 103).

10 Hardt, *Deleuze*, 59.

11 DI, 39; EP, 39; DR, 57; cf. NP, 23.

12 EP, 172. As defined in the *Catholic Encyclopaedia*, 'immanence is the quality of any action which begins and ends within the agent'.

13 DR, 32. What holds the notion of being together, for Aristotle, is not the singularity of an exclusive sense but rather relations of analogy that apply across its various senses, and that group them around the most essential or eminent of these meanings (namely, the meaning of being as substance). Cf. Aristotle, *Metaphysics*, 1030a-b.

14 Deleuze, 'Bergson's Conception of Difference', DI, 42tm. Michel Henry will arrive at a similar conclusion: the manifesting or 'revelation of absolute being is not separate from it, is nothing external to it, nothing unreal, is not an image of being but resides in it, in its reality as identical to it, as being itself' (Henry, *Essence de la manifestation*, 859).

15 Bergson, *Creative Evolution*, 271, 250.

16 Bergson, *Creative Evolution*, 212. On the spiritualist orientation of Bergson's work, see in particular Jankélévitch, *Henri Bergson*, 86, 95, 247–52.

17 Bergson, *Creative Evolution*, 248–9.

18 Bergson, *The Two Sources of Morality and Religion*, 101.

19 TP, 382–3.

20 DI, 30tm; Leibniz, Letter to von Hessen-Rheinfels 12 April 1686, in Leibniz, *Philosophical Texts*, 99.

21 WP, 59–60; TP, 254–5; 'The Actual and the Virtual', 149tm.

22 See for example C2, 83; NP, 72.

23 NP, 24. Alain Badiou is perfectly right, therefore, to describe Deleuze as 'the most radical thinker of the One since Bergson' – so long as we remember that this 'One is already in itself nothing other than the power by which its immanent modes occur', that it figures as 'the infinite reservoir of dissimilar productions', that it is only 'immutable qua perpetual mutation' (Badiou, *Deleuze*, 80, 68–9, 91; cf. Hallward, 'Deleuze and Redemption from Interest' [1997]; 'Deleuze and the World Without Others' [1997]).

24 C1, 9, quoting Bergson, *Creative Evolution*, 340; cf. PS, 130. The most influential critique of Bergsonian continuity as a limit imposed upon creativity *in the present* remains Gaston Bachelard's *The Dialectic of Duration*, first published in 1936. Bergson's insistence on temporal continuity, Bachelard argues, necessarily excludes the dimension of the transformative 'instant' or 'event', and ensures that 'the present can create nothing' (Bachelard, *Dialectic*, 58, 24–5). Badiou's critique of Deleuze involves a similar argument and a comparable valorisation of discontinuity and of 'interruption' (Badiou, *Deleuze*, 64–5).

25 Bergson, *Creative Evolution*, 309.

26 Bergson, *Matter and Memory*, 16; Bergson, *The Creative Mind*, 141.

27 Bergson, *Matter and Memory*, 183.

28 Bergson, *Creative Evolution*, 7.

29 NP, 4; B, 74. One of Deleuze's main criticisms of Bergson is simply that his way of privileging the intensive and the spiritual over the extensive or spatial wrongly attributes to 'quality everything that belongs to intensive quantities' (DR, 239).

30 TP, 51. As Uexküll explains, in this way 'the whole rich world around the tick shrinks and changes into a scanty framework consisting, in essence, of three receptor cues and three effector cues' (Uexküll, 'A Stroll through the Worlds of Animals and Men', 12).

31 NP, 8. From a Nietzschean perspective, any given 'object itself is force, expression of a force' and 'all reality is already quantity of force' (NP, 6, 40). Since any given 'force is appropriation, domination, exploitation of a quantity of reality' (3), so then 'difference in quantity is the essence of force and of the relation of force to force' (43). This is why Nietzsche suggests that 'the attempt should be made to see whether a scientific order of values could be constructed simply on a numerical and quantitative scale of force. All other "values" are prejudices, naiveties and misunderstandings. They are everywhere reducible to this numerical and quantitative scale' (Nietzsche, *Will to Power* §710, quoted in NP, 43).

32 EP, 197, 183, 191; cf. DR, 77, TP, 257.

33 Leibniz, in DR, 84; cf. LB, 58, 110. Compared to Leibniz, Spinoza is simply the more insistently univocal of the two (EP, 333).

34 Bergson, *Creative Evolution*, 265–70.

35 Bergson, *The Two Sources of Morality and Religion*, 220–1; cf. B, 112.

36 Bergson, *Two Sources*, 229, 99, 311, 232.

37 C1, 9, quoting Bergson, *Creative Evolution*, 340; cf. PS, 130.

38 Bergson, *Duration and Simultaneity*, 47, quoted in B, 82.

39 Bergson, *Two Sources*, 234, 255.

40 Bergson, *Two Sources*, 255–7.

41 Bergson, *Two Sources*, 257.

42 DI, 13–14. Deleuze will return to a number of these themes, almost word for word, in a review of Michel Tournier's 1967 novel *Vendredi* (LS, 301–21). See below, Chapter 4, section III.

43 Dickens, *Our Mutual Friend*, 443–5, 446–7.

44 'Immanence: A Life…' (1995), PI, 28–9; cf. Agamben, *Potentialities*, 229.

45 TP, 265. Deleuze and Guattari draw here, as elsewhere, on Maurice Blanchot's exploration of the impersonal third person French pronoun *on* (as in *on meurt, on parle*); cf. Blanchot, *L'Entretien infini*, 556–7.

46 Meister Eckhart takes the point to its logical conclusion: 'If a person turns away from self and from all created things, then – to the extent that you do this – you will attain to oneness and blessedness in your soul's spark, which time and place never touched. This spark is opposed to all creatures; it wants nothing but God, naked, just as he is' (Eckhart, *Sermons and Treatises*, vol. 2, 105).

2 Actual Creatures, Virtual Creatings

1 D, 125. In their revised version of this account, which makes up the ninth plateau of *A Thousand Plateaus*, Deleuze and Guattari present the field of individuation in terms of two 'poles'. On the one hand, there are actually or rigidly individuated elements. On the other hand there is 'an abstract machine of mutation' which, itself absolutely deterritorialised, is 'what draws the lines of flight' and 'assures the connection-creation of flows'. Multiple and individual creatings then take place between these two poles, across 'a whole realm of properly molecular negotiation, translation, and transduction' through which, in one and the same time, creatings come to be consolidated in creatures or else extinguished in 'black holes', and creatures come to identify with their constituted actuality or else escape it through counter-actualisation (TP, 223–4).

2 Corbin, *Histoire*, 78–9.

3 Leibniz, *Theodicy*, 51.

4 WP, 42. This difference between sustainable creation and the risk of anarchic chaos is itself fundamental to the difference between Spinoza and Leibniz on the one hand and Descartes on the other – and after them, between the Deleuze who follows the former, and the Badiou who follows the latter. Unlike Leibniz, Descartes accepts no internal rules of reason that might govern creation, i.e. that might constrain God to create in a certain way. The Cartesian god creates literally ex nihilo, through an unregulated power of invention that is both eternal and spontaneous. From a Leibnizian perspective, such a conception of creation absolutises it in a way that blunts its difference from chaos, i.e. from a world of pure contingency or discontinuity. As Bergson will later put it, this would be 'a world that dies and is reborn at every instant, the world which Descartes was thinking of when he spoke of continued creation' (*Creative Evolution*, 22). Creation as discontinuous, abrupt, and thus potentially unsustainable or abstract, vs. creation as continuous, sustained, and thus potentially indistinct or inconsequential: in a nutshell, this is the whole difference between Badiou and Deleuze.

5 Spinoza, *Ethics* IP29S.

6 Spinoza, *Ethics* IIP45.

7 Spinoza, *Ethics*, VP29S. Whereas the object of an actual mind is its actual or existent body, the idea of a body's essence is itself eternal (cf. Donagan, *Spinoza*, 197–200).

8 Spinoza, *Ethics* VP36S. This conclusion is the key to understanding Spinoza's famous *conatus* principle, which might easily be misinterpreted as an affirmation of merely individuated actuality. According to Spinoza, all individuals naturally strive to persevere in being what they are, or in doing all that they can do. An actual mind will instinctively strive, first and foremost, to affirm itself, the existence of its actual body and its appetites and desires (IIIP9-P10). Insofar as an individual acts as passively individuated, its striving is drastically limited by its own weakness and by the interference of other individuals. However, the force by which any given singular thing 'perseveres in existing follows from the eternal necessity of God's nature' (IIP45S), not from its 'own' particularity. Though 'desire is the very essence of man' (IVP18D), what we desire is precisely to know ourselves as aspects of divine nature. Our 'mind's power, or nature, or its great striving, is to understand things' just as God understands them, i.e. by an immediate intuition of the essence that creates them (VP25D; cf. IVP28).

9 Deleuze, 'Bergson's Conception of Difference', DI, 44, 42; cf. SP, 97–8.

10 Bergson, *Matter and Memory*, 31, 158; cf. C1, 63–4; C2, 20, 45.

11 Bergson, *Matter and Memory*, 138–9.

12 See in particular Ansell-Pearson's *Germinal Life* (1999) and his *Philosophy and the Adventure of the Virtual* (2002).

13 Bergson, *Matter and Memory*, 106.

14 'The objective is that which has no virtuality – whether realised or not, whether possible or real, everything is actual in the objective' (B, 41).

15 Bergson, *Matter and Memory*, 151.

16 C2, 80; cf. C2, 54–5; 98; B, 56–9.

17 Bergson, *Matter and Memory*, 140.

18   Our tendency to think of the virtual in terms of the actual is a literally fundamental illusion. Although he understands its implications in a completely different way, Bergson agrees with Kant's assertion that 'reason deep within itself engenders not mistakes but inevitable illusions, only the effect of which could be warded off [...]. The illusion is based in the deepest part of intelligence: it is not, strictly speaking, dispelled or dispellable, rather it can only be repressed' (B, 20–1).

19   As de Beistegui points out, the distinction of actual from virtual does not violate univocity but establishes it, since only this distinction 'can provide a genetic account of actual systems' without reference to any classical distinction between form and matter (de Beistegui, *Truth and Genesis*, 272–3).

20   Bergson, 'Memory of the Present and False Recognition', *Key Writings*, 147.

21   'If it was not already past at the same time as present, the present would never pass on' (C2, 79; cf. B, 58–60, DR, 76–82; PS, 57–9).

22   See in particular DeLanda, *Intensive Science and Virtual Philosophy* (2002); Massumi, *A User's Guide to Capitalism and Schizophrenia* (1992); Massumi, *Parables for the Virtual* (2002); and Ansell-Pearson's *Germinal Life* (1999). I will briefly take up the case of biology and complexity theory towards the end of this chapter. Several mathematical theories, in particular a version of calculus that Deleuze adapts from Leibniz in an especially dense section of *Difference and Repetition*, provide other important arenas for the distinction of the virtual and actual: Daniel Smith provides characteristically clear accounts in his essays 'Badiou and Deleuze on the Ontology of Mathematics' [2004] and 'Deleuze's Philosophy of Mathematics' [2005]).

23   'The Actual and the Virtual', *Dialogues II* (2002 ed.), 149–150tm. Moreover, the closer the process of actualisation comes to that of creation pure and simple, so then virtual and actual tend towards a single indistinction, a single process of 'crystallisation' — and this singular process is itself virtual, precisely (151).

24   'Immanence: A Life...', PI, 28–9.

25   See for instance DR, 211–12; CC, 153.

26   As is now well known, Antonio Negri has long sought to develop a comparably neo-Spinozist account of constituent power, rigorously distinguished from every constituted form of government or state. See in particular Negri, *Insurgencies* (1992).

27   Bergson, *Creative Evolution*, 248–9.

28   DeLanda, *Intensive Science*, 15.

29   The first or extensive kind of multiplicity 'is a multiplicity of exteriority, of simultaneity, of juxtaposition, of order [...], it is a numerical multiplicity, *discontinuous and actual*. The other type of multiplicity appears in pure duration: it is an internal multiplicity [...], a *virtual and continuous* multiplicity that cannot be reduced to numbers' (B, 38).

30   EP, 110. This is why 'parallelism, strictly speaking, is to be understood [...] only from the viewpoint of an immanent God and immanent causality' (109); see below, Chapter 4, section II.

31   Spinoza, *Ethics* IIP11, IIP13.

32   Spinoza, *Ethics* IIP7S.

33   Spinoza, *Ethics* IIP2; IP15S1. The fact that human minds usually think of 'infinite, unique, and indivisible' extension as divisible, according to Spinoza (again in anticipation of Bergson), is just a result of habit and facility, in particular of our habitual reliance on the imagination, rather than the intellect (IP15S5).

34   Woolhouse, *Descartes, Spinoza, Leibniz*, 50.

35   RF, 215. If Deleuze privileges an apparently causal logic in Spinoza (for whom to know something is to know its cause), this is of course because Spinoza equates causation with creation itself. As absolute power of creation, God is the cause of all things. Spinoza's achievement is thus precisely to 'free expression from any subordination to emanative or exemplary causality' (EP, 180), i.e. from any transitive relation between a cause (over here) and its effect (over there). What Spinoza provides, and what remains missing in Descartes, is a principle of 'reason through which self-causality can be arrived at in itself, and directly grounded in the concept or nature of God' (EP, 164).

36   Deleuze, 'Bergson's Conception of Difference', DI, 51tm. 'A thing in itself and in its true nature is the expression of a tendency prior to being the effect of a cause', since 'causes are always

derived retroactively from the product itself' (34). Nietzsche had already anticipated the point: 'Cause and effect – a dangerous concept so long as one thinks of something that causes and something upon which an effect is produced' (Nietzsche, *Will to Power*, §552).

37 WP, 156. An immanent act of creating inheres in the creatures to which it gives rise, but is not itself, of course, a creature – 'this is why we cannot say that sense exists, but rather that it inheres or subsists' (LS, 21).

38 LS, 100–1; cf. FC, 121; TP, 71–2.

39 'Immanence: A Life', PI, 31–2.

40 Bogue, *Deleuze on Literature*, 23; cf. LS, 4.

41 LS, 182. 'The event has a different nature than the actions and the passions of the body. But it results from them, since sense is the incorporeal effect of corporeal causes and their mixtures. It is always therefore in danger of being snapped up by its cause. It escapes and affirms its irreducibility only to the degree […] that it is linked, at the surface, to a quasi-cause which is itself incorporeal' – i.e. an event (LS, 94).

42 Arguably, there is no single issue more difficult to untangle in the whole of Deleuze's oeuvre than this relation, in *Logic of Sense*, between surface and depth. There isn't space here to do more than suggest the outlines of a possible interpretation, in three moments.

In a first moment, Deleuze appears to insist unequivocally on the primacy of the causal depths, conceived as 'formless, fathomless nonsense', as the 'terrible primordial order' (LS, 82) that is suffered in schizophrenia and that was explored by Nietzsche and Artaud (129, 93). The experience of depth passes through the collapse of surface and sense.

In a second and more emphatic moment, however, 'all height and depth [are] abolished' in favour of the surface and the '*savoir-faire* of the pure event' (LS, 141). 'Surface is the transcendental field itself, and the locus of sense and expression. Sense is that which is formed and deployed at the surface' (125). The creative force of 'free and unbound energy' that Nietzsche helps us to discover 'is not an undifferentiated abyss, it leaps from one singularity to another', from one sense-event to another (107). Surface now seems to prevail over depth: 'no, one does not fall into an undifferentiated ground, into groundless depth, when one undoes the individual and the person […]. Deeper than any other ground is the surface and the skin' (140–1). Deleuze will eventually ask the question directly: 'How can we maintain both that sense produces even the states of affairs [i.e., bodies, causes] in which it is embodied, and that it is itself produced by these states of affairs or the actions and passions of bodies (an immaculate conception)?' His answer again confirms the primacy of surface and of incorporeal events: 'individuation in bodies, the measure in their mixtures […] – this entire order presupposes sense and the pre-individual and impersonal neutral field within which it unfolds' (124).

But this answer will only become unambiguous, I think, when in a third and final moment, the moment of *Anti-Oedipus*, he and Guattari eliminate the whole problem of a relation between depth-cause and surface-creation in favour of an exclusive affirmation of the latter. In *Anti-Oedipus*, all of the psychoanalytic concepts that Deleuze struggles so hard to retain in the final section of *Logic of Sense,* and that effectively mediate between surface and depth – castration, lack, the sublimation of drives, Oedipus itself – are finally ditched as mere obstacles to any properly immanent theory of production or creation. From now on, the univocity of being will inhere within a single *plane* of reality. One symptom of this shift is particularly telling: Artaud's schizophrenic 'body without organs', the paradigm of heroic depth and obscurity in *Logic of Sense*, will figure as 'plane of immanence' and 'surface of inscription' in *Capitalism and Schizophrenia*. Asked about *Logic of Sense* five years after it was published, Deleuze responded tersely: 'I've undergone a change. The surface–depth opposition no longer concerns me' (DI, 261; cf. RF, 60; N, 144).

43 Cf. LS, 67–70. Deleuze and Guattari's own use of the term 'rhizome' makes it operate as a non-sense word in much the same way. The name rhizome proliferates in much the way a rhizome itself does; rhizome is a word which denotes its sense, it is a non-sense which distributes sense all through the pages of *A Thousand Plateaus* – 'the rhizome is a map' (TP, 12); 'the rhizome is an antimemory' (14); 'becoming is a rhizome' (239); 'a haecceity is a rhizome' (263); 'the phylum is a kind of rhizome' (415); 'a rhizome is made of plateaus' (21), etc. – so as to articulate that more inclusive

sense-event which governs the whole creative field: 'RHIZOMATICS = SCHIZOANALYSIS = STRATOANALYSIS = PRAGMATICS = MICROPOLITICS' (22).

44 LB, 44–5. All existent monads are by definition compatible with all other monads. The monad Adam, for instance, with his singular qualities of 'being the first man' and 'being guilty of original sin', is 'compossible with all the monads whose singularities converge with its own' (LB, 64). Such convergence is what defines the world that we and Adam share. The monad Adam the non-sinner is not a contradiction in itself but implies a wholly alternative world, incompossible with our own. If Deleuze himself, unlike Leibniz, affirms such incompossibility as the ultimate horizon of a philosophy of pure difference, i.e. of an absolutely unfettered creation, this is because he is a *more* rather than less non-relational thinker than Leibniz; I'll come back to this point briefly in Chapter 6, section V.

45 DI, 94tm. 'We call the determination of the virtual content of an Idea differentiation; we call the actualisation of that virtuality into species and distinguished parts differenciation' (DR, 207).

46 EP, 99. Or as Eckhart puts it: 'He who possesses the whole world with God would have no more than if he had God by himself' (Eckhart, *Sermons and Treatises*, vol. 1, 284).

47 LS, 81. Virtual or creative 'intensity remains implicated in itself and continues to envelop difference at the very moment when it is reflected in the extensity and the quality that it creates, which implicate it only secondarily' (DR, 240).

48 DR, 105; cf. CB, 91–2, 114–15.

49 Artaud, *Oeuvres complètes*, vol. 3, 76, quoted in C2, 170–2.

50 'How Do We Recognise Structuralism', DI, 184–9; cf. DR, 105–7; LS, 71.

51 DI, 28. As Bergson puts it, our errors arise from 'our habit of transposing into fabrication what is creation' (*Creative Evolution*, 95).

52 'The Actual and the Virtual', 151tm.

53 TP, 71ff; 'The Actual and the Virtual', 149.

54 Bergson, 'Introduction to Metaphysics', *Creative Mind*, 190.

55 DR, 170–82. It was in order to measure effectively virtual quantities that Leibniz and Newton first developed the calculus of differential ratios (I draw here on the much simplified explanation provided by Davis and Hersh in their textbook *The Mathematical Experience*, 242–5). Calculus allows us to measure things like the acceleration of moving objects, i.e. the rate at which an object's speed changes over time. The paradigmatic example is the acceleration of a falling stone as it drops from a given height towards the ground. Simple observation shows that gravity makes the stone accelerate at a rate of around 32 feet per second, or 20 miles per hour). It is then very easy to measure the *average* speed of our stone, which is to say the amount of space it traverses over a particular length of time: the relationship between the changing position of the stone to its changing speed can be (approximately) expressed according to a simple equation, $s = 16t^2$, where s is the number of feet travelled by the stone and t is the number of seconds that have elapsed since it began to fall. By definition, the measurement of this kind of relationship remains a function of what Deleuze would call actual or 'extended' quantities. But what about the measurement of the stone's speed at any given instant – its 'instantaneous velocity'? Since there is surely an essential difference between a moving stone and a motionless stone, there must be *some* way of expressing this motion even during the briefest conceivable instant. How fast is our stone travelling, for instance, exactly one second after it begins to fall, at the precise point where $t = 1$?

Leibniz introduced the useful but problematic notion of infinitesimal (or immeasurably small) numbers to 'measure' instantaneous speeds of this kind. Infinitesimals are numbers that are smaller than any finite or measurable quantity but that are nonetheless presumed to be larger than zero. Infinitesimals could thus serve to express non-extended or intensive quantities. An infinitesimal increase of t is symbolised as 'dt'. Since it is infinitesimal, this quantity dt is not *measurably* or *actually* different from t itself but it will convey something of its pure 'moving', so to speak. It conveys the moving forward of t from one second to the instant *immediately* after one second – it conveys a quantity so immediately close to one second itself as to be only virtually discernible from it. The corresponding infinitesimal increase of s will be written as ds, and the relationship between these vanishingly small quantities can then be expressed as ds/dt. Now given our original equation of $s = 16t^2$, if $t = 1$ then a little algebraic fiddling tells us that ds/dt is equal to $32 + 16dt$. Assuming that we can pay no attention to the infinitesimal quantity $16dt$ (which is effectively indistinguishable from zero), this confirms that at the precise point where t is equal to 1 second, our stone is indeed falling at a rate of 32 feet per second.

As Berkeley famously pointed out (in his 1734 essay *The Analyst*), however, it seems mathematically incoherent simply to accept the status of a positive number like $16dt$ as if it were equal to zero. His objection to infinitesimals as 'the ghosts of departed quantities' proved difficult to answer until in the early 1870s Weierstrass and his colleagues abandoned the attempt to compute things like velocities as ratios, and began instead to define them in terms of tendencies towards a *limit*. The basic idea is that although the limit itself cannot be numerically measured (as distinct from zero), the tendency towards it *is* measurable, so long as we are content to approximate the movement towards this limit in terms of finite increments. Rather than an immeasurably small difference like dt, we will deal instead only with very small finite quantities (say, a trillionth of a second). It is then a relatively easy matter to match such small but finite increments of time, symbolised as Δt, with correspondingly small amounts of space traversed (Δs). In our example, $\Delta s/\Delta t$ will now equal $32 + 16\Delta t$. If we then set Δt to a quantity that is very nearly equal to zero, it is easy to confirm what we already know, that the speed at $t = 1$ will be (almost exactly) 32 feet per second. By tackling the problem this way, we drop any reference to mysteriously intensive or virtual quantities, and restore mathematics to a purely actual dimension.

Development of the theory of sets initiated by Weierstrass's contemporaries Cantor and Dedekind subsequently provided the foundations for all the actual numbers required by calculus and indeed by the whole of modern mathematics. Cantor or Leibniz, Badiou or Deleuze: the argument continues.

56 Ansell-Pearson, *Germinal Life*, 170; B, 98.

57 Not unlike Deleuze and Guattari, Hansen notes, complexity theorists like Brian Goodwin and Stuart Kaufman tend to emphasise fluid 'population thinking and transversal communication' and thereby break the 'fixation of biology on species and organisms'. But the 'revised picture of evolution they produce involves a cooperation between such molecular factors (which are themselves subject to selection) and the contribution they make as "components" of higher forms like organisms (also subject to selection). Indeed, on the model presented by complexity theory, these two levels freely interact with one another in the process of morphogenesis that yields organismic forms. For Deleuze & Guattari, by contrast, the point of a molecular reading of Darwinism is to eliminate the need and possibility for such interaction [...]. What Deleuze & Guattari seek is an understanding of the complex, relational causality that underlies the emergence of organismic effects from the molecular standpoint, that is, from a perspective or on an ontological level at which the organism has no causal autonomy.' By contrast, 'complexity theory presents a forceful reaffirmation of the importance of the organism as an integral and irreducible factor in morphogenesis: neither the result of external processes of random selection nor a mere epiphenomenon of molecular genetics, the organism attains its proper status as "the fundamental unit of life," a "natural kind" rather than an historical accident' (Hansen, 'Becoming as Creative Involution?', §29, §41).

58 EP, 208. One of the ways in which Spinoza disagrees with Leibniz, and one of the reasons why Deleuze ultimately thinks of himself as more Spinozist than Leibnizian, is that he refuses to weaken the virtual sufficiency of modal essences by attributing to them any inherent tendency to come into actual existence. For Spinoza, 'modal essences are not "possibles"; they lack nothing, are all that they are, even if the corresponding modes do not exist. They thus involve no tendency to come into existence' (EP, 230).

59 Deleuze, 'Cours Vincennes: Leibniz', 15 April 1980.

60 Understood as anti-creative, the conventional notion of 'God is the sole guarantor of the identity of the self [...]. The death of god essentially signifies, and essentially entails, the dissolution of the self' (LS, 294). Conversely, this 'God survives as long as the *I* enjoys a subsistence, a simplicity and an identity which express the entirety of its resemblance to the divine' (DR, 86; cf. TP, 159).

3 Creatural Confinement

1 FC, 87tm; EP, 263; 289–90.

2 Nietzsche, *Beyond Good and Evil*, §225. Nietzsche's own concern, of course, lies with 'human beings who are new, unique, incomparable, who give themselves laws, who create themselves' (Nietzsche, *Gay Science*, §335). Creators are people who 'justify all impermanence', and their 'fervent will to create' is the only thing that justifies human existence (Nietzsche, *Thus Spoke Zarathustra* II §2).

3 Eriugena, *Periphyseon* V 977A–978B.

4 AO, 29; cf. 119; cf. CC, 9, 14; C1, 125; SM, 15–16; N, 195.

5 Corbin, *Histoire de la philosophie islamique*, 357; Corbin, *Philosophie iranienne*, 118; cf. Jambet, *Logique des Orientaux*, 38. Eckhart anticipates the main point: 'I can never see God except in that in which God sees himself' (Eckhart, *Sermons and Treatises*, vol. 1, 298). Or as Michel Henry puts it, rather than initiation through a text, an image or a representation, it is 'Truth and Truth alone that can offer us access to itself [...]. More radically, divine essence consists in Revelation as self-revelation, as revelation of itself on the basis of itself. Only one to whom that revelation is made can enter into it, into its absolute truth.' There is then 'no separation between the seeing and what is seen, between the light and what it illuminates' (Henry, *I Am the Truth*, 9–10, 24).

6 I began to develop this more general reading of the field in my 'The One or the Other: French Philosophy Today' (2003). Despite all the obvious differences that distinguish Deleuze from Levinas, for instance, a version of the verbal and temporal logic that privileges a creating over the created applies to both thinkers. Levinas' pre-original or pre-ontological *saying [dire]* – a bearing witness to infinite transcendence as such – stands in immeasurable excess over whatever can actually be *said* [dit]. The saying animates the said whose articulation betrays it, and the task of philosophy is then to strive to minimise this 'indispensable' betrayal. See in particular Levinas, *Otherwise Than Being*, 5–7; 'Truth of Disclosure and Truth of Testimony,' in *Basic Philosophical Writings*, 103–6.

7 Bergson, *The Creative Mind*, 140–1. If as Bergson so often says, 'nowhere is the substantiality of [Real or creative] change so visible, so palpable as in the domain of inner life' (148), this is precisely because what lives in inner life is not an actual body but virtual and indivisible spirit.

8 Bergson, *Creative Evolution*, 128.

9 Bergson, *The Creative Mind*, 153.

10 Bergson, *Creative Evolution*, 306.

11 Bergson, *Matter and Memory*, 198.

12 Bergson, *Matter and Memory*, 185.

13 C1, 68, 66. This is why 'the experimental cinema tends toward a perception as it was before men (or after)', 'towards an any-space-whatever released from its human coordinates' (C1, 122; cf. 81; TP, 280; CC, 36–9).

14 'The becoming-animal of the human being is real, even if the animal the human being becomes is not [...]. You do not become a barking molar dog, but by barking, if it is done with enough feeling, with enough necessity and composition, you emit a molecular dog' (TP, 238, 275).

15 ES, 88. Why is difference primary here? Because if only distinct perceptions of impressions are given, then at this most basic level of experience we cannot 'separate what is not distinguishable, or distinguish what is not different'. Difference serves therefore as the 'constitutive principle giving a status to experience' (87). What is primary is a differing 'idea as it is given in the mind, without anything transcending it'. Such ideas are not *in* the mind but are the mind: 'the mind is identical with the idea' (28).

16 ES, 98. In Hume no less than in Bergson, the subject is a category of practical action or utility, and not of insight or knowledge. 'What is denounced and criticised is the idea that the subject can be a knowing subject' (ES, 120–1).

17 NP, 55, 42, 84, 128. Nietzsche, Spinoza and Leibniz all agree on this: passive or reactive force 'expresses nothing' and is the 'mere limitation of active force [...]. Only active force is strictly real, positive and affirmative' (EP, 223; cf. NP, 147).

18 NP, 35. 'To have *ressentiment* or not to have *ressentiment* – there is no greater difference, beyond psychology, beyond history, beyond metaphysics' (35).

19 For women as much as men, all 'human becomings begin with and pass through becoming-woman', since virtually to become woman is the first and simplest stage in the process whereby we cease actually being molar man – a process that continues and intensifies when we further become animal, then molecular, and then eventually, imperceptible (TP, 277; cf. 31–3, 248, 273).

20 B, 106–7; cf. Bergson, *Creative Evolution*, 264.

21 Why is this 'transformation the completion of nihilism? It is because, in transmutation, we are not concerned with a simple substitution, but with a conversion. Nihilism reaches its completion by passing through the last man, but going beyond him to the man who wants to perish. In the man who wants to perish, to be overcome, negation has broken everything which still held it back, it has defeated itself, it has become a power of affirming, a power which is already superhuman' (NP, 175).

22 Nietzsche, *Thus Spoke Zarathustra*, quoted in NP, 175; NP, xii.

23 Deleuze relies here, in part, on Michel Serres, *Le Système de Leibniz*, 648–57.

24 FC, 132, quoting Foucault, *The Order of Things*, 383.

25 Cf. AO, 54, 73, 269; TP, 129–30.

26 AO, 305. See in particular 'L'Interprétation des énoncés', in RF, 80–103.

27 'The history of the long error is the history of representation, the history of the icons' (DR, 301).

28 C1, 61. 'Bodies in themselves are already a language', and 'language is always the language of bodies' (PS, 92).

29 C2, 286 n.8, quoting Pasolini, *L'Expérience hérétique*, 170, 199. Through cinema 'it is the whole of the real, life in its entirety, which has become spectacle' (C2, 84), so long as we remember that this spectacle is nothing other than the universe as such, 'the universe as cinema in itself, a metacinema' (C1, 59).

30 C1, 60, quoting Bergson, *Matter and Memory*, 38tm.

31 B, 25; cf. 57, DR, 56–7; AO, 26; TP, 369.

32 C2, 7tm (Deleuze's emphases). Likewise Godard: his 'violently hallucinatory' work affirms 'an art of description which is always being renewed and always replacing its object' (C2, 10).

33 C2, 130–1; cf. Sam Gillespie, *The Mathematics of Novelty*, 265.

34 RF, 199; C2, 21tm. Deleuze's texts are littered with occasional reminders of the type, 'there is nothing metaphoric about the becoming-animal' (K, 35) or 'the desiring-machine is not a metaphor' (AO, 41; cf. AO, 141, 293; DR, 190; TP, 69, 345; D, 3). In *Proust and Signs*, metaphor is affirmed only because it is equated, this one time, with creative metamorphosis itself, and thereby 'becomes utterly spiritual' (PS, 46–50).

35 K, 22; 70; TP, 77, NP, 42. Cf. Lecercle, *The Violence of Language*, 179; Lecercle, *Philosophy through the Looking-Glass*, 114, 161–2, 183.

36 C2, 226, 174, 173. Deleuze refuses 'irony' or 'aesthetic distance' for the same reason. Irony is a figure of transcendence and of confinement with actuality (LS, 137–9). 'Irony appears each time language deploys itself in accordance with relations of eminence, equivocity, or analogy', i.e. in conformity with 'the whole comparative play of self, world and God' (LS, 247).

37 'Letter to a Harsh Critic,' N, 6tm.

38 In the preface he wrote for the 1984 English translation of his book on Kant, Deleuze summarised this aspect through 'four poetic formulas': 'time is out of joint' (Shakespeare), 'I is another' (Rimbaud), 'the Good is what the Law says' (Kafka), 'a disorder of all the senses' (again Rimbaud). More importantly, in *Difference and Repetition* Deleuze explores a 'problematic' version of what Kant called the 'ideas of reason' (regulative notions to which there corresponds no actual object: the ideas of our free self, world and God). The notions of the virtual, of an event, of a life or living, etc., might all be considered 'problems' in this sense. Unlike Kant's ideas, however, Deleuze affirms such problems precisely insofar as they *do* allow for the immediate and adequate intuition of reality as it is in itself.

Some of the most sophisticated and original new work on Deleuze centres on precisely this aspect of his relation to Kantian and post-Kantian philosophy. See in particular Christian Kerslake 'The Vertigo of Philosophy' (2002); Kerslake, 'Deleuze, Kant and the Question of Metacritique' (2004); Daniel Smith, *Difference and Genesis: Gilles Deleuze and the Legacy of Post-Kantian Philosophy* (forthcoming). My reply to Kerslake, 'To Have Done with Justification', appeared in *Radical Philosophy* 114 (2002).

39 DR, 85–6; cf. DR, 194, 199; KT, viii–ix; Kant, *Critique of Pure Reason*, B157–158, B428–431. It might well be argued that, when he comes to acknowledge that the operation of the cogito is itself fully dependent on the existence of God, Descartes himself already anticipates much of Kant's argument here. In any case, Kant's critique of Descartes only goes so far: according to Deleuze, both philosophers remain trapped within the logic of recognition that is central to any theory of representation, and 'for Kant as for Descartes, it is the identity of the Self in the "I think" which grounds the harmony of all the faculties and their agreement on the form of a supposed Same object' (DR, 133).

40 C2, 82–3. 'From the Greeks to Kant [...], the subordination of time to movement was reversed' (C2, preface to the English edition, xi; cf. CC, 40–2; DR, 88–9).

41 Cf. Monique David-Menard, *La Folie dans la raison pure* (1990).

42 NP, 88. As Pierre Zaoui notes, to the degree the neo-Spinozist 'certainty imposes itself by itself (unlike Cartesianism and the whole of critical rationalism), the problem of critique is not the first task of philosophy'. Rather than 'judge, legitimate or distribute', critique provides only a preliminary service to philosophy: it destroys the illusions that get in the way of immediate certainty (Zaoui, 'La Grande Identité Nietzsche-Spinoza, quelle identité?', 75–6).

43 LB, 120. Badiou is again perfectly right to present Deleuze (no less than himself) as a 'classical' or 'pre-critical' thinker, i.e. one who insists on the identity of being and thought. 'Not only is it possible to think Being, but there is thought only insofar as Being simultaneously formulates and pronounces itself therein' (Badiou, *Deleuze*, 20; cf. 45).

44 Deleuze, 'Immanence: A Life...', 26; cf. LS, 102, 109. For the same reason, the expression of virtual sense 'may occur only within an [...] impersonal transcendental field, freed from the form of a synthetic personal consciousness or a subjective identity', in line with Sartre's 'decisive' argument in his *Transcendence of the Ego* (LS, 98–9tm; cf. WP, 47). Only on this condition can we see what Deleuze means when he says that 'the transcendental field is, however close two sensations may be, the passage from one to the other as a becoming, as increase or decrease of power (virtual quantity)' ('Immanence: A Life...', 25).

45 Spinoza, *Ethics* VP24.

46 'Jean Hyppolite's *Logic and Existence*' [1954], DI, 18.

47 LS, 211; LS, 182. 'Univocity means the identity of [...] event and sense' (LS, 180; cf. C2, 99–100), and 'what renders language possible is the event' (LS, 182).

48 EP, 42, 62. In *Logic of Sense*, Deleuze transposes this configuration more or less unaltered. 'On the one hand, sense [*sens*] does not exist outside the proposition which expresses it'. Sense 'inheres or subsists' but does not exist. 'On the other hand, it does not merge at all with the proposition, for it has an *objectité* which is quite distinct. What is expressed has no resemblance whatsoever to the expression. Sense is indeed attributed, but it is not at all the attribute of the proposition [...]. "Green" designates a quality, a mixture of things, a mixture of tree and air where chlorophyll coexists with all the parts of the leaf. "To green," on the contrary, is not a quality in the thing, but an attribute which is said of the thing. This attribute does not exist outside of the proposition which expresses it' (LS, 21). Green is a merely actual quality; to green is a virtual or creative event.

49 LS, 182; cf. EP, 114–15; LS, 137.

50 This is just a condition of the virtuality of sense. 'There is only one kind of word which expresses both itself and its sense', and such a virtual word can only be a 'nonsense word: abraxas, snark or blituri' (DR, 155). Like so many variants on a divine name, such a word *makes* rather than has sense. 'Nonsense enacts a *donation of sense*' (LS, 69).

4 Creative Subtraction

1 Bergson, *The Two Sources of Morality and Religion*, 309.

2 TP, 262. Likewise, although your molecular creating is actualised in a molar creature, nevertheless you are not in equal parts molecular and molar. Rather, 'all becomings are molecular: the animal,

flower, or stone one becomes are molecular collectivities, haecceities, not molar subjects, objects, or forms that we know from the outside' (TP, 275). In somewhat the same way, our natural but mistaken tendency is to 'postulate the contemporaneity of subject and object, whereas one is constituted only through the annihilation of the other' (LS, 310).

3 B, 49; Bergson, *Creative Evolution*, 11. 'Psychology is now only an opening into ontology, a spring-board for an "installation" in Being' (B, 76; cf. NP, 116). Such for instance is the properly Bergsonian achievement of Resnais's cinema: 'throughout Resnais's work we plunge into a memory which over-flows the conditions of psychology', a 'memory-world' (C2, 119).

4 Take for example the relation between states and nomads. It remains 'a vital concern of every state not only to vanquish nomadism but to control migrations and, more generally, to establish a zone of rights over an entire "exterior"' (TP, 385). The priority of the nomadic 'war machine', by contrast, is to de-populate and dis-establish, to sever the links that bind people to place, to 'make the desert grow'. If the state then intervenes to block the nomadic project, its only option is to destroy the state. 'If war necessarily results, it is because the war machine collides with states and cities, as forces (of striation) opposing its positive object [...]. It is at this point that the war machine becomes war: anni-hilate the forces of the state' (TP, 417).

5 Foucault, *Remarks on Marx*, 31.

6 For a fuller account of Badiou's subtractive conception of being see my 'Depending on Inconsistency' (2005).

7 CC, 1, 76–7. At one point, Deleuze asks: 'what remains of souls once they are no longer attached to particularities, what keeps them from melting into a whole? What remains is precisely their "original-ity", that is, a sound that each one produces, like a ritornello at the limit of language, but that it produces only when it takes to the open road (or to the open sea)…'. (CC, 87).

8 DR, 258; cf. DR, 28; LS, 106–7. That creatures themselves must accomplish their own emanci-pation is consistent with the anti-Cartesian naturalism that Deleuze affirms after Spinoza and Leibniz. If natural movements are controlled by 'mechanical laws', these laws cannot be external and indifferent to what they determine, as if they simply obeyed a transcendent will. The laws only 'work' because they resonate with the internal workings of natural bodies themselves. Even mechanical determination, in other words, must be consistent with that capacity to be affected which determines the essence of any given body (cf. EP, 229).

9 Hegel, *Lectures on the History of Philosophy*, vol. 3, 281; cf. Macherey, *Hegel ou Spinoza*, 11–13, 29, 39. Even Hegel himself concedes, however, that 'it may really be said: you are either a Spinozist or not a philosopher at all' (*op. cit.*, 283).

10 I'm thinking here, for instance, of readings of Deleuze that seek to present him as the prophet of an exuberant bodily or 'fleshy materialism', that emphasise his concern for biological processes or exotic cultural encounters, that privilege his interest in complex processes of material emergence and physical transformation, or that look to his work for resources that might guide practical forms of political and sometimes even 'communitarian' empowerment. Even Brian Massumi, certainly one of Deleuze's most sophisticated and resourceful readers, betrays some signs of this ambivalence when, after recognising that 'our true destiny' is collective 'dissipation' (Massumi, *User's Guide*, 141), he goes on to emphasise the worldly orientation of Deleuzian philosophy. 'We have to live our immersion in the world [...]. That's what Deleuze is saying belief is about, a belief in the world. It's not a belief that's "about" being in the world, it is a being in the world. Because it's all about being in this world, warts and all…' (Massumi, 'Navigating Movements' [2003]).

11 I included slightly more substantial discussions of Ishraq in my *Absolutely Postcolonial* (2001), and of Corbin and Jambet in *The One or the Other* (2003).

12 Jambet, *Logique des Orientaux*, 110, 142, 163.

13 C1, 59–60. As Oliver Davies rightly suggests, there is a good basis for comparison here between Deleuze and Plotinus, considered as thinkers attempting to present 'a radical and unconditioned dif-ference which resist[s] any kind of representational constraint' (Oliver Davies, 'Thinking Difference: A Comparative Study of Gilles Deleuze, Plotinus and Meister Eckhart,' 76). In Plotinus, vision of the One beyond being is precisely a vision that 'floods the eyes with light, but it is not a light showing some

other object' (*Aenneads*, VI, 7, 36), simply the immediate revelation of a 'direct intuition' (III, 8, 9), a 'presence overpassing all knowledge' (VI, 9, 3–4, quoted in Davies, 77–9).

14 Al-Suhrawardi, *Le Livre de la Sagesse Orientale*, §129–30.

15 Al-Suhrawardi, *L'Archange empourpré*, 431.

16 Al-Suhrawardi, *L'Archange*, 57. Deleuze reads the work of T.E. Lawrence along similar lines, as grounded in a realisation that 'light is the opening that makes space', as striving to become adequate to the Arabian desert as an infinitely open space emptied of all worldly opacity and constraint (CC, 115).

17 Al-Suhrawardi, *L'Archange*, 101–2; cf. Corbin, *En Islam iranien*, vol. 2, 22.

18 Jambet, *Logique*, 38; cf. Corbin, *Histoire*, 357; Corbin, *Philosophie iranienne et philosophie comparée*, 118.

19 Jambet, *Logique*, 118, 224–5.

20 Ali Al-Hujwiri, *The Kashf al-Mahjub*, 367, quoted in Schimmel, *Mystical Dimensions of Islam*, 6.

21 Jambet, *Logique*, 131–2.

22 See in particular 'On Detachment', in Eckhart, *Sermons and Treatises*, vol. 3, 117–29.

23 Eckhart, *Sermons and Treatises*, vol. 1, 284. 'Anything, however small, adhering to the soul, prevents us from seeing God', for 'as long as you mind yourself or anything at all you know no more of God than my mouth knows of colour or my eye of taste' (293; 144).

24 Eckhart, *Sermons and Treatises*, vol. 1, 17. 'No creatures can reach God in their capacity of created things' (187).

25 Cf. al-Suhrawardi, *L'Archange*, 172.

26 DI, 25, quoting Bergson, 'The Life and Work of Ravaisson', *The Creative Mind*, 225–6tm.

27 Corbin, *Histoire*, 292, my emphasis.

28 Corbin, *Le Paradoxe du monothéisme*, 200.

29 Henry, *I Am the Truth*, 104.

30 NP, 83–5; cf. CC, 51–2.

31 Benjamin, 'Theologico-Political Fragment' (1920/1921), *One-Way Street*, 155–6; 'Critique of Violence', *ibid.*, 151, 153; cf. 'Theses on the Philosophy of History' §10, *Illuminations*, 258.

32 Benjamin, *The Origin of German Tragic Drama*, 182, 232–3; cf. Wolin, *Benjamin*, 52–9.

33 Weil, *Waiting for God*, 133.

34 Weil, *Gravity and Grace*, 33.

35 Since God only 'gave me Being in order that I should give it back to him', so then my distinct 'existence is made up only of God's waiting for [my] acceptance not to exist.' And by letting go of our afflicted existence we accomplish our supreme goal – 'to make something created pass into the uncreated' (Weil, *Gravity and Grace*, 32–8).

36 Badiou, 'Deleuze: *The Fold*,' 62–8; Badiou, *Deleuze*, 150; Badiou, *L'Etre et l'événement*, 522. For more on Badiou's critique of Deleuze, see my *Badiou: A Subject to Truth*, 174–80.

37 Badiou, 'Deleuze: *The Fold*,' 63–4. On the other hand, Badiou goes perhaps a little too far in the other direction when he describes the ultimate orientation of this philosophy of life as 'ascetic' and hence as indistinguishable from a philosophy of death, a philosophy animated by the 'identity of thinking and dying' (Badiou, *Deleuze*, 63; 13–14). This is to downplay the difference between creative or experimental counter-actualisation and mere renunciation or extinction, and thus risks aligning Deleuze more with Eckhart than Spinoza, more with Schopenhauer than Nietzsche.

38 Žižek, *Organs without Bodies*, 24. As part of his wide-ranging critique of a movement of post-theological thought that includes both Deleuze and Lacan, Conor Cunningham goes so far as to read Deleuze as a 'sophisticated nihilist', in line with his assumption that 'nihilism says […] that creation is nothing and remains so' (Cunningham, *Genealogy of Nihilism*, 242).

39 Žižek, *Organs without Bodies*, 20–1. Žižek's dismissal of *Anti-Oedipus* (and with it much of Deleuze's subsequent work) is consistent with Baudrillard's earlier attack on that 'production paradigm' he discerns at the heart of both Foucault and Deleuze's work (Baudrillard, *Forget Foucault*, 21–2).

40 Spinoza, *Theologico-Political Treatise*, in Spinoza, *The Political Works*, iv, 83.

41 Spinoza, *Ethics* IIP7S.

42 Spinoza, *Ethics* IIP43, 45.

43 Spinoza, *Emendation of the Intellect* §95–96, in *Collected Works* (1985), vol. 1, 39–40.

44 EP, 22. To have an idea of a winged horse, for instance, is to affirm wings of a horse (Spinoza, *Ethics* IIP49S).

45 Spinoza, *Ethics* IIP11D, IIP11C.

46 EP, 133, 299–300. 'Ideas are all the more perfect, the more reality or perfection they express in their object; ideas which the mind forms "absolutely" thus express infinity' (15).

47 EP, 137–8; cf. SP, 70, 73.

48 Spinoza, *Ethics* IIP29C.

49 Cf. Spinoza, *Ethics* IIP30–31.

50 EP, 303, 308; cf. 116; Spinoza, *Ethics* VP25D.

51 Spinoza, *Ethics* IIP40S2; VP36S.

52 EP, 283, 308–9; cf. 226–7.

53 EP, 226; cf. SP, 125. This is why Deleuze and Guattari, though never short on practical advice, eschew all programmatic or global prescriptions in favour of tactical tips: 'lodge yourself on a stratum, experiment with the opportunities it offers, find an advantageous place on it, find potential movements of deterritorialisation, possible lines of flight, experience them and experiment with them…' (TP, 161tm; cf. D, 47–8).

54 Spinoza, *Ethics* IIP27–9.

55 A fuller version of this important sequence runs as follows. We are modes of a single creative substance or God. Our virtual or eternal essence is a facet of this substance. This essence comes into existence, furthermore, when it is actualised in the attributes of thought (as an actual idea or mind) and of extension (as an actual body). Because the attributes are parallel and because the essence of a mode is the same for its actualisation in every attribute, our actual mind is then the idea of our actually existing body and conversely, our body is the object of this idea (Spinoza, *Ethics* IIP11–13; cf. SP, 86). Like any idea, the idea that we express immediately follows from the idea of God, and is sustained by the autonomous power of thought as an attribute of God; like any object, our existent body conforms to the laws of material extension. To begin with, our actual minds and bodies are passive and ignorant of what they are or express.

However, although the parallelism of the attributes ensures that access to the third and highest kind of knowledge is not a straightforward process of 'idealisation' or bodily renunciation, nevertheless our access to the idea that expresses what we are is itself the achievement of thought or intellect. Although we are actualised as both body and mind, only the mind is capable of thinking or 'conceiving' the essence that causes or creates us. The essence of our body 'appears only insofar as it is expressed by the idea that constitutes the essence of the mind (the idea that we are)', for 'the essences of modes have a cause through which they must be conceived; hence there is an idea that expresses the essence of the body and that makes us conceive this essence through its cause', i.e., 'in God' (SP, 91; Spinoza, *Ethics* VP22D). Or again, 'whatever the mind understands under a species of eternity, it understands not from the fact that it conceives the body's present actual existence, but from the fact that it conceives the body's essence under a species of eternity' (*Ethics* VP29). It's this essence that exceeds the body, and that can thus survive it when it dies (*Ethics* VP20S).

Leaving aside the much-debated question as to whether Spinoza's definition of an attribute as 'what the intellect perceives of a substance, as constituting its essence' (*Ethics* ID4) already presumes a certain primacy of thought over extension, this primacy is clearly presumed during the final stages of the redemptive sequence itself, i.e. the sequence that leads from inadequate to adequate ideas, from bondage to beatitude. The intellectual love of God is the concern of the mind 'without relation to the body' (V20S), and the 'idea which expresses the essence of the body under a species of eternity is a certain mode of thinking, which pertains to the essence of the mind, and which is necessarily eternal' (V23S). In keeping with the prevailing reception of his work, however, most critics who engage in detail with Deleuze's Spinozism choose to privilege instead the apparent primacy of body and affect. Gillian Howie, for example, accuses Deleuze of promoting 'an extreme form of materialism', whereby the mind is effectively *defined* by its object, by 'the body or the physical alteration of the body' (Howie, *Deleuze and Spinoza*, 100; cf. Hardt, *Deleuze*, 82; Norris, *Spinoza and the*

Origins of Modern Critical Theory, 59, 65). In my opinion these readings pay too little attention to the fact that, although the object of the idea that constitutes a mind is its body, what constitutes the essence of this idea is of course its (divine) cause, not its object.

56   LS, 283; cf. NP 13; AO, 132.

57   AO, 63; cf. TP, 107; DR, 16.

58   Cf. TP, 46, 218–19; 229; 381.

59   DR, 281; cf. 260–1; LS, 307.

60   LS, 311–13. Few post-Lacanian psychoanalysts are more distant from a Deleuzian conception of things, consequently, than Jean Laplanche, for whom 'the unconscious is only maintained in its radical alterity by the other person (*der Andere*): in brief, by seduction. When the alterity of the other person is blurred, when it is reintegrated in the form of my fantasy of the other, of my "fantasy of seduction", the alterity of the unconscious is put at risk' (Laplanche, 'Unfinished Copernican Revolution,' *Essays on Otherness*, 71).

61   MS, 61; cf. 'From Sacher-Masoch to Masochism', 128; CC, 84–5.

62   MS, 66; 'From Sacher-Masoch to Masochism,' 129–30.

63   TP, 509–10tm. 'The movement of the earth is deterritorialisation itself' (D, 37).

64   TP, 381–2. For the same reason, while 'minorities are objectively definable states, states of language, ethnicity, or sex with their own ghetto territorialities, they must also be thought of as seeds, crystals of becoming whose value is to trigger uncontrollable movements and deterritorialisations of the mean or majority' (TP, 106).

65   TP, 243–4. 'Ahab chooses Moby-Dick, in a choosing that exceeds him and comes from elsewhere' (TP, 244).

66   K, 19–21. In addition to Deleuze's own examples, Flaubert's late story about Saint Julian (in his *Three Tales*) might be read along comparable lines. A psychoanalyst may be tempted to interpret this story as an effort to come to terms with unendurable contradictions: a child who is divided between mother and father, a hero who cannot be both warrior and saint, a bed that is the place of both murder and hospitality, and so on (see for instance Shoshana Felman's brilliantly compressed interpretation of 'Flaubert's Signature: "The Legend of Saint Julian the Hospitable"'). Read from a Deleuzian perspective, by contrast, the story is free to regain its full escape velocity. In a first moment, our hero builds an assemblage that coordinates a multiplicity of diverse components in a single hunting machine (body, weapon, dog, horse, prey), a machine that allows him to act and react with superhuman speed. So long as this machine is geared towards hunting as such, however, it remains trapped within a destructive molar frenzy, a sort of butchery gone mad. But once Julian bends it towards his deterritorialisation, in a second moment, it allows him to wander without purpose or constraint, and eventually to become responsive rather than merely reactive. Rather than immediately kill the animals he perceives he is able to engage in a becoming-other than himself, and his final encounter with the leper leads directly to his liberation from both self and world.

67   TP, 188. See in particular D, 138–40.

68   'Becoming isn't part of history; history designates only the set of preconditions, however recent, that one leaves behind in order to "become", that is, to create something new' (N, 171tm; cf. N, 30; TP, 23, 393–4; C2, 258; CB, 97).

69   Corbin: 'History is not the place in which supreme divine consciousness develops […] History as such dissolves or vanishes' in the face of theophany (Corbin, *Histoire*, 58; Corbin, *Le Paradoxe du monothéisme*, 55). And Henry: the absolute 'does not produce itself in history' and remains independent of historical development. 'The idea that the absolute might reveal itself progressively, bit by bit, is absurd' (Henry, *Essence de la manifestation*, 203–4, 859).

70   'Jean Hyppolite's *Logic and Existence*' [1954], DI, 17.

71   WP, 110, 96. Or as Žižek puts it, 'the emergence of the New occurs when a work overcomes its historical context' (Žižek, *Organs without Bodies*, 11).

72   TP, 142. Only once history is equated with the construction of virtual or creative 'problems' is it possible to accept that 'humanity makes its own history, and the becoming conscious of that activity is like the conquest of freedom' (B, 16).

73 TP, 393. Nomadology is 'the opposite of a history' (TP, 23).

74 Deleuze's favourite sentence in *Anti-Oedipus* is well-known: 'No, we've never seen a schizophrenic' (N, 12; cf. AO, 380). Christopher Miller confirms, at their expense, the ahistorical status of Deleuze and Guattari's nomads in his article 'The Postidentitarian Predicament in the Footnotes of *A Thousand Plateaus*' (1993).

75 Kerslake, 'Transcendental Cinema', 8.

5 Creation Mediated: Art and Literature

1 Bergson, *Laughter*, 160.

2 AO, 87. 'The only end of writing is life' (D, 6; cf. 50; CC, 11, 16).

3 WP, 203, referring to D.H. Lawrence, 'Chaos in Poetry'.

4 TP, 186–7. See in particular D, chapter 2.

5 Deleuze, 'The Exhausted' (1992), in CC, 152–74. Cf. Blanchot, 'La Solitude essentielle', *L'Espace littéraire*; 13–32; Blanchot, *L'Entretien Infini*, 304–5.

6 As Ronald Bogue has shown, Deleuze draws here on Henri Maldiney's essays, collected in *Regard Parole Espace* (1973). Maldiney himself builds on Erwin Straus's distinction of perception and sensation, whereby perception is conceived as a secondary, rationalised organisation of a primary and chaotic domain of sensation, a domain in which I am indistinguishable from what I sense, caught up in the flux of the world, prior to any stable differentiation of subject from object. Maldiney then distinguishes between three major moments in the 'rhythm' of aesthetic form: after the initial chaos of pure sensation, actual forms consolidate through the 'systolic' condensation of visual elements into clear and distinctive shapes, before then dissolving anew (e.g. with Cézanne) through the diastolic eruption of forces that exceed shape and resonate across the entire field of the 'whole'. Cf. Bogue, *Deleuze on Music, Painting and the Arts*, 116–21.

7 'The diagram is a violent chaos in relation to the figurative givens, but it is a germ of rhythm in relation to the new order of the painting' (FB, 102).

8 Sylvester, *Interviews with Francis Bacon*, 17; cf. 101–2.

9 Bergson, *The Creative Mind*, 137.

10 C2, 126–8. Deleuze adapts part of his crystalline theory of individuation from Gilbert Simondon's *L'Individu et sa genèse physico-biologique* (1964), a book that plays an important role in *Difference and Repetition*; see in particular DR 86–9. It is worth quoting Bogue's useful summary, since it confirms the priority of a virtual form over its subsequent actualisation. 'Crystallisation begins when a "seed" crystal is introduced into a substance which is in an amorphous, metastable state, a state characterised by Simondon as an internal resonance of singularities. The seed crystal communicates its shape to a molecule of the substance, which then communicates the shape to another, and so on. (In some substances, several different kinds of crystals may be formed, the seed crystal determining which one will be actualised). The process of individuation occurs between each crystal and the contiguous amorphous substance, always at the surface of crystal, the individually formed crystals being the products of individuation and marking the cessation of the process of individuation. Individuation, therefore, precedes the individual' – with the notable exception, of course, of the virtual seed crystal itself (Bogue, *Deleuze and Guattari*, 62; cf. Pearson, *Germinal Life*, 91).

11 Deleuze mentions, as examples, the encounter in *Last Year in Marienbad*, the accident in *L'Immortelle*, the key in *Trans-Europe Express*, the betrayal in *The Man Who Lies*. In each case, 'the three implicated presents are constantly revived, contradicted, obliterated, substituted, re-created, fork and return' as so many incompossible possibilities. In the process they give rise to a direct image of time itself, rather than an indirect image of time mediated through an intelligible succession of movements (C2, 101).

12 AO, 69; PS, 181–2; RF, 30–1, 38–9.

13 'The work of art always constitutes and reconstitutes the beginning of the world, but also forms a specific world absolutely different from the others and envelops a landscape or immaterial site quite distinct from the site where we have grasped it' (PS, 110).

14 PS, 39, referring to Proust, *A la Recherche du temps perdu*, vol. 1, 347; vol. 2, 48; cf. LB, 80.

15 PS, 50. 'The superiority of art over life consists in this: all the signs we meet in life are still material signs, and their meaning, because it is always in something else, is not altogether spiritual' (PS, 40–1).

16 Proust himself, of course, consistently privileges art over philosophy, i.e. a philosophy of representation. But since it leads to the affirmation that 'only pure thought discovers essence' so then Deleuze happily suggests that 'Proust's critique of philosophy is eminently philosophical' (PS, 100).

17 PS, 42–3. Like both Proust and Leibniz, Deleuze doesn't hesitate to make the obvious connection, and to link the expression of essence to the old metaphysical problem of the immortality of the soul. 'Essences, perhaps, have imprisoned themselves, have enveloped themselves in these souls they individualise. They exist only in such captivity', yet by exceeding the individuals that they animate they suggest that 'we are immortal in some fashion' (PS, 44).

18 PS, 74–5. Consider for instance the shifting effect of Vinteuil's musical phrase when, in Swann's ears, it passes from the regime of love to the regime of art. Vinteuil's phrase at first territorialises Odette's face in relation to the Bois de Boulogne, 'as if it reassured Swann that the Bois de Boulogne was indeed his territory, and Odette his possession' (TP, 319). Such reassurance in fact only condemns Swann to the subsequent torment of jealousy and anxiety. The worldly Swann finds Odette's face everywhere, in paintings, in music, in places, but this multiplication offers no escape from its passionate re-capture. 'Odette's face races down a line hurtling toward a single black hole, that of Swann's passion.' By itself, love offers no way out of this impasse. Swann's salvation begins when, his passion exhausted, he 'attends a reception where he sees the faces of the servants and guests disaggregate into autonomous aesthetic traits, as if the line of picturality regained its independence [...]. Then Vinteuil's little phrase regains its transcendence and renews its connection with a still more intense, asignifying, and asubjective line of pure musicality.' Swann thus escapes the 'black hole of involuntary memory' through art, 'uniquely through art'. The more pure the art the more it is dedicated to such 'blazing life lines' that burn away all lived constraints. Art generates 'positive deterritorialisations that never reterritorialise on art, but instead sweep it away with them toward the realms of the asignifying, asubjective, and faceless' (TP, 186–7).

19 'Jean Hyppolite's *Logic and Existence*', DI, 18. Deleuze's only argument with Hyppolite's Hegel here, and again in anticipation of *Difference and Repetition*, turns on whether dialectical contradiction can rightly claim to be the limit of absolute difference, or whether it should instead be acknowledged only as a limited form of difference.

20 Deleuze's examples include a famous scene on the train when the narrator runs from one side of the carriage to the other, witness to a proliferation of divergent landscapes, and the scene in which he kisses Albertine for the first time: as he approaches, her face dissolves and multiplies in many Albertines, each more intangible than the last (RF, 38–9).

6 Creation Unmediated: Philosophy

1 Bergson, *Two Sources*, 255.

2 If, then, painting devotes its 'clinical' resources to the exploration of hysteria, music is here associated with the more profound and more pressing demands of a 'galloping schizophrenia'. Deleuze cites the example of Mozart's *Requiem*: 'The beats of the timpani in the *Requiem* are sharp, majestic, and divine, and they can only announce to our surprised ears the coming of a being who, to use Stendhal's words, surely has relations with another world' (FB, 54–5, quoting Marcel Moré).

3 PS, 97, 111. 'To think is to create – there is no other creation – but to create is first of all to engender "thinking" in thought' (DR, 147).

4 'Cours Vincennes: Leibniz', 15 April 1980; WP, 5, 11; N, 25, 32, 136; DI, 22, 141; RF, 292.

5 Philip Goodchild makes a case for the opposite conclusion, arguing that 'the question of philosophy in Deleuze's work is subordinated to the desire for life', and even to an ultimately religious desire for 'transcendent' life (Goodchild, *Deleuze and the Question of Philosophy*, 19, 158–69).

6 To be sure, Deleuze often insists that philosophy cannot proceed independently of art and science, and that it has no privileged status. 'Philosophy obviously cannot claim the least superiority, but also creates and expounds its own concepts only in relation to what it can grasp of scientific functions

and artistic constructions' (Preface to the English edition [1994], DR, xvi; cf. WP, 8, 198; RF, 353). No doubt every conceptual extraction operates within the situation that confronts it. No less than any of his other books, however, the general argument of *What is Philosophy?* makes the properly *ontological* hierarchy of the disciplines abundantly clear.

7 WP, 208tm. Alternatively – although it amounts to the same thing – science, art and philosophy are the 'three aspects under which the brain becomes subject, Thought-brain'. And as brain becomes subject, so too 'the concept becomes object as created, as event or creation itself' (WP, 210–11).

8 WP, 156. Deleuze's privileged scientific references – an eclectic collection ranging from Maïmon and Saint-Hilaire through Bergson and Whitehead to Simondon and Prigogine – have at least one thing in common: they restore a creative dynamism to the plane of reference as such. See for instance TP, 484–5; WP, 130, 154.

9 WP, 197, my emphasis.

10 Bergson, *The Creative Mind*, 157.

11 Bergson, *The Creative Mind*, 138.

12 Bergson, *Creative Evolution*, 268.

13 Bergson, *Two Sources*, 239.

14 Kant, *Critique of Pure Reason*, Bxxx.

15 EP, 67, 22tm; cf. DR, 40.

16 NP, 176. 'Sovereign affirmation is inseparable from the destruction of all known values, it turns this destruction into a total destruction' (NP, 176).

17 CC, 126–35. 'Becoming is not "judged" […], it is "just" and possesses its own law in itself' (NP, 28). The violent 'demonstrations' that make up the fifth part of Spinoza's *Ethics*, for example, 'are perfectly adapted to essences insofar as they surpass any order of discursivity or deduction […]. The geometric method of Book V is a method of invention that will proceed by intervals and leaps […], perhaps it surpasses all demonstration inasmuch as it operates in the "undecidable"' (CC, 149).

18 'The mode of the event is the problematic […], events bear exclusively upon problems and define their conditions' (LS, 54); consequently, 'the problem as problem is completely determined' (DR, 280).

19 NP, 32. 'The system of the future […] must be called a divine game, since there is no pre-existing rule, since the game bears already upon its own rules, all of chance being affirmed each time and for all times' (DR, 116). This is why Mallarmé 'presents the child Igitur invoking his ancestors who are not men but Elohim, a race which was pure, which "raised its purity to the absolute, in order to be it"' (NP, 32).

20 DR, 197, 199. In *What is Philosophy?*, concepts will be defined as 'the outcome of throws of the dice' (WP, 35).

21 Eckhart, *Sermons and Treatises*, vol. 1, 298.

22 PS, 99; DR, 85–6; DR, 199, 194; cf. KT, viii–ix.

23 C2, 263; EP, 158; cf. EP, 115, 131, 160.

24 EP, 269; cf. SP, 69–70. Modern cinema is likewise 'automatism become spiritual art'; through cinema, 'the moving machine becomes one with the psychological automaton pure and simple' (C2, 263).

25 PV, 11. 'Three centuries ago certain fools were astonished because Spinoza wished to see the liberation of man, even though he did not believe in his liberty or even in his particular existence. Today new fools, or perhaps the same ones reincarnated, are astonished because the Foucault who had spoken of the death of man took part in political struggle' (FC, 90tm).

26 Spinoza, *Political Treatise*, in *Political Works*, 367, 383; cf. EP, 266–7; ES, 43, 131.

27 WP, 11, 199, 210. On this point, Deleuze and Guattari are again directly in line with a Nietzschean prescription: 'What dawns on philosophers last of all: they must no longer accept concepts as a gift, not merely purify and polish them, but first make and create them' (Nietzsche, *Will to Power*, §409).

28 C2, 280. Deleuze's concern is with 'concepts specific to cinema, but which can only be formed philosophically. They're not technical notions (like tracking, continuity, depth or flatness of field, and

so on), because technique only makes sense in relation to ends which it presupposes but doesn't explain' (N, 58).

29   Deleuze, 'Bergson's Conception of Difference', DI, 36.

30   CC, 148–51; SP, 127. As Pascal asks, 'Do you believe that it is impossible for God to be infinite and indivisible?' – 'Yes.' – 'Very well, I will show you something infinite and indivisible: it is a point moving everywhere at an infinite speed. It is one and the same everywhere and wholly present in every place' (Pascal, *Pensées*, §420).

31   Conceptual personae serve to crystallise and orient the creation of concepts – Deleuze and Guattari's examples include Socrates and the figure of the friend as conceptual personae for Plato, or Dionysus and Zarathustra (along with a different version of Socrates) for Nietzsche. Conceptual personae are the explorers of 'thought's territories, its absolute deterritorialisations and reterritorialisations' (WP, 69). Or again, if 'philosophy's sole aim is to become worthy of the event, it is precisely the conceptual persona who counter-effectuates the event' (WP, 160).

32   WP, 59. Philosophy always 'posits as prephilosophical […] the power of a One-All like a moving desert that concepts come to populate. Prephilosophical does not mean something preexistent but rather *something that does not exist outside philosophy*, although philosophy presupposes it' (WP, 41). This particular obligation or privilege of thought, we might note in passing, indicates perhaps the deepest and most interesting point of convergence between the philosophies of Deleuze and Badiou. What Badiou calls a truth-procedure is nothing other than a rigorous way of drawing the consequences of a pure implication – although with Badiou this always concerns the implication of *inconsistency*, precisely, rather than of consistency. Cf. Hallward, 'Depending on Inconsistency' (2005).

33   DR, 228tm. Just as music lends us an 'impossible ear' by rendering audible forces (time, intensity, the virtual…) that are themselves inaudible, so too philosophy's concern is with 'impossible thought, that is, the effort to render thinkable, with complex materials of thought, forces that not themselves thinkable' (RF, 146). Or as Deleuze and Guattari put it elsewhere: 'Modern philosophy tends to elaborate a material of thought in order to capture forces that are not thinkable in themselves […]. The forces to be captured are no longer those of the earth, which still constitute a great expressive Form, but the forces of an immaterial, nonformal, and energetic Cosmos' (TP, 343).

34   LS, 63, 165–6; 'On Four Poetic Formulas…', KT, vii–viii.

35   C2, Preface to the English edition, xi; cf. CC, 40–2; DR, 88–9.

36   Spinoza, *Ethics* ID8Exp.

37   See in particular EP, 175–6, 214–15; DR, 254–9.

38   If what we experience is the 'affect' of time, this is not because we experience time in our 'own' way but because 'time itself, pure virtuality, divides itself in two as affector and affected'; in the process, time defines itself as 'affection of self by self' (C2, 83). The formula recalls Michel Henry's conception of spiritual life as pure auto-affection (Henry, *I Am the Truth*, 104–7).

39   PS, 169, 129–30. Philosophy's own time obeys a similarly transversal logic. Since 'philosophy is becoming, not history', it proceeds via 'the coexistence of planes, not the succession of systems' (WP, 59).

40   Readers familiar with Nietzsche's own version of eternal return will know that he had something rather different in mind – the eternal return of the *same*, precisely, and the same understood as *the same in all its actuality*. Deleuze transforms Nietzsche's concept by orienting it to the virtual return of differings alone. What returns is not sameness but difference, the infinite repetition of difference. 'Eternal return cannot mean the return of the Identical because it presupposes a world (that of the will to power) in which all previous identities have been abolished and dissolved […]. Returning is the becoming-identical of becoming itself' (DR, 41).

41   NP, 24. As Todd May explains, 'everything returns, everything recurs, but what recurs does not do so in the form of actualised identities but in the form of the virtual difference that constitutes those identities' (May, *Deleuze*, 62).

42   DR, 41–2. 'The eternal return has no other sense but this: the absence of any assignable origin – in other words, the assignation of difference as the origin, which then relates different to different in order to make it (or them) return as such' (DR, 125).

43 LS, 179–80; DR, 300; cf. NP, 86.

44 Deleuze, 'Bergson's Conception of Difference' [1956], DI, 40–3.

45 AO, 314, my emphasis; cf. TP, 479.

46 Hume, *Treatise of Human Nature*, 46, quoted in ES, 99.

47 'The AND is not a specific relation, it is that which subtends all relations, the path of all relations, which makes relations shoot outside their terms [...]; it is a quite extraordinary thought, and yet it is life' (D, 57). 'AND is [...] the destruction of all identities' (N, 44).

48 Spinoza, *Political Treatise* III, 2, quoted in EP, 266; cf. Spinoza, *Ethics* IVP18S.

49 EP, 232–3. When it comes to an affirmation of 'the immanence of being [...], Spinoza stands alone. One finds it only in him. This is why I consider myself a Spinozist, rather than a Leibnizian, although I owe a lot to Leibniz' (Deleuze, letter to Martin Joughin, quoted in 'Translator's Preface', EP, 11).

50 LB, 81, 137. 'All that Spinozism needed to do for the univocal to become an object of pure affirmation was to make substance turn around the modes – in other words, to realise univocity in the form of repetition in the eternal return' (DR, 304; cf. 40).

51 Tim Clark arrives at a similar conclusion, when he notes that Deleuze's effort to 'pluralise Spinozism' results in the reconfiguration of 'something like Whiteheadian pure potentiality in a radically decentred form' – a 'chaosmology' sustained by 'a vision of multiple "little divinities" effecting random syntheses of differential elements within an immanent space of possibilities' (Clark, 'A Whiteheadian Chaosmos', 192).

52 'Gueroult's General Method for Spinoza' (1969), DI, 152; DI, 303n.21.

53 B, 29; cf. 92–3.

54 FB, 42, 44. A similarly non-relational configuration governs inter-figural and inter-essential relations themselves. Cf. FB, 65–6; PS, 90–1.

55 DI, 186–8. '*As a general rule, the real, the imaginary and their relations are always engendered secondarily by the functioning of the structure, which starts by having its primary effect in itself*' (DI, 191).

Conclusion

1 Paul, *Second Letter to the Corinthians*, 5:16–17. 'Adapt yourselves no longer to the pattern of this present world', Paul advises his followers in Rome, 'but let your minds be remade and your whole nature thus transformed', for 'you are on the spiritual level if *only* God's Spirit dwells within you' (Paul, *Letter to the Romans*, 12:2, 8:9).

2 Miguel de Beistegui makes this similarity the basis for his compelling analysis of Heidegger and Deleuze as contributors to a common philosophical project attuned to the 'two-sidedness' of being, i.e. to the irreducible gap between presentable ontic qualities of being and the ontological 'event of presence itself, which is nothing like a thing, yet the eventing of which opens onto the presence of things themselves' (de Beistegui, *Truth and Genesis*, 17). So Heideggerian a reading, however, runs two significant risks. On the one hand, it risks conceiving the eventfulness of being as altogether other than (and thus transcendent of) presentable being, such that the infinite difference between them becomes the 'very measure of being', along with the basis for an ethics attuned to the vertigo of 'placelessness' and the 'abyss' (338–9). On the other hand, after DeLanda, it risks reducing Deleuze's concern with difference to merely 'natural processes of differentiation', i.e. to the spatio-temporal mechanics of material actualisation, of emergent properties, complex systems, etc. (337; cf. 258–76).

3 Agamben, *Means Without End*, 7–9.

4 Agamben, *The Coming Community*, 35; cf. Agamben, *Idea of Prose*, 82; *The Open*, 92.

5 Agamben, *Potentialities*, 183–4.

6 Such is the properly messianic imperative: 'another world and another time must make themselves present in *this* world and time'. Unlike Deleuze, Agamben's concern is less with forms of becoming that remain external to history so much as with the properly historical effects of a temporality that remains missing *within* history, that is present in history in the form of 'deferral and procrastination' (Agamben, *Potentialities*, 168).

7 Foucault, 'Polemics, Politics and Problematisations', in *The Foucault Reader*, 388. I develop this distinction of Foucault from Deleuze in more detail in my 'The Limits of Individuation, or How to Distinguish Deleuze from Foucault' (2000).

8 Foucault, *History of Sexuality: An Introduction*, 95. 'Nothing is fundamental [...], there are only reciprocal relations' (Foucault, 'Space, Knowledge and Power,' *Foucault Reader*, 247).

9 Foucault, 'On the Archaeology of the Sciences' [1968], *Essential Works*, vol. 2, 332–3.

10 Foucault, 'A Preface to Transgression', *Essential Works*, vol. 2, 80; Foucault, 'La folie, l'absence d'œuvre' [1964], *Dits et écrits*, vol. 1, 420.

11 Foucault, 'The Thought of the Outside', *Essential Works*, vol. 2, 155. The outside 'has nothing to offer but the infinite void that opens beneath the feet of the person it attracts, the indifference that greets him as if he were not there' (155).

12 Foucault 'The Thought of the Outside', 150, 166.

13 Foucault, 'On the Ways of Writing History' [1967], *Essential Works*, vol. 2, 291.

14 Defending Deleuze against Badiou's accusation that his philosophy lacks a specifically political dimension, Nicholas Thoburn, for instance, argues that 'Deleuze's project is precisely concerned to develop a politics of invention that is adequate to capital', a 'politics of life' that might allow us to confront contemporary forms of exploitation; a Deleuzian micro-politics is not concerned with a true or just 'representation of a people' but with their 'creation' or deterritorialisation (Thoburn, *Deleuze, Marx and Politics*, 5–6, 8; cf. Patton, *Deleuze and the Political*, 9; Hardt and Negri, *Empire*, 28). Rather like Thoburn, Jason Read embraces Deleuze's work as a contribution to the renewal of a Marxist politics. For Read, Deleuze helps revitalise a distinctively political conception of the classical Marxist notion of a mode of production, considered precisely as a mediating instance that links material and machinic conditions with forms of consciousness or subjective life (Read, *Micro-Politics of Capital*, 6, 54–5). Along somewhat similar lines, what John Protevi draws from his enthusiastic engagement with 'Deleuzian historical-libidinal materialism' are principles designed to explain, at a maximum difference from any idealist metaphysics, the 'material self-ordering' or emergent complexity of socio-political bodies (Protevi, *Political Physics*, 2–3).

According to Protevi, Deleuze encourages us to undertake 'the empirical study of forceful bodies politic in their material production' (*Political Physics*, 2); according to Thoburn, Deleuze's work is marked by a 'continual and inventive engagement with the forces of the world' (*Deleuze, Marx and Politics* 6). But the whole question is precisely whether the political 'forces of the world' are best confronted in terms of evanescent creations, lines of flight, deterritorialisation, minor identities, and continuous variation or flux, rather than in terms of decisive confrontations and principled prescriptions. In line with a tradition that includes Badiou, Sartre, Fanon and Lenin, I have sketched an initial defence of this more confrontational approach to politics in my 'Politics of Prescription' (2005) and 'The Politics of the Front' (forthcoming).

Of the various other affirmations of a Deleuzian politics, Jean-Jacques Lecercle's nuanced appraisal of Deleuze and Guattari as 'para-Marxist' offers perhaps the most promising approach. Lecercle recognises the forms of 'displacement' that lead from Marx to Deleuze (e.g. from history to geography, from ideology to assemblage, from party to group, etc.), but is able to draw on Deleuzian pragmatics in order to develop an analysis of language-events on the model of Lenin's conception of slogans (see in particular Lecercle, 'Deleuze, Guattari and Marxism' [2005], 41, 50). To my mind, however, even Lecercle exaggerates the materialist and 'embodied' orientation of Deleuze's conception of both practice and language.

15 DI, 279–80; RF, 13; cf. TP, 351ff. Adorno makes a similar point in a rather different context. If like Kant you try to separate the *constituens* (that is, a purely transcendental consciousness) from the '*constitutum* – that is, the world in its broadest sense' – then you simply render the *constituens* indeterminate and abstract, if not unimaginable. The only alternatives are then either (a) to try to encompass both the constituting and the constituted in a single 'monstrous, gigantic, absolute' term (subject for Fichte, cosmos for Schelling), or else (b) to adopt *some* sort of dialectical approach, one that realises that 'there is in short neither a *constituens* nor a *constitutum*, but [that] instead these two elements mutually produce one another' (Adorno, *Kant's* Critique of Pure Reason, 147–8). Deleuze's

whole effort, we might say, was to renew a putatively post-dialectical version of the monstrous approach.

16   TP, 90. 'A society, a social field does not contradict itself; instead, what is primary is that it flees, it flees, to begin with, in every direction. What is primary are its lines of flight' (RF, 116; cf. N, 171).

17   See for example Eyal Weizman's suggestive analysis of recent Israeli Defence Force tactics in his 'Walking Through Walls: Soldiers as Architects in the Israeli-Palestinian Conflict', *Radical Philosophy* 136 (March 2006), 8–22; cf. Weizman, *The Politics of Verticality*, forthcoming from Verso in 2006.

18   WP, 213tm. The paradigm here is again Spinoza, for whom God's power simply expresses the infinite perfection of his essence: 'God acts and produces only through his essence, and not through an understanding or a will' (DI, 153). Badiou concludes his review of Deleuze's book on Leibniz with a similar point: whereas Leibniz affirms a concept of mind affirmed as presence, force or 'strength, and not action' (LB, 119), Badiou insists any viable notion of militant and transformative truth must conceive it as 'action and not presence' (Badiou, 'Deleuze: *The Fold*', 69).

Bibliography

Adorno, Theodor W. *Kant's* Critique of Pure Reason, ed. Rolf Tiedemann, trans. Rodney Livingstone. Cambridge: Polity, 2001.

Agamben, Giorgio. *The Coming Community*, trans. Michael Hardt. Minneapolis: University of Minnesota Press, 1993.

—*The Idea of Prose*, trans. Michael Sullivan. Albany: State University of New York Press, 1995.

—*Potentialities: Collected Essays in Philosophy*, trans. Daniel Heller-Roazen. Stanford: Stanford University Press, 1999.

—*Means without End: Notes on Politics*, trans. Vincenzo Binetti and Cesare Casarino. Minneapolis: University of Minnesota Press, 2000.

—*The Open: Man and Animal*, trans. Kevin Attell. Stanford: Stanford University Press, 2004.

Ansell-Pearson, Keith, ed. *Deleuze and Philosophy: The Difference Engineer*. London: Routledge, 1997.

—*Germinal Life: The Difference and Repetition of Deleuze*. London: Routledge, 1999.

—*Philosophy and the Adventure of the Virtual: Bergson and the Time of Life*. London: Routledge, 2002.

Aristotle. *Metaphysics*, in *The Complete Works of Aristotle*, volume 2, ed. Jonathan Barnes. Princeton: Princeton University Press, 1984.

Artaud, Antonin. O*euvres Complètes*, vol. 3, ed. Paule Thévenin. Paris: Gallimard, 1961.

Bachelard, Gaston. *The Dialectic of Duration*, trans. Mary McAllester Jones. Manchester: Clinamen, 2000.

Badiou, Alain. *L'Etre et l'événement*. Paris: Seuil, 1988.

—*Gilles Deleuze: The Clamor of Being*, trans. Louise Burchill. Minneapolis: University of Minnesota Press, 2000.

—'Gilles Deleuze, *The Fold: Leibniz and the Baroque*', trans. Thelma Sowley. *Gilles Deleuze: The Theatre of Philosophy*, ed. Constantin Boundas and Dorothea Olkowski. New York: Columbia University Press, 1994. 51–69

Baudrillard, Jean. *Forget Foucault*, trans. Nicole Dufresne. NY: Semiotext(e), 1987.

Beistegui, Miguel de. *Truth and Genesis: Philosophy as Differential Ontology*. Bloomington: Indiana University Press, 2004.

Benjamin, Walter. *The Origin of German Tragic Drama,* trans. George Steiner. London: Verso, 1977.

—*Illuminations: Essays and Reflections,* ed. Hannah Arendt, trans. Harry Zohn. New York: Schocken Books, 1969.

—*One-Way Street and Other Writings,* trans. Edmund Jephcott and Kingsley Shorter. London: Verso, 1979.

Bergson, Henri. *Matter and Memory,* trans. Nancy Margaret Paul and W. Scott Palmer. New York: Zone Books, 1988.

—*Creative Evolution,* trans. Arthur Mitchell. New York: Henry Holt, 1911. Reprinted by Dover Publications, 1998.

—*Laughter: An Essay on the Meaning of the Comic,* trans. Cloudsley Brereton and Fred Rothwell, in *Comedy,* ed. Wylie Sypher. Baltimore: Johns Hopkins University Press, 1980.

—*The Creative Mind,* trans. Mabelle L. Andison. NY: Carol Publishing, 1992.

—*Duration and Simultaneity,* trans. Leon Jacobson. Indianapolis: Bobbs-Merrill, 1965.

—*The Two Sources of Morality and Religion,* trans. R. Ashley Audra and Cloudesley Brereton, with W. Horsfall Carter. NY: Doubleday, 1954.

—*Key Writings,* ed. Keith Ansell-Pearson and John Mullarkey. London: Continuum, 2002.

Blanchot, Maurice. *L'Espace littéraire.* Paris: Gallimard, 'Folio', 1955 (1988 printing).

—*L'Entretien infini.* Paris: Gallimard, 1969.

Bogue, Ronald. *Deleuze and Guattari.* New York: Routledge, 1989.

—*Deleuze on Cinema.* London: Routledge, 2003.

—*Deleuze on Literature.* London: Routledge, 2003.

—*Deleuze on Music, Painting, and the Arts.* London: Routledge, 2003.

Boundas, Constantin. 'Introduction', in *The Deleuze Reader,* ed. Constantin Boundas. New York: Columbia University Press, 1992.

Boundas, Constantin, and Dorothea Olkowski eds. *Gilles Deleuze and the Theater of Philosophy.* New York: Routledge, 1994.

Bryden, Mary, ed. *Deleuze and Religion.* London: Routledge, 2001.

Buydens, Mireille. *Sahara: L'esthétique de Gilles Deleuze.* Paris: Vrin, 1990.

Clark, Tim. 'A Whiteheadian Chaosmos: Process Philosophy from a Deleuzean Perspective.' *Process Studies* 28: 3-4 (Fall-Winter, 1999): 179-194.

Corbin, Henry. *En Islam iranien,* 4 vols. Paris: Gallimard, 1971–1972.

—*L'Imagination créatrice dans le soufisme d'Ibn 'Arabî.* Paris: Flammarion, 1977.

—*Le Paradoxe du monothéisme.* Paris: Livre de Poche, 1981.

—*Philosophie iranienne et philosophie comparée.* Paris: Buchet-Chastel, 1985.

—*Histoire de la philosophie islamique.* Paris: Gallimard, 'Folio', 1986.

Cunningham, Conor. *A Genealogy of Nihilism: Philosophies of Nothing and the Difference of Theology.* London: Routledge, 2002.

Davies, Oliver. 'Thinking Difference: A Comparative Study of Gilles Deleuze, Plotinus and Meister Eckhart', in *Deleuze and Religion,* ed. Mary Bryden. London: Routledge, 2001. 76–86.

DeLanda, Manuel. *Intensive Science and Virtual Philosophy.* London: Continuum, 2002.

Deleuze, Gilles. *Empirisme et subjectivité.* Paris: PUF, 1953. *Empiricism and Subjectivity,* trans. Constantin Boundas. NY: Columbia University Press, 1991.

—'From Sacher-Masoch to Masochism' [1961], trans. Christian Kerslake. *Angelaki* 9:1 (April 2004): 125–133.

—*Nietzsche et la philosophie*. Paris: PUF, 1962. *Nietzsche and Philosophy*, trans. Hugh Tomlinson. Minneapolis: University of Minnesota Press, 1983.

—*La Philosophie critique de Kant*. Paris: PUF, 1963. *Kant's Critical Philosophy*, trans. Hugh Tomlinson and Barbara Habberjam. Minneapolis: University of Minnesota Press 1984.

—*Proust et les signes* [1964]. Paris: PUF, 1976, fourth edition. *Proust and Signs*, trans. Richard Howard. London: Continuum, 2000.

—*Le Bergsonisme*, Paris: PUF, 1966. *Bergsonism*, trans. Hugh Tomlinson and Barbara Habberjam. NY: Zone, 1988.

—*Présentation de Sacher-Masoch*. Paris: Minuit, 1967. *Masochism: An Interpretation of Coldness and Cruelty*, trans. Jean McNeil. NY: Zone, 1989.

—*Différence et répétition*. Paris: PUF, 1968. *Difference and Repetition*, trans. Paul Patton. NY: Columbia University Press, 1994.

—*L'Idée d'expression dans la philosophie de Spinoza*. Paris: Minuit, 1968. *Expressionism in Philosophy: Spinoza*, trans. Martin Joughin. NY: Zone, 1990.

—*Logique du sens* Paris: Minuit, 1969. *The Logic of Sense*, trans. Mark Lester with Charles Stivale. NY: Columbia University Press, 1990.

—*Spinoza: philosophie pratique* [1970]. Paris: Minuit, 1981. *Spinoza: Practical Philosophy*, trans. Robert Hurley. San Francisco: City Light Books, 1988.

—*Dialogues*, avec Claire Parnet [1977]. Paris: Flammarion, 'Champs' 1996. *Dialogues*, trans. Hugh Tomlinson and Barbara Habberjam. NY: Columbia University Press, 1987.

—'Un Manifeste de moins', in Carmelo Bene and Gilles Deleuze, *Superpositions*. Paris: Minuit, 1979. 87–131.

—'Cours Vincennes: Leibniz', 15 April 1980, available online at http://www.webdeleuze. com/php/texte.php?cle=48&groupe=Leibniz&langue=1.

—*Francis Bacon: Logique de la sensation*, vol. 1. Paris: Editions de la Différence, 1981. *Francis Bacon: The Logic of Sensation*, trans. Daniel W. Smith. London: Continuum, 2003.

—*Cinéma 1: L'Image-mouvement*. Paris: Minuit, 1983. *Cinema 1: The Movement-Image*, trans. Hugh Tomlinson and Barbara Habberjam. Minneapolis: University of Minnesota Press, 1986.

—*Cinéma 2: L'Image-temps*. Paris: Minuit, 1985. *Cinema 2: The Time-Image*, trans. Hugh Tomlinson and Robert Galeta. Minneapolis: University of Minnesota Press, 1989.

—*Foucault*. Paris: Minuit, 1986. *Foucault*, trans. Seán Hand. Minneapolis: University of Minnesota Press, 1988.

—*Le Pli: Leibniz et le baroque*. Paris: Minuit, 1988. *The Fold: Leibniz and the Baroque*, trans. Tom Conley. Minneapolis: University of Minnesota Press, 1993.

—*Périclès et Verdi: La Philosophie de François Châtelet*. Paris: Minuit, 1988.

—*Pourparlers, 1972–1990*. Paris: Minuit, 1990. *Negotiations*, trans. Martin Joughin. NY: Columbia University Press, 1995.

—*Critique et clinique*. Paris, Minuit, 1993. *Essays Critical and Clinical*, trans. Daniel W. Smith and Michael A. Greco. Minneapolis: University of Minnesota Press, 1997.

—'The Actual and the Virtual' [1996], in Deleuze and Parnet, *Dialogues II*. London: Continuum, 2002. 148–152.

—*Pure Immanence: Essays on a Life*, trans. Anne Boyman. NY: Zone, 2001.

—*L'Ile déserte et autres texts: Textes et entretiens 1953–1974*, ed. David Lapoujade. Paris, Editions de Minuit, 2002. *Desert Islands and Other Texts 1953–1974*, trans. Michael Taormina. Cambridge: Semiotext(e), 2004.

—*Deux Régimes de fous. Textes et entretiens 1975–1995*, ed. David Lapoujade. Paris, Editions de Minuit, 2003.

Deleuze, Gilles, and Félix Guattari. *L'Anti-Oedipe. Capitalisme et schizophrénie*. Paris: Minuit, 1972. *Anti-Oedipus. Capitalism and Schizophrenia*, trans. Robert Hurley, Mark Seem and Helen R. Lane. Minneapolis: University of Minnesota Press, 1977.

—*Kafka: pour une littérature mineure*. Paris: Minuit, 1975. *Kafka: For a Minor Literature*, trans. Dana Polan. Minneapolis: University of Minnesota Press, 1986.

—*Mille plateaux. Capitalisme et schizophrénie*. Paris: Minuit, 1980. *A Thousand Plateaus. Capitalism and Schizophrenia*, trans. Brian Massumi. Minneapolis: University of Minnesota Press, 1986.

—*Qu'est-ce que la philosophie?* Paris: Minuit, 1991. *What is Philosophy?*, trans. Hugh Tomlinson and Graham Burchell. NY: Columbia University Press, 1994.

David-Menard, Monique. *La Folie dans la raison pure: Kant lecteur de Swedenborg*. Paris: Vrin, 1990.

Davis, Philip J., and Reuben Hersh. *The Mathematical Experience*. Harmondsworth: Penguin, 1980.

Descombes, Vincent. *Modern French Philosophy*, trans. L. Scott-Fox and J.M. Harding. Cambridge: Cambridge University Press, 1980.

Dickens, Charles. *Our Mutual Friend*. London: Everyman's Library, 1994.

Donagan, Alan. *Spinoza*. Chicago: University of Chicago Press, 1989.

Eckhart, Meister. *Sermons and Treatises*, ed. Maurice O'Connell Walshe, 3 vols. Rockport: Element Books, 1992.

Eriugena, John Scottus. *Periphyseon (The Division of Nature)*, ed. and trans. Inglis Patrick Sheldon-Williams and John O'Meara. Montréal: Bellarmin, 1987.

Felman, Shoshana. 'Flaubert's Signature: "The Legend of Saint Julian the Hospitable"', in *Flaubert and Postmodernism*, ed. Naomi Schor and Henry F. Majewski. Lincoln: University of Nebraska Press, 1984.

Flaubert, Gustave. *Three Tales*, trans. Roger Whitehouse. Harmondsworth: Penguin, 2005.

Foucault, Michel. *The Order of Things*, trans. Alan Sheridan. London: Tavistock, 1970.

—*The Foucault Reader*, ed. Paul Rabinow. NY: Pantheon, 1984.

—*History of Sexuality, volume 1: An Introduction*, trans. Robert Hurley. Harmondsworth: Penguin, 1981

—*Remarks on Marx: Conversations with Duccio Trombatori*, trans. R. James Goldstein and James Cascaito. New York: Semiotext(e), 1991.

—*Dits et écrits*, ed. Daniel Defert and François Ewald, 4 vols. Paris: Gallimard, 1994.

—*Essential Works of Foucault 1954–1984*, ed. Paul Rabinow, 3 vols. NY: New Press, 1997–2000.

Gillespie, Sam. *The Mathematics of Novelty: Badiou's Minimalist Metaphysics*. Warwick University PhD, 2004.

Goodchild, Philip. *Gilles Deleuze and the Question of Philosophy*. London: Associated University Presses, 1996.

Hallward, Peter. 'Deleuze and Redemption from Interest'. *Radical Philosophy* 81 (January 1997): 6–21.

—'Deleuze and the World Without Others'. *Philosophy Today* 41:4 (Winter, 1997): 530–544.

—'The Limits of Individuation, or How to Distinguish Deleuze from Foucault'. *Angelaki* 5:2 (August 2000): 93–112.

—*Absolutely Postcolonial: Writing Between the Singular and the Specific*. Manchester: Manchester University Press, 2001.

—'To Have Done with Justification: A Reply to Christian Kerslake'. *Radical Philosophy* 114 (June 2002): 29–31.

—*Badiou: A Subject to Truth*. Minneapolis: University of Minnesota Press, 2003.

—ed. *The One or the Other? French Philosophy Today*. Special issue of *Angelaki* (8:2, August, 2003).

—ed. *Think Again: Alain Badiou and the Future of Philosophy*. London: Continuum Press, 2004.

—'Depending on Inconsistency: Badiou's Answer to the "Guiding Question of All Contemporary Philosophy"'. *Polygraph* 17 (Spring 2005): 7–21

—'The Politics of Prescription'. *South Atlantic Quarterly* 104:4 (Autumn 2005): 771–91.

Hansen, Mark. 'Becoming as Creative Involution? Contextualizing Deleuze and Guattari's Biophilosophy'. *Postmodern Culture* 11:1 (September 2000), available online at http://www3.iath.virginia.edu/pmc/text-only/issue.900/11.1hansen.txt.

Hardt, Michael. *Gilles Deleuze: An Apprenticeship in Philosophy*. Minneapolis: University of Minnesota Press, 1992.

Hardt, Michael, and Antonio Negri. *Empire*. Cambridge: Harvard University Press, 2000.

Hegel, Georg W.F. *Science of Logic*, trans. A.V. Miller. NY: Humanity Books, 1999.

—*Lectures on the History of Philosophy*, trans. E. S. Haldane and F. H. Simson, 3 vols. London: Kegan Paul, 1896.

Henry, Michel. *L'Essence de la manifestation* [1963]. Paris: PUF, 1990.

—*Marx: A Philosophy of Human Reality*, trans. Kathleen McLaughlin. Bloomington: Indiana University Press, 1983.

—*I Am the Truth: Toward a Philosophy of Christianity*, trans. Susan Emanuel. Stanford: Stanford University Press, 2003.

Howie, Gillian. *Deleuze and Spinoza: Aura of Expressionism*. Houndmills: Palgrave, 2002.

Hume, David. *Treatise of Human Nature*, ed. L.A. Selby-Brigge. Oxford: Clarendon Press, 1888.

Inwood, M. J. *Hegel*. London: Routledge & Kegan Paul, 1983.

Jambet, Christian. *La Logique des Orientaux. Henry Corbin et la science des formes*. Paris: Seuil, 1983.

—*La Grande Resurrection d'Alamût*. Lagrasse: Verdier, 1990.

—'The Stranger and Theophany'. *Umbr(a)* 2005: 27–41.

Jankélévitch, Vladimir. *Henri Bergson*. Paris: PUF, 1959.

Kant, Immanuel. *The Critique of Pure Reason*, trans. Paul Guyer and Allen Wood. Cambridge: Cambridge University Press, 1998.

Kerslake, Christian. 'The Vertigo of Philosophy'. *Radical Philosophy* 113 (2002): 10–23.

—'Deleuze, Kant and the Question of Metacritique'. *The Southern Journal of Philosophy* 42 (2004): 481–508.

—'Transcendental Cinema: Deleuze, Time and Modernity'. *Radical Philosophy* 130 (March 2005): 7–19.

—*Deleuze and the Unconscious*. London: Continuum, 2006.

—*The Problem of Immanence in Kant and Deleuze*, forthcoming.

Laplanche, Jean. *Essays on Otherness*, ed. John Fletcher. London: Routledge, 1999.

Lawrence, D.H. 'Chaos in Poetry', in Lawrence, *Selected Literary Criticism*, ed. Anthony Beal. London: Heinemann, 1955.

Lecercle, Jean-Jacques. *Philosophy through the Looking-Glass: Language, Nonsense, Desire*. La Salle: Open Court, 1985.

—*The Violence of Language*. London: Routledge, 1990.

—*Deleuze and Language*. Houndmills: Palgrave Macmillan, 2002.

—'Deleuze, Guattari, and Marxism'. *Historical Materialism* 13:3 (2005): 35–55.

Leibniz, Gottfried W. *Philosophical Texts*, ed. and trans. R.S. Woolhouse and Richard Francks. Oxford: OUP, 1998.

—*Theodicy*, ed. Austin Farrer. La Salle: Open Court, 1985.

Levinas, Emmanuel. *Basic Philosophical Writings*, ed. Adriaan Peperzak et al. Bloomington: Indiana University Press, 1996.

—*Otherwise Than Being*, trans. Alphonso Lingis. The Hague: Martinus Nijhoff, 1981.

Macherey, Pierre. *Hegel ou Spinoza*. Paris: Editions La Découverte, 1990.

—*In a Materialist Way: Selected Essays*, ed. Warren Montag. London: Verso, 1998.

Maldiney, Henri. *Regard, Parole, Espace*. Lausanne: Editions L'Age d'Homme, 1973.

Massumi, Brian. *A User's Guide to Capitalism and Schizophrenia*. Cambridge, MIT Press, 1992.

—*A Shock to Thought: Expressions after Deleuze & Guattari*. London: Routledge, 2002.

—*Parables for the Virtual: Movement, Affect, Sensation*. Durham: Duke University Press, 2002.

—'Navigating Movements'. *21C Magazine* 2 (2003), available online at http://www.21cmagazine.com/issue2/massumi.html.

May, Todd. *Gilles Deleuze: An Introduction*. Cambridge: Cambridge University Press, 2005.

Mengue, Philippe. *Deleuze: Le système du multiple*. Paris: Kimé, 1995.

Miller, Christopher. 'The Postidentitarian Predicament in the Footnotes of *A Thousand Plateaus*: Nomadology, Anthropology, and Authority'. *Diacritics* 23:3 (1993): 6–35.

Negri, Antonio. *Insurgencies: Constituent Power and the Modern State*, trans. Maurizia Boscagli. Minneapolis: University of Minnesota Press, 1999.

Nietzsche, Friedrich. *Basic Writings of Nietzsche*, ed. Walter Kaufmann. New York: Modern Library, 2000.

—*The Will to Power*, ed. Walter Kaufman, trans. Walter Kaufman and R.J. Hollingdale. NY: Vintage, 1968.

Norris, Christopher. *Spinoza and the Origins of Modern Critical Theory*. Oxford: Blackwell, 1991.

Pascal, Blaise. *Pensées*, trans. A.J. Krailsheimer. Harmondsworth: Penguin, 1966.

Pasolini, Pier Paolo. *L'Expérience hérétique*. Paris: Payot, 1976.

Patton, Paul, ed. *Deleuze: A Critical Reader*. Oxford: Blackwell, 1996.

—*Deleuze and the Political*. London: Routledge, 2000.

Plotinus. *The Aenneads*, trans. Stephen Mackenna. London: Faber and Faber, 1969.

Prigogine, Ilya, and Isabelle Stengers. *La Nouvelle alliance*. Paris: Gallimard, 1986.

Protevi, John. *Political Physics: Deleuze, Derrida, and the Body Politic*. London: Athlone Press, 2001.

Proust, Marcel. *A la Recherche du temps perdu*, 3 vols. Paris: Gallimard, 'Bibliothèque de la Pléiade', 1954.

Read, Jason. *The Micro-Politics of Capital: Marx and the Prehistory of the Present*. Albany: State University of New York Press, 2003.

Sartre, Jean-Paul. *The Transcendence of the Ego*, trans. Forrest Williams and Robert Kirkpatrick. NY: Noonday Press, 1957.

Schimmel, Annemarie. *Mystical Dimensions of Islam*. Chapel Hill: University of North Carolina Press, 1975.

Serres, Michel. *Le Système de Leibniz*. Paris: PUF, 1982.

Simondon, Gilbert. *L'Individu et sa genèse physico-biologique*. Paris: PUF, 1964.

Smith, Daniel. 'The Doctrine of Univocity: Deleuze's Ontology of Immanence', in *Deleuze and Religion*, ed. Mary Bryden. London: Routledge, 2001. 167–183.

—'Badiou and Deleuze on the Ontology of Mathematics', in *Think Again: Alain Badiou and the Future of Philosophy*, ed. Peter Hallward. London: Continuum, 2004. 77–93.

—'Deleuze's Philosophy of Mathematics', in *Virtual Mathematics: The Logic of Difference*, ed. Simon Duffy. Manchester: Clinamen Press, 2005.

—*Difference and Genesis: Gilles Deleuze and the Legacy of Post-Kantian Philosophy* (forthcoming).

Spinoza, Benedict de. *The Collected Works of Spinoza*, vol. 1, ed. and trans. Edwin Curley. Princeton: Princeton University Press, 1985. References to the *Ethics* conform to Curley's standard abbreviations: '*Ethics* IIIP57S', for instance, refers to *Ethics*, Book III, proposition 57, scholium.

—*The Political Works*, ed. A.G. Wernham. Oxford: OUP, 1958.

Suhrawardi, Shihab al-Din Yahya al-. *Le Livre de la Sagesse Orientale*, trans. and ed. Henry Corbin. Lagrasse: Verdier, 1986.

—*L'Archange empourpré, Quinze traités et récits mystiques*, trans. and ed. Henry Corbin. Paris: Fayard, 1976.

Sylvester, David, and Francis Bacon. *Interviews with Francis Bacon*. London: Thames and Hudson, 1993.

Thoburn, Nicholas. *Deleuze, Marx, and Politics*. London: Routledge, 2003.

Uexküll, Jakob von. 'A Stroll through the Worlds of Animals and Men: A Picture Book of Invisible Worlds' [1934], trans. Claire Schiller, in *Instinctive Behavior: The Development of a Modern Concept*, ed. Claire Schiller. New York: International Universities Press, 1957. 5–80.

Weil, Simone. *Waiting for God*, trans. Emma Craufurd. New York: Capricorn Books, 1951.

—*Gravity and Grace*, trans. Emma Craufurd and Mario von der Ruhr. London: Routledge Classics, 2002.

Wolin, Richard. *Walter Benjamin, An Aesthetic of Redemption*. Berkeley: University of California Press, 1994.

Woolhouse, R. S. *Descartes, Spinoza, Leibniz: The Concept of Substance in Seventeenth-Century Metaphysics*. London: Routledge, 1993.

Zaoui, Pierre. 'La grande identité Nietzsche-Spinoza, quelle identité?'. *Philosophie* 47 (September 1995): 64–84.

Žižek, Slavoj. *Organs without Bodies: Deleuze and Consequences*. New York: Routledge, 2004.

Zourabichvili, François. *Deleuze: Une Philosophie de l'événement*. Paris: PUF, 1995.

Index

absolute, the 100
absolute creation 5–6, 136, 149, 163
absolute difference 153
abstract lines 82
action-images 113–14
active forces 63–4
actual, the 31–6, 36, 37, 41, 47–54, 55, 63, 79, 82, 83, 87, 162
'Actual and the Virtual, The' (Deleuze) 36
actualisation 36–40, 41, 42, 44, 47, 50, 52–3, 143
actuality 101–3
Adorno, Theodore W. 12
affirmation 134–7, 138, 141, 150, 153, 156
Agamben, Giorgio 160
Aion 146–7
aleatory points 37
Althusser, Louis 48
Anti-Oedipus (Deleuze and Guattari) 10, 56, 67, 68, 75, 87
Aristotle 14, 37, 72, 141
art 34, 72, 85, 104–13, 120–2, 122–6, 127–9, 130, 131–2, 132, 133, 140, 157
Artaud, Antonin 67, 72, 102, 108, 117, 161
artistic creation 107–10
artists 105, 106, 108–10, 151–2
automaton, the 137–8

Bacon, Francis 4, 85, 100, 107, 112–13, 120, 157

Badiou, Alain 58, 81–2, 86
Barthes, Roland 157
Bataille, Georges 161
Baudrillard, Jean 58
Beckett, Samuel 3, 85, 92, 102, 108, 109
becoming 3, 109, 140, 153
'becoming-animal' 61
being 1, 12–13, 27, 81–2, 87, 141, 149, 152
    and creation 127, 145
    and creativity 8, 8–11, 15–18
Bene, Carmelo 80
Benjamin, Walter 4, 86
Bergson, Henri 4, 5, 6, 7, 8, 12, 14–15, 17, 21, 22–3, 30, 31–2, 34, 35, 37, 38, 45, 50, 51, 57, 58, 59–60, 63, 69, 70, 71, 80, 85, 95, 101, 105, 113, 114, 132–3, 141, 146, 147, 149
Blanchot, Maurice 91, 92, 98, 109, 136
body, virtual 61
'Body without Organs' (BwO), the 98–9, 156
Boehme, Jacob 9
Bogue, Ronald 43
Bopp, Franz 66
brain, the 60, 142
Burial of the Count of Orgaz (painting, El Greco) 110–11
Byzantine art 110

capitalism 68–9, 102–3
Capitalism and Schizophrenia (Deleuze and Guattari) 75, 102, 156, 162

Carrol, Lewis 107
Cassavetes, John 115
causality 41–5
'Causes and Reasons of Desert Islands'
    (Deleuze) 23–4
Cézanne, Paul 110
chance 135–6
chaos 29, 130, 132, 145
Chronos 146, 147
Chrysippus 77
cinema 4, 70, 90, 102, 113–17, 128, 140
Colourism 115
concepts 139–46
consciousness 64, 70
continuous variation 48
Corbin, Henry 4, 57, 83, 85, 100, 160
counter-actualisation 43, 44, 67, 79, 82, 82–3,
    87, 91, 92, 94, 99–100, 102, 106, 112, 124,
    125, 131–2, 143
counter-effectuation 132
creatings 2, 5, 11, 16, 17, 26, 27, 37, 41, 50,
    64, 79, 100, 120–1, 136
    conceptual 139–40
    virtual 27, 28, 35, 87, 104, 163
creation 28, 29, 37, 44–5, 46, 55, 56, 59, 63,
    76, 80, 84, 86, 91, 104–5, 151, 164
    absolute 5–6, 136, 149, 163
    and being 127, 145
    and chaos 130, 145
    dimension of 144–5
    lines of 135
    speed 131
    and time 146, 147, 148, 149
creative autonomy 49
creative determination 48
creative expression 76–7
creative force 56
creative time 147, 148, 149
creativity 1, 3, 15, 41
    absolute 57
    and being 8, 8–11, 15–18
    and thought 2
creatural concerns 57
creatural condition, the 88
creatural configuration, the 95
creatural confinement 55–78
creatural force 80
creatural time 101

creatures 27, 29, 29–30, 35
critical philosophy 59

dark precursor, the 37
Darwin, Charles 7, 66, 95, 162
De Landa, Manuel 4, 38
De Sica, Vittorio 115
death 91–2
Derrida, Jacques 141
Descartes, René 13, 73, 85, 134, 141, 145,
    150–1
desire 67–8
determination 33, 37
deterritorialisation 23–4, 95–9, 99–100, 101,
    103, 154, 157, 162
Dickens, Charles 24–5
difference 145–6, 149, 150, 152–8, 154, 162
Difference and Repetition (Deleuze) 14, 51, 56, 98,
    102, 123, 135, 147, 150, 151, 157
differential ratios 51–2
differentiation 1, 12–15, 16, 27, 37, 50, 84–5,
    135, 158, 163
Dionysus 82
dualism 82–7, 157
duration 80

Eckhart, Meister 5, 9, 84, 85, 137
El Greco 110–11
Epicurus 142
Eriugena, John Scottus 5, 37, 56
espace quelconque 106–7, 115–16, 138
Essays Critical and Clinical (Deleuze) 108
essence 120, 122–5, 149
Ethics (Spinoza) 134–5, 156
events 41–4, 45–7, 146–7, 148, 152
evolution 52–3, 65, 66
exclusion 47
Expressionism 115
extension 39–40, 56
extinction 87, 100
extra-worldly 57
extraction 132

false problems 31–2
Fellini, Federico 115
Figure at a Washbasin (painting, Bacon) 112
Foucault, Michel 49, 58, 66, 67, 80, 101, 102,
    158, 160–1

frame of reference 127
free will 138–9
freedom 145, 163

Girard, René 92
God 2, 4, 5, 9–10, 11–12, 21, 29, 30, 31, 39, 46, 53, 54, 56, 57, 66, 67, 76, 78, 83–4, 85, 86, 87–90, 96, 133, 134, 135, 136–7, 147, 156
Godard, Jean-Luc 102, 115
Gothic art 110
Guattari, Félix 10, 16, 19, 23, 28, 29, 34, 36, 39, 40, 41, 44, 47, 49, 52, 56, 58–9, 61–2, 67–9, 71, 72, 75, 79–80, 83, 87, 92, 95–9, 99, 101, 102, 103, 107, 109, 127, 130, 131, 139, 140, 142, 144–5, 145, 153, 156, 162, 163–4
Gueroult, Martial 156

habit 63
haecceity 40
al-Hallaj 85
Hansen, Mark 52
Hardt, Michael 13
Hardy, Thomas 109
Heart of Glass (Herzog) 116
Hegel, Georg W. F. 6, 15, 72, 82, 83, 100, 134, 140, 149
Heidegger, Martin 8, 11–12, 140, 141, 160
Henry, Michel 4, 85, 100, 160
Herzog, Werner 116
history 100–3
Hollywood 113
Holy Family (painting, Michelangelo) 111
al-Hujwiri 84
human condition, the 20, 56, 58–9, 62–5, 66–7
Hume, David 13, 62–3, 69, 154
Husserl, Edmund 72, 145
Hyppolite, Jean 76, 125

Ibn al-'Arabi 5
ideas 46, 47, 50
identity 28–9, 30
illusion 50–1
image, and movement 70
'imaginal world', the 85
'Immanence: A Life...' (Deleuze) 24
In Search of Lost Time (Proust) 46–7, 117–20, 121, 122–3, 125

incompatibility 47
individuals 30–1
individuation 19–20, 30–1, 45, 47, 49–50, 53–4, 79, 82, 84–5, 92, 100, 124, 143, 154, 156, 158
inequality 18–21
infinite, the 67, 132
infinite speed 141–2, 145, 146
infinity 142
intelligibility, levels of 118–22
intuition 129
Ishraq 83–5
Iven, Jorge 45

Jambet, Christian 4, 83, 84, 160
Jet of Water (painting, Bacon) 113
Joyce, James 108

Kafka (Deleuze and Guattari) 156
Kafka, Franz 98, 103, 107, 109, 117
Kandinsky, Wassili 111
Kant, Immanuel 6, 11, 12, 13, 57, 66, 73–6, 80, 129, 134, 141, 145, 147, 163
Kerslake, Christian 102
Klossowski, Pierre 91, 102
knowledge 11–12

Lacan, Jacques 48, 58, 94, 157, 158
Lamarck, Jean-Baptiste 66
language 67, 107–8
Lawrence, T.E. 39, 109
Leibniz, Gottfried W. 7, 12, 16, 19–20, 29, 46, 50, 53, 54, 72, 74, 91, 123, 135, 138–9, 141, 143–4, 155, 163
Lévi-Strauss, Claude 48, 157, 158
Levinas, Emmanuel 11–12, 58
liberty 139
life 1, 25–6, 36, 55, 59–62, 64, 105, 163, 164
'line of flight' 58, 95, 99
literature 97–8, 106, 107–8, 109, 117–20, 121, 122–3, 125, 128–9, 136
Logic and Existence (Hyppolite) 76
logic of difference 152–8
Logic of Sense, The (Deleuze) 41, 43, 44, 45, 54, 67, 76, 87, 94, 123, 135, 157
love 119, 125
Lyotard, Jean Francois 102
lyrical-abstractionists 115

Mallarmé, Stéphane 67
Marx, Karl 7, 66, 103, 162
masochism 93–5
Massumi, Brian 4
Matter and Memory (Bergson) 32, 59
Melville, Herman 97–8, 106, 109
memory 33, 34
Michaux, Henri 102, 142
Michelangelo 110, 111
Miller, Arthur 109, 158
mind 63
Moby Dick (Melville) 97–8, 106
modal essences 46
modern painting 111
'molar' poles 58
monads 46, 50, 53, 123, 139, 141, 143–4, 155–6
Mondrian, Piet 85, 111–13
movement, and image 70
multiplicity 16–17, 38–9, 100, 152, 153, 154–5
music 121, 128
mysticism 21, 22–3, 84, 132, 161

natural phenomenology 86
negation 65
Nicholas of Cusa 145
Nietzsche, Friedrich Wilhelm 3, 4, 19, 28, 39, 56, 62, 63–5, 69, 71, 74, 80, 82, 85, 96, 101, 109, 120, 135, 149, 163
Nietzsche and Philosophy (Deleuze) 56
nomads 83, 98, 101, 162
nonsense 37
nouvelle vague cinema 113

objectivism 122
Oedipus 67–9, 103, 158
'Omnitudo' 15–18, 144
One, the 145
'One Manifesto Less' (Deleuze) 80–1
organic form, limits imposed by 59–62
organising principle 130–3
orientation 83
other, the 92–3
Our Mutual Friend (Dickens) 24–5
overman (*Übermensch*), the 64
Ozu, Yasujiro 113, 115–16

Painting (painting, Bacon) 112

paradoxical element, the 37
Parmenides 8, 11
Pascal, Blaise 143
Pasolini, Pier Paolo 70
past, the 32–5, 59–60
Péguy, Charles Pierre 67
phantasms 94
Philonenko, Alexis 50–1
philosophy 20–1, 35–6, 56, 57, 59, 67, 71, 81, 101, 104, 127–9, 130, 132, 139, 140, 143, 144, 145, 150, 159
plane of immanence 144, 161
Plato 50, 81, 92, 123, 134, 140, 141, 145
Plotinus 57
political philosophy 56, 139, 162
Pollock, Jackson 85, 111
potentiality 160
'Preface to Transgression' (Foucault) 161
present, the 32, 35
Prigogine, Ilya 4
Proust, Marcel 4, 46–7, 85–6, 94, 98, 107, 109, 117–20, 120, 121, 122–3, 125, 128, 129, 147, 149, 155
Proust and Signs (Deleuze) 56, 118, 123, 151
psychoanalysis 59, 67, 153
'Purloined Letter, The' (Poe) 158

Rain (film) 45
reality 55, 59–60, 69–70, 100, 104, 108, 134, 157
redemption 86
relation, theory of 154–5
repetition 70–1, 151
representation 59, 69–72, 76, 77, 92
Resnais, Alain 71, 115, 128
reterritorialisation 103, 157
return, the 149–51
Ricardo, David 66
Robbe-Grillet, Alain 70, 116
Rodin, Auguste 106
Rosset, Clément 4, 58
Roussel, Raymond 136, 161

Sacher-Masoch, Leopold von 4, 93–5
Sartre, Jean Paul 58
Schlegel, Friedrich von 66
Schopenhauer, Arthur 82, 85
science 41, 66, 108, 130–2, 132, 143

Scotus, Duns 9
scripture 77–8
self 61
sensation 105–6, 107, 108, 131, 157
sense 42, 76–7
sensory-motor schema 114–15
signification 76
signs 118–22, 128
Simondon, Gilbert 102, 153
Sollers, Philippe 98, 158
Spinoza, Benedict de 2, 4, 5, 6, 8, 9–10, 12, 13,
    13–14, 14, 15, 19, 27, 30, 38–9, 46, 50, 53,
    54, 57, 69, 73, 74, 76, 77–8, 82, 83, 85, 87–8,
    91, 101, 106, 120, 125, 134–5, 137, 138, 139,
    142, 143, 145, 146, 147, 149, 155, 156, 160,
    163
state, the 68
Stengers, Isabelle 4
Stoic ethics 43, 77
structuralism 157–8
subjectivism 122–3
subjectivity 73, 137
subtraction 87
al-Suhrawardi, Shihab al-Din Yahya 83–5, 116

terminology 2
Thomas Aquinas 9
thought 2, 128, 129, 130, 137–8, 142–3, 145,
    159–60, 163
'Thought from the Outside' (Foucault) 161
thoughtlessness 55–6
Thousand Plateaus, A (Deleuze and Guattari) 40,
    71, 83, 95, 127
time 22, 45, 100, 101, 105, 113, 114, 116, 126,
    146–52
Tournier, Michel 93

'transcendental', the 74–5
transmutation 135
transubstantiation 106
Truffaut, Francois 115
truth 104

Uexküll, Jacob von 19, 95
univocal ontology 71–2, 107–10
'unlimited finity' 66–7
unpresentable, the 21–3
unthought, the 37

values 28
Van Gogh, Vincent 110
Vendredi (Tournier) 93
Venus in Furs (Sacher-Masoch) 94
Vermeer, Jan 121
virtual, the 21–3, 30–54, 55, 79, 143, 162, 164
virtual creatings 27, 28, 35, 87, 104, 163
virtual determination 48–9, 100
virtual difference 145–6
virtual extraction 91
virtual sense 44
visual art 110–13
vitalism 163–4

Water running from a Flowing Tap (painting, Bacon)
    113
Weil, Simone 4, 86
What is Philosophy (Deleuze and Guattari) 40,
    130, 139, 140
whole, the 126
Wittgenstein, Ludwig 12
work 66, 68

Žižek, Slavoj 87, 94